The Complete Book of
NEEDLECRAFTS

The Complete Book of
NEEDLECRAFTS

Introduced by Caroline Ollard

BLACK CAT

Acknowledgments

The photographs on the following pages are by courtesy of: British Architectural Library, RIBA 164 (inset); Camera Press, London 14-15, 16, 17, 18, 19, 20, 37, 44, 46, 59, 98, 170, 173, 193, 195, 212; J. & P. Coats, Edinburgh 10, 11. The remainder of the photographs were taken by the following photographers: Jan Baldwin, Tom Belshaw, Tim Bishop, Brian Boyle, Allan Grainger, Chris Harvey, Hank Kemme, Monique Leluhandre, Di Lewis, Liz Mc Aulay, Polly Mitchell, Tino Tedaldi, Jerry Tubby and Nick Wright.
The artwork was drawn by the following artists: Muriel Best, Amanda Bloom, Lindsay Blow, Andy Earl, Sharon Finmark, Eugene Fleury, Jill Gordon, Susanne Lisle, Coral Mula, Colin Salmon, Amanda Severne, Sue Sharples, Sara Silcock, Sheila Tizzard, Catherine Ward and John Woodcock.

Front cover: Jan Baldwin, Tom Belshaw, Monique Leluhandre, Spike Powell and (top right) Camera Press
Half title page: Jan Baldwin
Title page: Monique Leluhandre
Page 8: Di Lewis

First published 1986 in Great Britain by Orbis Publishing Limited, London
Reprinted 1988 by Macdonald & Co (Publishers) Ltd under the Black Cat imprint

Macdonald & Co (Publishers) Ltd
3rd Floor
Greater London House
Hampstead Road
London NW1 7QX

a member of Maxwell Pergamon Publishing Corporation plc

ISBN 0-7481-0093-8
Printed in Hungary

Contents

Introduction

When you open this magnificent compendium of needlecrafts, the chances are you literally won't know where to start. If you are a complete beginner, don't worry; you will probably find that your ideal needlecraft will 'choose' you! Just enjoy the colours, patterns, different styles and techniques which appear in the collection of pretty things on these pages. If you are already a keen stitcher, the array of home, fashion, childrens' and gift items is bound to spark ideas, suggesting more and more combinations of stitch and texture.

The Complete Book of Needlecrafts is truly comprehensive. There are clear instructions on how to plan, begin, stitch and finish your work in five fascinating 'media' – embroidery, needlepoint, quilting, appliqué and patchwork – each of which rejoices in the simplest of equipment and in being easy to carry around. All the traditional stitches and patterns are here. Some are treated conventionally; others have taken a new direction and throughout the book you will see the traditional juxtaposed with, or combined with, a modern approach. Once you have discovered the possibilities you will be keen to explore them for yourself. There are a wealth of appealing projects too, ranging from simple, small-scale items to the more complex 'once in a lifetime' pieces, and the special Design Extra boxes show you how to ring the changes by developing your awareness of colour and pattern.

Whether you enjoy the versatility of embroidery on fabric or the more disciplined concept of needlepoint on a canvas framework, there are plenty of clearly illustrated stitches to get you started. Quilting and appliqué are delightful crafts which have been popular at different times but in fact they are perfect partners: see how closely the techniques complement each other. Patchwork is one of the most well-loved needlecrafts with one of the humblest beginnings – a *real* 'rags to riches' story.

All these crafts can be readily combined in designs of your own. Or you can borrow ideas from one craft and apply them to another. You may not consider yourself an artist, but all needlework is a form of 'painting' with thread and yarn on canvas or fabric – or painting with the fabric itself, as in patchwork and appliqué. Motifs and borders, for example, offer a wonderful way of making a plain item into something beautiful – stamped with your personal style. Seminole patchwork borders, quilted cable designs or Florentine needlepoint wave patterns, you can use them on almost anything you like.

As you gain in confidence, finding out which are your favourite techniques, you will be acquiring the knowhow to make unique gifts, beautifully and economically. All you need is a needle, thread or yarn, fabric or canvas – and this book!

Caroline Ollard

Caroline Ollard, 1986

Embroidery

It is the rich, worldwide tradition of embroidery which makes it such a fascinating craft. People have decorated fabrics with stitching for centuries and embroidery is certainly one of the most ancient needlecrafts.

Many of the designs given in the following pages have their roots in styles popular over the last few centuries. Some are treated traditionally, some are given a new look. For example, one of the oldest techniques represented is blackwork, which came to sixteenth-century England from Spain and is based on Moorish patterns. Chapter 9 suggests an update for blackwork designs – in the kitchen!

Embroidery stitches are numerous and it is impossible to cover them all here. However, all the well-known stitches, as well as some less familiar techniques, are included. Each chapter introduces a new way of working, starting with the basic surface stitches. Looped and knotted stitches follow, in various simple and combined forms. From counted thread stitches and others which rely on neatness and regularity for their effect, you can progress to the more complex drawn thread and pulled thread stitches and the techniques of smocking, tambour beadwork and goldwork.

Clear step-by-step diagrams and simple instructions guide you through the various techniques. Working charts, trace patterns and diagrams provide all that is needed to complete both large and small projects. And full-colour photographs and drawings bring the work up close for you to see the detail.

You don't have to be a perfectionist to enjoy this craft. Tiny stitches on fine fabric do make awe-inspiring heirlooms as we can see in pieces from the past, but with embroidery almost anything goes! Bold designs and vivid colours, chunky threads and fabrics all have their place. Needlecraft shops and departments are rich storehouses of threads of every possible hue – wools, cottons, silks, metallic threads and exciting extras like beads and sequins.

The following chapters will guide you in your choice as well as your selection of equipment such as pins and needles, fabrics and frames. Each project has a comprehensive list of things you will need and discusses alternatives where applicable. Do not despair if you are miles from a needlecraft stockist. There are plenty of shops with mail-order services as well as specialist mail-order suppliers.

CHAPTER 1

Introducing materials and basic stitches

Embroidery covers a vast range of decorative skills using fabrics and threads of every kind. Once you have mastered even a few simple stitches, you have opened the door to a whole new world of creativity.

1   2   3   4

Handling beautiful fabrics and threads is a joy in itself, but there is a very special satisfaction in making attractive and useful articles for yourself, your family and your home while enjoying a creative and relaxing hobby.

Much of the charm of embroidery lies in the fact that you need little equipment and there is hardly any setting out and clearing up to do. You are also working with textures and colours to produce your own unique combination of design, fabric, thread and technique. Embroidery is a surprisingly suitable hobby for people with a hectic lifestyle as the work can be picked up in odd moments – the problem is putting it down again!

It is always worth buying the best equipment – good quality tools are a

sound investment and a lasting pleasure to use.

Start with the most expensive item – a pair of small sharp embroidery scissors. You will also need a longer-bladed pair for cutting fabric, and an old pair for cutting paper.

Choose a smooth thimble to fit your middle finger, and buy a tape measure and a box of fine steel pins. Collect transparent plastic boxes (from haberdashers) for storing threads, and find a needlebook or piece of flannel for your needles.

Threads

Many threads both natural and man-made are manufactured especially for embroidery. You can also incorporate knitting and weaving yarns, metal threads or raffia.

Choosing and using thread Keep in mind the intended use for the embroidery. Does it need to be washed or dry-cleaned? Will it have to stand up to a lot of wear.

Choose threads accordingly, noticing the differences between them – thin or thick, twisted or loose. Bear in mind the contrast between the thread and the background – shiny threads show up against a dull background. Don't use too long a thread in the needle. 50cm/20in is enough for most purposes. If a thread wears thin or fluffs up, replace it immediately with a fresh length. You will often find you need to use only a few strands of the total thickness of some threads. Separate the strands carefully – rub the ends of the required strands and pull gently to avoid tangles.

Four basic stitches

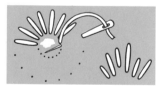

Straight stitch

This is a single stitch, made in any direction. Straight stitches can be grouped in geometric shapes, used in lines, scattered about singly or with other stitches, or used to make broad effects like brush strokes.

Back stitch

Work from right to left. Bring the needle up a stitch away from the beginning of the line, take a stitch an equal distance behind and in front. Pull thread through. For the next stitch the needle goes down where it first came up.

Stem stitch

Work from left to right, or upwards. Take a long stitch forward and a shorter, slanting stitch back. The more pronounced the slant, the thicker the line. Keep the thread under the needle.

Chain stitch

Work from right to left, or downwards. Bring the thread out at the beginning of the line, hold the thread down with the left thumb while the needle is reinserted into the same spot and brought out again a short distance away. Draw it through over the loop of thread under your thumb. The needle always goes down again into the same hole.

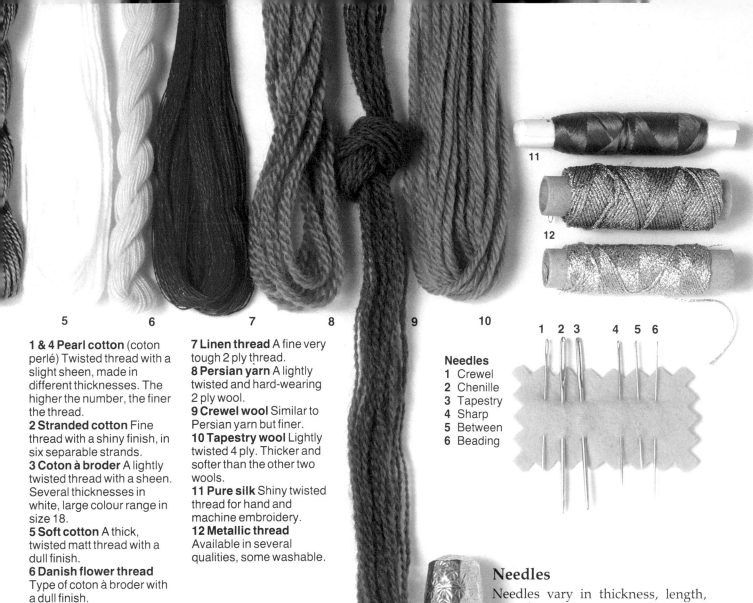

5 6 7 8 9 10

1 & 4 **Pearl cotton** (coton perlé) Twisted thread with a slight sheen, made in different thicknesses. The higher the number, the finer the thread.
2 **Stranded cotton** Fine thread with a shiny finish, in six separable strands.
3 **Coton à broder** A lightly twisted thread with a sheen. Several thicknesses in white, large colour range in size 18.
5 **Soft cotton** A thick, twisted matt thread with a dull finish.
6 **Danish flower thread** Type of coton à broder with a dull finish.

7 **Linen thread** A fine very tough 2 ply thread.
8 **Persian yarn** A lightly twisted and hard-wearing 2 ply wool.
9 **Crewel wool** Similar to Persian yarn but finer.
10 **Tapestry wool** Lightly twisted 4 ply. Thicker and softer than the other two wools.
11 **Pure silk** Shiny twisted thread for hand and machine embroidery.
12 **Metallic thread** Available in several qualities, some washable.

Needles
1 Crewel
2 Chenille
3 Tapestry
4 Sharp
5 Between
6 Beading

1 2 3 4 5 6

Needles

Needles vary in thickness, length, size of eye, sharpness and shape of point, depending on the fabric and type of stitchery. A number indicates the size: the higher the number, the finer the needle.

Crewel The basic all-round embroidery needle, with a fine point and a long eye to take several strands of thread. A packet of sizes 5-10 covers most types of surface stitchery on closely woven fabric.

Chenille A bigger needle with a large eye for thick threads and a sharp point. It is useful for taking couched threads to the back of the fabric.

Tapestry A blunt needle with a large eye. It is inserted between the threads of the fabric without piercing them. Used for needlepoint and counted thread work such as cross stitch, pulled and drawn thread work, and lacing on composite stitches.

Sharp A general sewing needle with a small eye.

Between Same as sharp, but shorter. It is a favourite quilting needle.

Beading A long, very fine needle with a tiny eye for small beads.

Two chain stitch variations

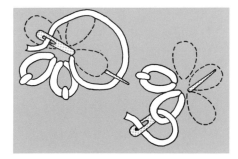

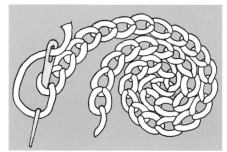

Detached chain stitch

This is also often called lazy daisy stitch as it is suitable for forming daisy-like flower motifs. Work a chain stitch in the normal way, but instead of reinserting the needle to form a second stitch, make a small stitch to catch down the loop of the first one and hold it in place. Work these in a circle for 'flowers' or separately for other effects.

Chain filling

Work the chain stitch in a line, but in a circular direction from the centre outwards, so that a solid round stitched area forms. This is useful for floral and other circle-based motifs.

11

Frames

A frame is not essential, but many stitches are easier to work on taut fabric, as they keep an even tension and there is no fear of puckering. If you use a frame, you work each stitch in two separate movements – right through the fabric to the back of the work and then out to the front again. (Stitches on hand-held work can be made in one action – the needle picks up successive stitch lengths of fabric.) Some frames come with table or floor stands so that you have both hands free for embroidery. The simplest type of frame for surface embroidery is the ring frame; others such as the rectangular slate frame are dealt with in chapter 5, page 26.

Ring frames come in various sizes,

measured by diameter, ranging from 7.5cm–30cm/3in–12in. They are suitable for working small designs and should be big enough to encompass the complete design.

Framing up Separate the two hoops.
1 Bind the inner ring with soft hem tape or bias strips of torn fabric. This stops your base fabric from slipping.
2 Lay the fabric over the inner ring, right side up, and press the outer ring in place.
Adjust the fabric evenly before tightening the screw.
If you need to move the ring along to a new area of fabric, protect the stitches already worked with a spare piece of soft fabric laid over the base fabric and cut away above the area you wish to work.

1

2

How to transfer designs

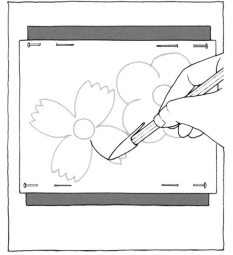

There are several ways to transfer embroidery designs on to fabric. Everyone has a favourite method, although often one method will be more suitable than another.

Trace and tack

This method will transfer a design on to most fabrics, and as it leaves no mark, the design can easily be altered.
Trace off the design on to tissue or tracing paper.
Lay the tracing on the right side of the fabric and pin in place. Outline the design with small running stitches through both paper and fabric.
Run the needle point along the lines of stitching to cut the tissue and tear it away carefully.

Dressmaker's carbon

This quick and easy method is suitable for marking designs on to smooth fabrics. The special carbon paper is available in several colours. Use a pale one for dark fabrics. Simply pin your traced design over the fabric with a sheet of dressmaker's carbon slipped in between, carbon side down. Then trace over the lines of the design with a fairly pointed implement such as a ballpoint with its cap on. For simple geometric designs, you could use a tracing wheel – a serrated-edged wheel mounted on a handle. The outline of the motif will appear on the fabric as a dotted line.

Window method

A simple motif can be traced directly on to most pale fabrics if both design and fabric are held up to the light as follows:
Trace off the design in bold black lines on to a piece of tracing paper and tape the tracing to a window pane with adhesive tape.
Then tape the fabric firmly in position over the tracing and trace the design on to the fabric using a sharp 2H pencil or a washable embroidery marker. (The marker can easily be sponged off if necessary.) Make sure the fabric is taut and positioned correctly over the traced design.

A pocketful of flowers

Breathe new life into a plain shirt with this fresh and pretty design of cornfield flowers. Work the motif in basic stitches on to a white or plain-coloured shirt with a breast pocket from which the flowers will appear to spring.

You will need

One skein each Coats Anchor stranded cotton in greens 0238 and 0267, red 046, blue 0132, yellow 0305 and black 0403
Crewel needle size 8 or 9
Tracing paper and tacking thread or dressmaker's carbon paper
Small ring frame if possible

Working the design

If you are using a new shirt, wash it first so that it does not shrink later and pucker your stitches.

If possible, mount the area to be worked on a ring frame. Thread the needle with three strands of the cotton. Don't knot it, but begin with some tiny neat back stitches which you will then cover up with your embroidery.

Work the cornflowers in straight rows of chain stitch sewn from the centre outwards. The poppy is worked in chain stitch filling, with the flower outlined and then filled in.

Use the trace design below for the flowers on the shirt above. Transfer it using one of the methods already described.

Next work the yellow corn in detached chain stitch and make your straight catching stitches long enough to look like the whiskers on the ears of corn. Use detached chain stitch again to work the black centre of the poppy. Then sew the bright green grass in stem stitch and the darker green stems in back stitch. The poppy bud is worked in green chain stitch and red straight stitches. At the lower edge of the design, extend your stitches 6mm/¼in inside the pocket.

Finishing off

Finish threads off by working a few small stitches in the back of the work and snipping off. Make sure the wrong side is neat and that you have not carried thread across white areas where it will show through on the right side.

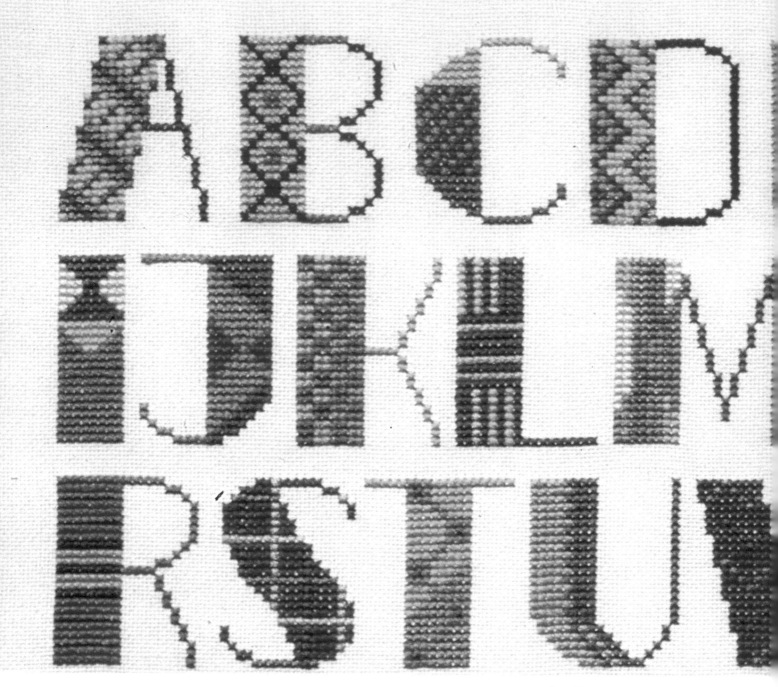

CHAPTER 2

Creative cross stitch

Cross stitch is the basis for traditional embroidery throughout much of the world, but it is also effective in contemporary work like these bold, bright letters. Stitch an initial – or sew the whole colourful alphabet.

Universally popular in Europe, particularly in Scandinavia and the Slav countries, cross stitch designs and motifs have been passed down with traditional folklore and every country has its own characteristic colours. It is one of the easiest of stitches – based on a single diagonal stitch made first in one direction and then in another to cross the first at right angles. These crosses are worked in groups to form strong blocks of colour, or else in lines to create outlines, letters and numerals.

Counted thread embroidery

Cross stitch is one of many stitches that are worked over counted threads – that is, the threads of the fabric are used to place the stitches. Evenweave fabric with regular, identical numbers of threads across both the warp and the weft is used. It comes in several weaves, from fine to coarse, ranging from ten to thirty threads to 2.5cm/1in. The size of stitch, and consequently of motif, depends on how many threads you are working over. The overall shape of

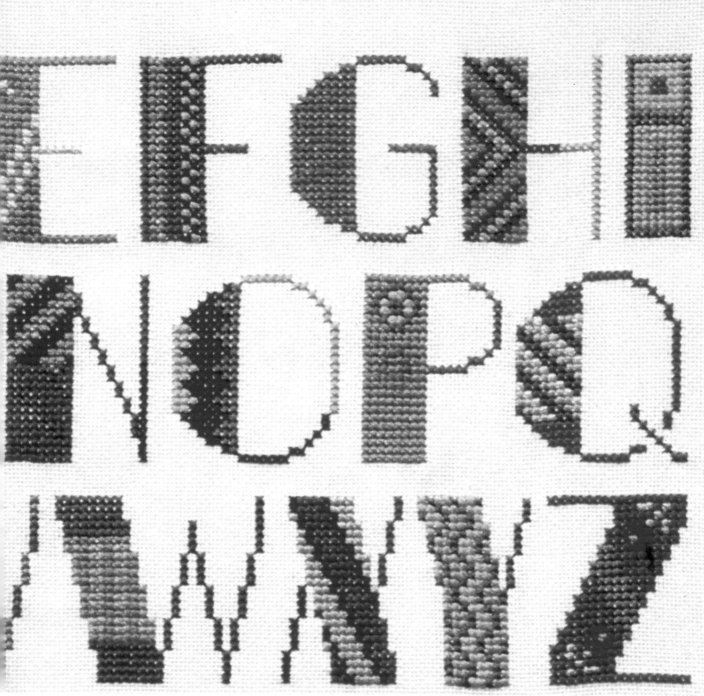

cross stitches should be square, covering the same number of threads vertically and horizontally. If you were to use a fabric of uneven weave, the stitches would be distorted.

Cross stitch can be sewn in many different scales, depending on the thread and fabric used, and the design being embroidered. To make a design larger, use a fabric with fewer threads to 2.5cm/1in and make larger crosses using thicker thread. Or, use more strands over more threads of the same fabric. To make a design smaller, reverse either of these processes.

Fabrics The most suitable fabric for cross stitch is an evenweave. Choose one where you can see clearly

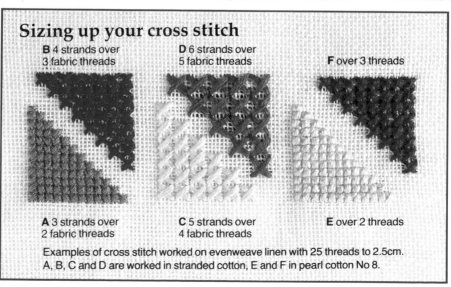

Sizing up your cross stitch

B 4 strands over 3 fabric threads

D 6 strands over 5 fabric threads

F over 3 threads

A 3 strands over 2 fabric threads

C 5 strands over 4 fabric threads

E over 2 threads

Examples of cross stitch worked on evenweave linen with 25 threads to 2.5cm. A, B, C and D are worked in stranded cotton, E and F in pearl cotton No 8.

enough to count the threads. Gingham and other checked fabrics are also convenient, as the stitch 'squares' are already marked out. (Make sure the needle goes into the same hole at each corner.)

Needles Use a blunt tapestry needle with a large eye, size 20 to 24 depending on the weave of the fabric.

Threads Many embroidery threads are suitable for cross stitch, particularly stranded cotton, coton à broder, Danish flower thread, No 8 pearl cotton and soft cotton. Pearl cotton is twisted and lustrous, and gives a particularly bold effect. At the coarser

end of the fabric scale, try crewel wool, or stranded Persian yarn on evenweave wool.

How to begin

Unlike freestyle embroidery designs, which are worked over a marked outline; no tracing is needed, although iron-on transfers marked out in crosses are available. Cross stitch is usually worked from a chart where each square denotes one cross stitch. You can work in horizontal rows, or in separate stitches, depending on the design.

When working in rows, lay down one set of diagonal threads first, then

add the crossing threads. For neatness, all the upper threads must lie in the same direction on one piece of work, unless you particularly wish to emphasize part of the design by the light catching threads running in the opposite direction.

Calculating the size of a design If you are working cross stitch from a chart, it is often hard to visualize the size of a finished design before you begin working it. This simple method of calculating the dimensions will save a few mistakes.

Work a 2cm/¾in row of cross stitches on the fabric. Count the

Working basic cross stitch

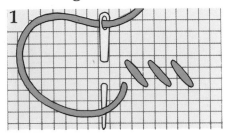 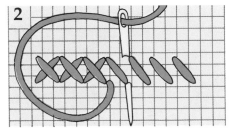 

To work horizontally
Working over two threads:
1 Bring the needle up on the right-hand side of the row at the bottom. Re-insert it two threads to the left and two threads up to form a diagonal half-cross. Bring the needle up again two threads along from where it first came up, and

continue along the row.
2 Work the upper crossing stitches by reversing the process and working from left to right. Bring the needle up on the left-hand side at the bottom. The needle should go through the same holes as on the first row, and the back of the work should have even vertical stitches.

To work diagonally
When working isolated stitches, or diagonal or vertical rows of a particular colour, it is easier to work individual complete crosses before passing on to the next stitch.

Below: Embroider initials on to a tiny bag and trim with twisted threads.

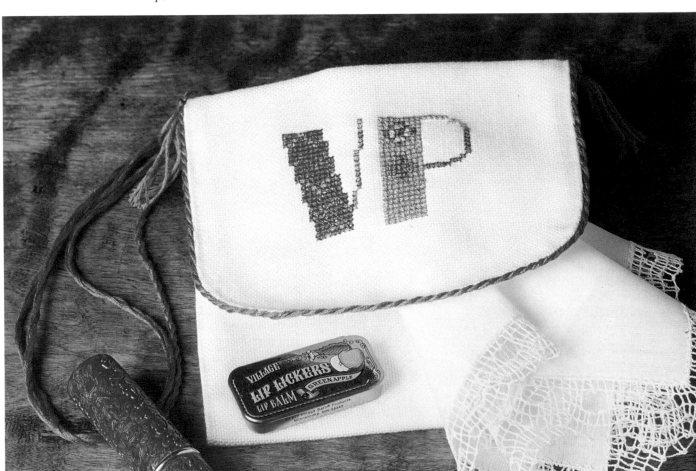

stitches. Now count the number of crosses on the chart in the length and width of the design to be copied. Divide each of these figures by the number of crosses in 2cm/¾in. Double each total to get the finished length and width of the stitched design for your particular fabric.

For example, a chart of 40 crosses long and 20 crosses wide on fabric with 10 crosses to 2cm/¾in will produce a design 8cm×4cm/6¼in× 1½in. On fabric with 5 crosses to 2cm/¾in this design measures 16cm× 8cm/6¼in×3¼in.

Cross stitch on fine fabrics

To work a cross stitch design on an uneven or close weave, or a very fine fabric such as organdie, tack a piece of fine, single thread canvas over the area to be worked. Sew the cross stitches over the canvas, pulling fairly tightly to avoid loose stitches later, and carefully cut the canvas close to the motif.
Pull away the canvas threads. It is best to remove all the threads running in one direction first.

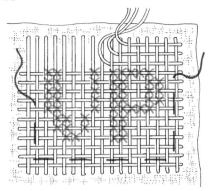

Colourful alphabet in cross stitch

Personalize a present with one, two or several of the brilliantly coloured letters on pages 14 and 15. They could find a home on many different items – pin cushions, needlecases, tops of trinket boxes or tiny bedroom cushions. You could stitch your favourite child's name and frame it, or for a beautiful nursery sampler picture, sew the whole alphabet, using the large picture as a layout guide. Or, using a piece of fine canvas as described above, stitch a name or initial on to T-shirts, sweatshirts, towels, dungarees or baby clothes. The letters are worked entirely in cross stitch using stranded cotton thread in a range of glowing colours. You can use the shades in the picture or choose your own. The colour of the background fabric should complement the bright colours. Each letter will be about 4.5cm/1¾in high when finished, but you can make them as large or as small as you like by changing the base fabric and thread.

You will need
Coats Anchor stranded cotton in at least four different shades
Evenweave fabric, 25 threads to 2.5cm/1in
Tapestry needle size 22 or 24
Small embroidery hoop if possible

Stitching the letters
Each letter includes a solid, multi-coloured area, and some plain lines. Work the cross stitches over two threads of the fabric using three strands of thread.

The big picture is your working guide for the colours and patterns. Charts are given below for the first three letters of the alphabet to show you how the patterns are built up. Work in horizontal rows where practical, turning the embroidery 90 degrees to work along the length of some of the letters; otherwise work vertically, or diagonally, in separate single stitches. Remember to work all the crossing threads in the same direction.
If more than one letter is to be worked, do not carry threads across on the wrong side; finish them off and start a new length for the next letter. Letters should be at least four fabric threads apart.

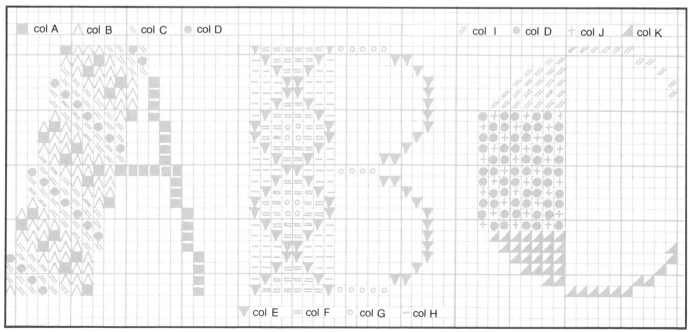

CHAPTER 3

Shimmering satin stitch

Satin stitch is beautifully smooth and glossy. It is useful for working many different kinds of motifs.
A swarm of honey bees has settled on this lovely bright table linen – learn basic satin stitch and French knots, and you will find them simple to embroider.

Satin stitch is a very commonly used stitch in embroidery, and is ideal for filling in solid areas of colour. Some preliminary practice will help you to get your stitches lying neatly side by side to obtain the silky finish which gives the stitch its name.

Working hints

All the stitches in each design, or part of a design, should lie in the same direction. The direction you choose will have quite an effect on the finished work because of the way the stitching catches the light. The stitch can be worked effectively and neatly on evenweave fabric.

When working satin stitch, always make sure the ends of the stitches cover any outlines marked on the base fabric, and make a clean edge. Always work with a frame to avoid drawing up the base fabric and keep all the stitches at the same tension so that there is no puckering when the frame is removed. If the motif is too large for a single row of satin stitches, use several rows worked neatly end to end or use encroaching satin stitch.

Below: These embroidered bees could be worked on any bright cotton fabric to match your kitchen colour scheme.

Three useful stitches

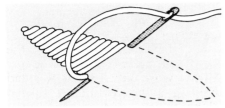

Satin stitch
Make a series of straight stitches lying close to each other. Bring the needle up and re-insert it on the other side of the motif being worked; bring the needle up again very close to where it first went in, being careful not to pull the first stitch too tight. Continue across the motif in this way.

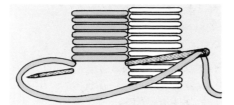

Encroaching satin stitch
When you need more than one row of satin stitch to cover an area, you can work the ends of the second row stitches between the ends of the stitches on the first row. The two rows will blend together smoothly. Encroaching satin stitch is often used for subtle tone variations in the shade of the thread.

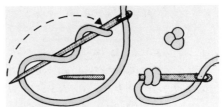

French knots
Bring the needle out where you want to make the stitch. Anchor the thread with your free thumb and circle the needle point twice round the thread. Keeping the thread anchored, re-insert the needle close to where it came up. Carefully pull it through to catch the knot down. Begin working next knot or secure with a backstitch.

Honey bee tablewear

The warm, honey-yellow gingham used to make this tablewear and matching apron is the perfect background for lively bees worked in simple embroidery stitches. Alternatively, you can use plain or striped fabric.

Placemat and napkin

The bee motifs make an attractive and inviting place setting when stitched on to a placemat and matching napkin. Use a bought mat and napkin, or make them up yourself.

You will need
For one placemat and one napkin (to work 23 to 25 bees)
Coats Anchor stranded cotton: 2 skeins black 0403, 1 skein each yellow 0298, grey 0398, green 0225
40cm/½yd of fabric (90cm/36in wide)
To work either one mat *or* one napkin: 1 skein in each shade
Tracing paper and dressmaker's carbon
Crewel needle

Working the mat and napkin
If you are making up your own table linen, work the embroidery first. Trace off bees of different sizes from the patterns overleaf on to tracing paper. Using dressmaker's carbon paper and a ball-point with its cap on, transfer as many bees as you want to the opposing corners of a rectangular piece of gingham fabric or on to a bought placemat. Position the bees at random wherever

you want them, or use the picture (below) as a guide. They should be at least 2cm/¾in away from edge of fabric if you are making your own mat. For the napkin, trace some different bees on to one corner of a square napkin, again making sure they are at least 2cm/¾in away from the edge of the fabric if making your own.
Mount the fabric in a ring frame (see the Professional Touch overleaf). With three strands of thread in the needle, work each bee's head in satin stitch so that stitches lie from head to tail. Add alternating yellow and black stripes for the body, using encroaching satin stitch to suggest softness.
Outline the end part of the body in black stem stitch. Use grey stem stitch for the wings, black for the legs, add black backstitched antennae and green French knots for the eyes.

Below: A matching mat and napkin set.

Tea-cosy

This tea-cosy really does look cosy. Shaped like beehives with embroidered bees buzzing round the entrances, both tea and egg-cosies are filled with wadding to keep your boiled egg and teapot snug. Make up your own simple cosies using fabric on which you have already embroidered the bees and the hive entrances. The outer seams are finished with a neat trim of bias binding.

You will need

For 1 tea-cosy, to work 15 bees and the hive entrance, Coats Anchor stranded cotton: 2 skeins black 0403, 1 skein each yellow 0298, grey 0398 and green 0225
Tracing paper and dressmaker's carbon
Crewel needle
40cm/½yd polyester wadding (8oz)
70cm/¾yd of fabric (90cm/36in wide or more) depending on size of teapot
1.50–2m/1½–2yd matching bias binding (25mm/1in wide)

Working the tea-cosy

Measure your teapot (or coffee pot if you prefer). Make up a standard tea-cosy pattern, and mark on to the fabric the outline of the two cosy pieces and the position of the bees and hive entrance. The hive entrance should be in the centre of the cosy, about 1cm/½in from the lower foldline of the cosy front. Embroider the motifs and then cut out the cosy. Fold the two pieces in half with wadding sandwiched in the middle, and tack it in place. Add about 12 horizontal lines of machine stitching through all layers. If you use gingham, follow the rows of checks to keep the lines straight, making bands of decreasing width to look like a beehive (see photograph on pages 18 and 19). When you come to an embroidered motif, interrupt the line of stitching.
Place the front and back of the cosy wrong sides together and stitch, finishing the seam with bias binding.

Egg-cosy

This charming egg-cosy is simple and quick to make. Adorned with just one bee, it makes a perfect small gift.

You will need

Coats Anchor stranded cotton:
  1 skein each of colours as for tea-cosy
Tracing paper and dressmaker's carbon
Crewel needle
20cm/¼yd polyester wadding (4oz)
20cm/¼yd fabric (90cm/36in wide)
40cm/½yd matching bias binding (25mm/1in wide)

Working the egg-cosy

The working method for the egg-cosy is similar to that for the tea-cosy, except that a lighter wadding is used. Follow the pattern (right) for the shape of the cosy. The pattern also shows you the position of the bee, hive entrance, machine-stitched rows, and bias-bound edging.

Apron

Honey bees are buzzing contentedly across the bib and pocket of the gingham apron. Use a bought apron, or make up a simple one with a neck-strap, waist ties, and gathered skirt. If you are making your own apron, embroider the pocket and bib piece first. The bee motifs are transferred and worked in exactly the same way as for the mats and napkins on the previous page.

You will need

For the embroidery:
Bought or made-up apron
To embroider 11–15 bees, Coats Anchor stranded cotton: 2 skeins black 0403, 1 skein each yellow 0298, grey 0398 and green 0225
Tracing paper and dressmaker's carbon
Crewel needle

If making your own apron, you will need 120cm/1⅜yd of 90cm/36in wide fabric and 110cm/1¼yd of 25mm/1in wide matching bias binding for the edging.

Left: The bib of an apron provides an effective area for embroidery and a toning border sets the bees off well.

Framing tricky corners

To embroider right into the corner of a napkin, mat or handkerchief, attach the work to a backing fabric but cut away the area behind the embroidery.

Lay a piece of firm cotton fabric over the inner ring of your ring frame (a piece of old sheet will do). Place the corner to be worked on top.

Press the outer ring in place. Work herringbone stitches round the edges of the corner, keeping both fabrics taut. Tack round the embroidery area, turn the hoop over, and carefully cut away the backing fabric within the tacking. When the work is completed, take it out of the frame and unpick the remainder of the backing fabric.

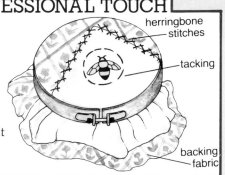

Trace patterns for bee motifs

These patterns are the right size for tracing and transferring to the fabric using dressmaker's carbon paper.

CHAPTER 4

Blanket and buttonhole stitch

Blanket stitch and its close relation, the more delicate buttonhole stitch, are traditional edging stitches. Apart from their obvious practical function, they can also be put to good decorative use. It's worth learning to work them neatly to get the best value from their versatility.

Blanket stitch is so called because it is a traditional edging for woollen blankets.

Blanket stitch *is* a good edging, particularly for non-woven fabrics such as felt, but can be worked just as well in the centre of a piece of fabric. The stitches can be used as motif outlines or straight lines – even as filling stitches. Delicate, feathery effects are possible, as well as bold, bright designs.

Basic stitch techniques

Like chain stitch, both belong to the family of stitches called looped stitches, where a loop is formed on the surface of the base fabric, and caught in place by another stitch.

Blanket stitches are worked a little way apart from one another, whereas buttonhole stitch is worked closely together and usually on a smaller scale – otherwise the two stitches are formed in exactly the same way. Work blanket and buttonhole stitches evenly for a neat appearance with regularly spaced stitches of identical length. They are all suitable for evenweave fabrics, whose regular threads can help you to work tidily.

Left: This multi-coloured embroidery includes blanket stitch edging and traditional peasant-style motifs.

Enlarging and reducing

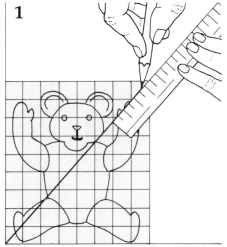

Successful embroidery can often depend on an accurate, well-marked design. Motifs, borders or pictures taken from books or prints may need to be enlarged or reduced according to the work in hand. A good method is to first mark the design with a squared grid. Then copy the design on to a grid of larger or smaller squares to make it larger or smaller. Use this method also for enlarging pattern pieces given on squared graphs.

To enlarge Make a tracing of the design and, using a ruler, mark a square or oblong frame closely

Blanket stitch

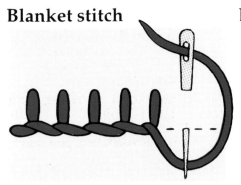

Work from left to right making every stitch the same height. Bring the needle out on the bottom line. If working the stitch as an edging, secure the thread underneath a little way in from the edge, and bring to the front.
Re-insert the needle on the top line, slightly to the right, and bring it out again directly underneath, on the bottom line. Pull the stitch through with the thread under the needle point to catch the loop.
Keep tension even throughout – do not pull any of the stitches too tight.

Buttonhole stitch

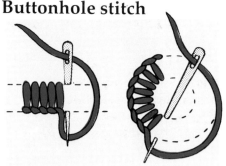

This stitch is worked in exactly the same way as blanket stitch, except that when you re-insert the needle on the top line, it should be close to the previous stitch.
Work all subsequent stitches very close together to form a smooth band.
Keep the stitches the same height, taking special care when working in curves or scallops.
Buttonhole wheels Work a tight circle of buttonhole stitch (caught loops on the outside) to form a useful round motif of any size.

Closed buttonhole stitch

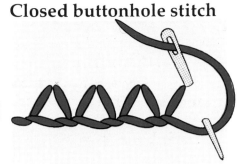

This buttonhole stitch variation is a very practical and attractive edging stitch and forms a triangular pattern.
Bring the needle out on the bottom line and re-insert it on the top line, slightly to the right. Bring it out again next to where it first came out (bottom line) and pull through, catching the loop under the point of the needle. Now re-insert on the top line, next to end of last stitch and bring the needle out on the bottom line, slightly to the right. Pull through, catching the loop.

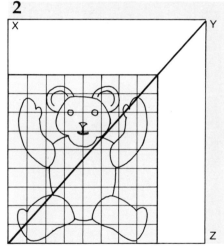

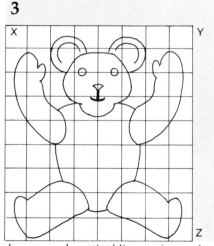

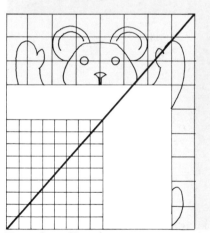

round it.
Mark this area off in regular squares – a simple method is to stick the tracing over a piece of graph paper.
1 Place the squared design in the bottom left-hand corner of a large sheet of paper. Draw a diagonal line from the bottom left to the top right-hand corner, and extend it on to the paper underneath.
2 On the plain paper, mark the level of the desired height for the design and extend the left-hand frame edge up to this height, X. Draw a horizontal line from X to cut the diagonal line at Y. From Y, draw a

downward vertical line as far as the bottom line (which should be extended to Z). You now have a scaled-up frame for the larger design. Remove the original design.
3 Mark the new large square or oblong off into the same number of squares as the small one. The squares will be proportionately larger.
Carefully copy the design, square by square, on to the large grid.
It is helpful to first mark where the main design lines intersect grid lines.

To reduce Use the same process in reverse to make a design smaller. Place a small sheet of paper in the lower left-hand corner of the squared-off large design and join opposite corners of the design to obtain the diagonal line. Decide on the new height and mark the top right-hand corner of the new grid. Join this point to the bottom and side lines.
Divide the area obtained into the same number of squares as the larger design and copy the design on to this small grid in the same way as for enlarging.

23

Peasant-style waistcoat for a child

You will need

40cm/16in black woollen coating fabric or blanketing (90cm/36in or wider) – non-woven fabrics are the most suitable

2 skeins each Coats Anchor stranded wool in red T3559, blue T3323, yellow T3535, 1 skein green T3507

Chenille needle size 2

Fine sewing needle and black polyester thread for making up

Tracing paper and coloured pens

This beautiful waistcoat made for a 6 to 8 year old (70cm/28in chest) is made up in a warm black fabric to show the bright embroidery yarn to best advantage. Work the embroidery in your hand – do not use a ring frame. There's no need to turn in the waistcoat edges – simply finish with blanket stitch. The design is embroidered in blanket stitch and chain stitch with a little satin stitch. Traditionally, this type of design was worked in one colour on smocks, usually in the same colour as the base fabric. In the 1920s it was taken up by Dorset women who called it 'Dorset feather stitchery'. They used buttonhole or blanket stitch almost exclusively, but the chain stitch added here complements it perfectly.

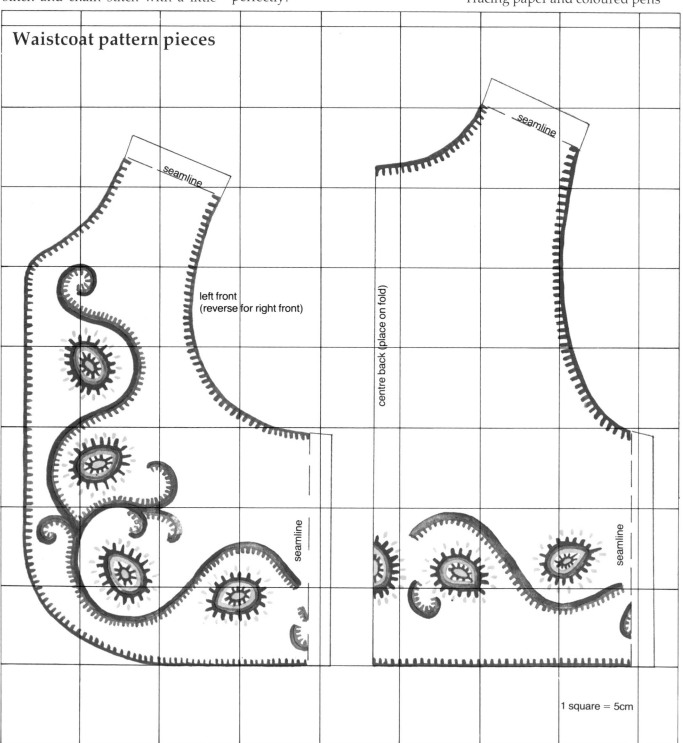

Waistcoat pattern pieces

left front
(reverse for right front)

centre back (place on fold)

seamline

seamline

seamline

seamline

1 square = 5cm

Preparing the waistcoat pieces

Enlarge the waistcoat pattern pieces and embroidery design as described on pages 22-23. Use squared dressmaker's graph paper for the enlarging (one square on chart = 5cm/2in), and then cut the pieces out in tracing paper – right and left fronts and a complete back. Mark shoulder and side seamlines. Mark the main lines of the embroidery design given for the left front and left half of the back on to the pattern pieces, using coloured felt-tips. (There is no need to mark any of the yellow parts of the design.) Reverse left front to trace design on right front. Fold back piece down centre back to trace design on to right half of back.

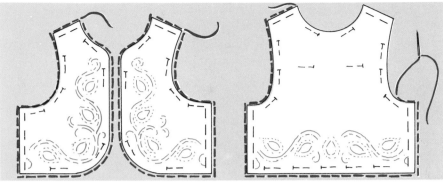

Transferring the design

Pin the three tracing paper pieces to the fabric, leaving ample space between them, particularly at side and shoulders. Tack along pattern cutting lines, then along main design lines of motifs. When the whole pattern is tacked in place, tear away the tracing paper, making sure all the tacking threads remain intact. Mark side and shoulder seamlines with tailor's chalk.

Working the design

The embroidery will be easier to work if you now cut the fabric into three separate pieces. Do not cut along final cutting lines, as the fabric may fray. Instead, cut the pieces out with about 1cm to spare all round.

With two strands of yarn in the needle, work the design in colours and stitches as shown. Use yarn in lengths of not more than 35cm/14in. Work the blanket stitch first, then the chain stitch, and finally the satin stitch and the yellow lazy daisies. Do not pull the stitches too tight. Remove tacking stitches.

Keep the wrong side of the work as neat as possible. Stop stitching about 1cm/½in short of the little red and blue 'curl' motif which comes over the side seam.

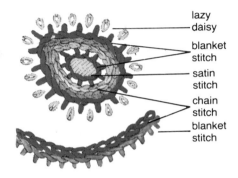

Joining seams

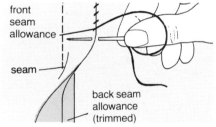

When all the embroidery except that at the side seams is done, cut along the side seam cutting lines and sew the side seams by hand or by machine. Trim the back seam allowance only to 1cm/½in and fold front seam allowance over it; secure with neat hemming stitches. Join shoulder seams in the same way. Now work the rest of the design over the side seams.

Working the edging

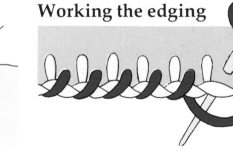

Cut out the armholes along tacked cutting lines and remove any remaining tacking. Follow colour chart, work blanket stitch round armhole edges. With four strands of contrast yarn in the needle, 'whip' the blanket stitch, catching in a little of the fabric between each blanket stitch to prevent fraying and give a secure edge to the waistcoat. (A whipping stitch is one that overcasts another stitch to make it more decorative. It does not always pass through the ground fabric.)

Now cut the lower, front and neck edges along cutting lines and work the border in the same way.

Above: The embroidery appears on the back of the waistcoat too. If you prefer, work the blanket stitch edging only.

CHAPTER 5

Six new sampler stitches

*Building up your repertoire of new embroidery stitches is
exciting – especially when you can use
them right away in a sampler picture. Add them to the basic
stitches you already know and work pictorial
subjects such as this elegant bowl of flowers.*

This chapter shows you how to work two knotted stitches, two flat stitches, and two looped stitches, all of which are particularly rewarding to work. Bullion knots, for instance, are slightly trickier than French knots but look most effective when worked correctly.

Coral stitch is a quick knotted line stitch. Fishbone stitch gives a close, flat effect, useful for working leaves and petals, while herringbone stitch can be worked closely or widely spaced according to the motif. Fly stitch and feather stitch are also versatile and decorative. Notice the different effects of working fly stitch singly, as an all-over stitch, or in rows. It is a good idea, when trying out new stitches, to practise first on a spare piece of fabric.

Right: Floral pictures have a universal appeal and this lovely embroidered version would be equally at home in a traditional or contemporary setting.

Rectangular embroidery frames

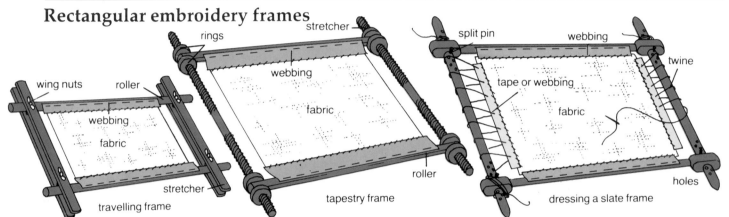

For medium or large-sized pieces of embroidery such as the picture (right) you will need a more substantial frame than a ring frame. There are three kinds of rectangular frame – the travelling (or rotating) frame, the tapestry frame, and the slate frame. Each has a roller, with webbing attached at the top and bottom. On all three the fabric is stretched in the same way, but they have different stretchers.

For beginners, the tapestry frame is a good choice. Try to buy one with its own stand.

Travelling frame The stretchers on this frame have a slot at each end and tension is produced by turning the rollers. Although it is of a convenient size – smaller than the other two types – it is difficult to achieve a good tension on it, especially with canvas.

Tapestry frame This has longer stretchers, with a thread. To obtain the tension, rings are screwed along them above and below each roller. The fabric used must be more than half the length of the stretchers. This popular frame can be bought with a table or floor stand.

Slate frame The stretchers are two pierced slats, which are inserted through slots in the rollers. To tension the fabric, split pins are inserted through holes in the slats, keeping the rollers apart. Slate frames are available with floor stands, which release both hands for working all the time.

Dressing a rectangular frame

The method of mounting light and heavy fabrics on a rectangular or square frame is slightly different. Light fabrics are best mounted on to calico first. Framing light fabrics is described on page 36.

Medium to heavy fabrics

Cut the fabric carefully along the grain to at least 5cm/2in larger than the desired finished size on each side. Find the centre points of the top and bottom edges and mark them. Make permanent marks with a laundry marker at the centre of the webbing on each roller.

Turn under a 5mm/¼in single hem at the top of the fabric and press. Lay it on the right side of the webbing, matching the centre marks, and pin it to the webbing from the centre outwards, stretching it as you go. Oversew it to the webbing with strong thread and remove the pins. Attach the opposite edge to the other roller in the same way.

Now fit the rollers and stretchers together, making the necessary adjustments to ensure that the fabric is kept absolutely taut. Reinforce the side edges by overcasting pieces of cotton tape or webbing over them. Tie a length of fine upholstery twine to one end of the right-hand stretcher. Using a large needle, lash the edge of the fabric to the stretcher by passing the twine through the tape and fabric and round the stretcher. Wind the twine several times round the end of the stretcher.

Lash the fabric to the left-hand stretcher in the same way. When you have finished, the fabric should be as tight as a drum. If it slackens during working, the rollers may be adjusted and the twine can be unwound and pulled tight again.

Bowl of flowers embroidered picture

Samplers do not have to be confined to cross stitch and alphabets. This one includes all the new stitches shown in this chapter, plus some which you will have used already. The design has a lovely flat, stencil-like quality. The use of voided (un-stitched) areas makes it even more effective and less time consuming. The picture area measures 33cm× 43cm/13in×17in.

You will need

50cm/½yd cream embroidery fabric (medium-weight linen or similar)
1 skein each DMC stranded cotton in 783 (gold) and 919 (dark terracotta)
2 skeins in 597 (blue-green)
3 skeins in 921 (light terracotta)
1 skein each DMC pearl cotton in 783, 919, 921 and 597
Greaseproof or tracing paper
Dressmaker's carbon paper
Pencil and ball-point pen
Rectangular embroidery frame
Crewel needles size 6

Transferring the design

Trace the main design outlines from the trace pattern on to the greaseproof or tracing paper.
Cut the linen to a rectangle at least 43cm×53cm/17in×21in. Press to remove any creases and lay on a flat surface. Place the carbon paper over the linen and pin the tracing centrally over the top.
Draw firmly over the main design lines, using a ball-point pen, to transfer the design to the fabric. Remove the tracing and carbon paper. If any parts of the design have not transferred clearly, go over them with a hard, sharp pencil.

Working the design

Mount the piece of fabric on the embroidery frame. Following the stitch guide, work the design in colours and threads as specified, using three strands of stranded cotton in the needle, and one of pearl cotton. The working order does not matter, but you may find it best to work the areas of satin stitch first (some of the main parts of the design).

Finishing off

When all the stitching is complete, check that the back of the work is neat, and remove it from the frame. Press it gently on the wrong side using a damp cloth and a warm iron. Before having the work framed – or framing it yourself – mount it on a piece of fairly thick white board (from art shops). Cut the board to the required size. Remember to allow for the frame overlap (usually 6mm/¼in). Trim fabric to 4cm/1½in larger all round than the board. Place work face down on a clean surface with the board centrally on top. Bit by bit, stretch fabric over the board, pinning it along the cut edge of the board and lacing opposite sides together across the back with a needle and strong thread. Tuck surplus fabric neatly under at the corners.

Trace pattern and stitch guide

Key to stitches and threads

double feather stitch (PC)

fishbone stitch (SC)

fly stitch (PC)

french knot (PC)

herringbone stitch (SC)

running stitch (PC)

satin stitch (SC)

stem stitch (PC)

straight stitch (SC)

coral stitch (PC except 2nd flower from left: SC)

back stitch (PC except water (SC))

bullion knot (PC)

blanket stitch (PC)

buttonhole stitch (SC)

SC = stranded cotton   PC = pearl cotton

Two knotted stitches

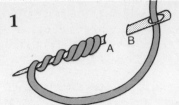 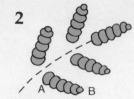

Bullion knots
1 Bring the needle up at A. Take a fairly large stitch from B to A but do not pull the needle through. Twist the thread six or seven times round the needle.

2 Pull the needle through, easing the twisted thread close to the fabric with your thumb. Re-insert the needle at B.

Coral stitch
Bring the thread through to the front of the fabric. Working from right to left, lay the thread along the stitching line, securing with your thumb. Now make a tiny stitch across the stitching line, a little distance away, under the laid-down thread and over the loop of thread to catch it in a knot. Continue making stitches an equal distance apart. Make them close together or spaced out, as you wish.

Two flat stitches

Fishbone stitch
Use this stitch to fill a shape with a central 'vein'.
1 Make a small stitch at the end of the shape, along the central vein. Bring the thread out to the right of the stitch on the outline of the shape, at A. Make a diagonal stitch, across the base of the first stitch. Bring the needle up at B, on the outline of the shape, to the left.
2 Make another stitch across the base of the last one, and continue in this way until the shape is filled.

Herringbone stitch
This is often worked between parallel lines, but may be used to fill a shape, as in the sampler. Bring the thread up on the bottom line and make a small running stitch along the opposite line, so that the thread lies diagonally across the fabric. Note that the stitch is worked from left to right, but the needle always points from right to left. Now make a small running stitch to the right of the first one, and along the bottom line. Continue, leaving a small space between running stitches.

Two looped stitches

  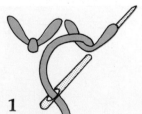 

Feather stitch
Bring the thread through to the front of the fabric. Make a loose stitch by inserting the needle level with this point, and bring it up lower down, so that when the thread is looped under the needle, it makes a V. Pull the needle through. Make stitches to right and left alternately.

Double feather stitch
Make three stitches to the right, then make two to the left, two to the right, and so on. Slope the needle from right to left when working to the right, and vice versa.

Fly stitch
Work this stitch singly, or in vertical rows.
1 Make a V-shaped stitch as for feather stitch, and make a running stitch to hold the V in place. This may be as long or as short as you wish and finishes a single fly stitch.
2 A continuous line is made by bringing the needle up to the left of the holding stitch and making the next V at its base as shown. Work the stitches close together, or space them by lengthening the holding stitch.

CHAPTER 6

Freestyle embroidery pictures

*You don't need an extensive knowledge of embroidery stitches
to create a beautiful piece. The direction
of the stitches and the threads used to work them play just
as important a part in the overall design.
Use them to convey the look of natural things, near and far.*

All the embroidery shown here is worked in a surprisingly simple range of stitches – in fact most of it is created using straight stitches – worked together, separately, horizontally, vertically, slanting, long, short – in every case, the effect comes from the way in which the embroiderer has chosen to work the stitches. Careful colour choice is also an essential.

The examples below show middle distance and landscape scenes.

Middle distance tree trunks

This beautiful study shows tree trunks worked in straight stitches using a single thread of stranded cotton. Mixed tones of subtle grey and green suggest moss or lichen on the trunks, and the stitches are worked in slightly varying diagonal lines to give a feeling of form.

In contrast, the sky is entirely in horizontal stitches and shaded with two blues and white to give a delicate 'wash' effect.

A beach landscape

There are only two stitches used to create this peaceful beach scene. A small amount of fly stitch in green (page 30) picks out the vegetation at the top of the beach. All the other effects are created with straight stitches – horizontal ones for the sea, a speckled effect (use seeding, page 50) in the middle ground, and blocks of short upright stitches amongst the fly stitches. The foreground pebbles are mottled with different shades of a medium silk thread. To give a three-dimensional effect some of them are raised from the fabric with small pieces of pelmet Vilene tacked to the ground fabric. The straight stitches are worked so that they lie close together over the top.

Below: Create a picture to be proud of with nature's own colours and carefully placed straight stitches. Keep the frames simple and in neutral tones.

Dandelion days panel picture

The design for this beautiful panel is based on the life-cycle of a dandelion. This humble flower, generally regarded as a weed, is full of interest from the moment of budding to the time when the last seedhead blows away. The finished panel is divided into six sections showing the flower at different stages from bud to seedhead. An exciting range of materials has been used, to portray the flowers as realistically as possible.

You will need

0.50m/½yd lightweight unbleached calico, or natural silk noil

1 skein each Coats stranded cotton in 0269 (dark green), 0266 (mid-green), 0264 (light green), 0307 (ochre) and 0300 (cream)

1 skein Danish flower thread in 123 (bright yellow)

10 artificial flower stamens (optional)

1m/1⅛yd each narrow – 3mm/⅛in – satin ribbon in yellow and mid-green

Oddment of parcel string

12cm/5in square white felt

Crewel needles sizes 7-9

Tacking thread

Tracing or greaseproof paper

Dressmaker's carbon paper

Rectangular embroidery frame

Green and white mounting card, craft knife and steel ruler

Preparing to work the design

Cut the fabric to a rectangle at least 45cm×36cm/18in×14in. Press to remove creases and lay on a flat surface.

Trace the design from the pattern on pages 34-35 and transfer to the fabric using the dressmaker's carbon paper (see page 12).

Mount the fabric on a frame as described on page 26, making sure it is drum-tight.

Working the embroidery

Refer to the Stitch and Colour Key on pages 34-35 throughout the embroidery.

First work all the thin, stitched grasses using long stem stitches. Make the lines flowing and graceful. (Note that thicker stems are worked with two strands.)

Next, apply the ribbon grasses – cut the ribbon to the required lengths following the trace pattern. Take care to keep them smooth and flat and anchor them on each side with tiny stitches at about 5mm/¼in intervals, using a single strand of mid-green thread.

Below: The finished picture measures 30cm×37cm/12in×14½in but if you do not wish to undertake the whole piece of work, stitch a single dandelion head - in full flower or at the seed stage – to make a charming picture.

Padding and stitching the flower centres

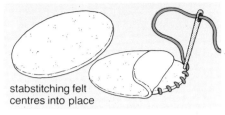

stabstitching felt
centres into place

Every dandelion head is padded with felt. Using the trace pattern, cut a piece of white felt to the shape required for each.

For panels 3, 4, 5 and 6, cut out two more pieces, each slightly smaller than the previous one. Sew the smallest in position first, using tiny stab stitches. Apply the second shape over the top in the same way, then the largest over the previous two. Always bring the needle up through the background fabric and down through the felt. This prevents it from tearing.

Now, following the key, cover the shapes in panels 1, 3, 4, 5 and 6 with closely-worked satin stitch. Stitch the tiny green sepals (Panels 1, 3 and 6) in slanting satin stitch, using two strands of thread. Shorten the stitches towards the tip.

Wrapping and couching the stems

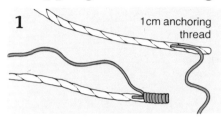

1cm anchoring thread

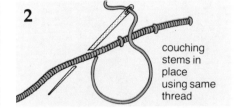

couching stems in place using same thread

To work the raised stems for the dandelions in panels 1, 2 and 3, cut lengths of parcel string for the cores following the trace pattern.

1 Cut three strands of mid-green thread, six times the length of the cut string. Begin wrapping from the top, first laying about 1cm/½in of thread along the string which you then cover to anchor it.

Wrap the string closely until the whole length is covered, making sure none of the core shows through. Fasten off the stranded cotton by threading it a short way back through the wrapping.

2 Now using the same thread, couch the prepared stems in position, keeping stitches 5mm/¼in apart. In panels 4, 5 and 6, work the dandelion stems in slanting straight stitches.

Petals and clocks

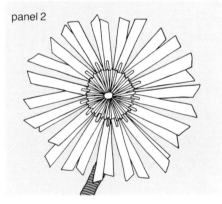

panel 2

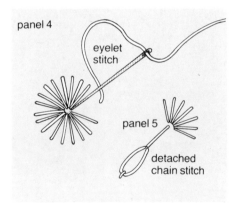

panel 4

eyelet stitch

panel 5

detached chain stitch

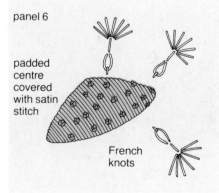

panel 6

padded centre covered with satin stitch

French knots

To work the petals in panels 1 and 3, use varying lengths of straight stitches and the Danish flower thread. Mix in a few artificial stamens (if available) at panel 1 and a little cream thread at panel 3.

In panel 2, cover the felt centre with yellow straight stitches, radiating out from the centre. Cut 15 lengths of yellow ribbon, 2.5cm/1in to 3.5cm/1½in long. Fold them in half roughly and stitch them in place around the centre with the shorter ones at the top, leaving the ends free. Use the Danish flower thread to work more straight stitches over the base of the ribbon loops and interspersed with the petals.

Panel 4 Round each padded flower head, work eyelets formed of many stitches radiating in to a centre point. Overlap them and let the stitches form the outside of the shape. Try to give a feeling of delicacy and transparency to the 'clock'.

Panel 5 Work three quarters of the 'clock' in eyelet stitch as before. Stitch three or four detached seeds flying off at different angles, with a straight stitch and a detached chain stitch under each.

Panel 6 Scatter French knots over the padded centre and add three or four seedheads blowing away.

Finishing off

Remove the fabric from the frame. Stretch the embroidery over the white mounting card, lacing it firmly across the back.

Draw out the rectangular windows on the green mounting card using the dimensions on the trace pattern. Use a sharp craft knife to cut them out. Position the card over the finished embroidery and frame – a perspex box frame is particularly suitable.

Trace pattern, stitch guide and colour key

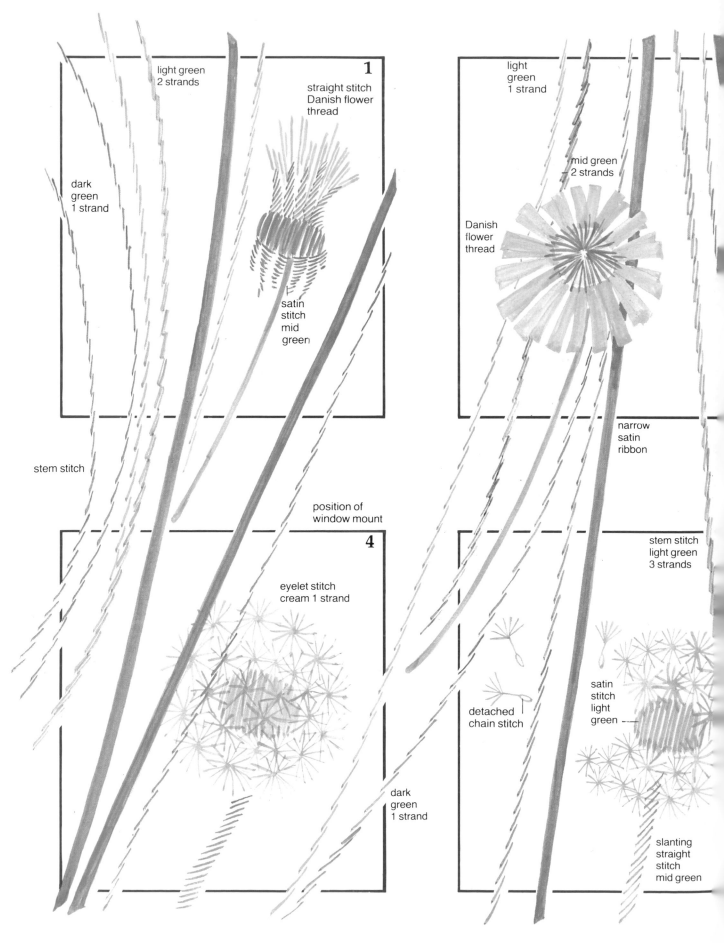

light green
2 strands

1

straight stitch
Danish flower
thread

dark
green
1 strand

satin
stitch
mid
green

stem stitch

light
green
1 strand

mid green
2 strands

Danish
flower
thread

narrow
satin
ribbon

position of
window mount

4

stem stitch
light green
3 strands

eyelet stitch
cream 1 strand

detached
chain stitch

satin
stitch
light
green

dark
green
1 strand

slanting
straight
stitch
mid green

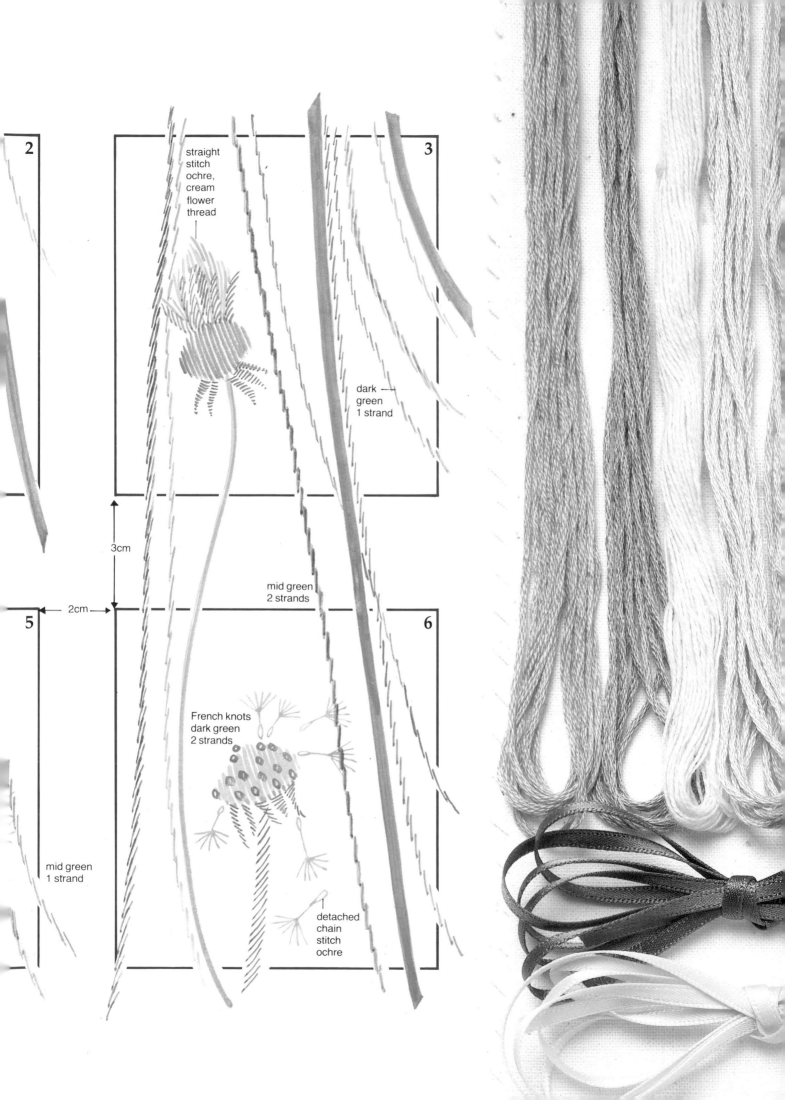

2

3

straight
stitch
ochre,
cream
flower
thread

dark
green
1 strand

3cm

mid green
2 strands

2cm

5

6

French knots
dark green
2 strands

mid green
1 strand

detached
chain
stitch
ochre

CHAPTER 7

Long and short stitches for a shaded effect

Long and short stitch, a close relation of satin stitch, allows you to create a silky, lustrous effect, as well as delicate colour-shading. It is ideal for this beautiful Chinese-style stitchery depicting glowing leaves and flowers typical of the far East.

Long and short stitch

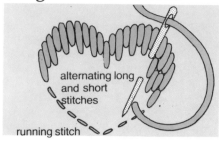

alternating long and short stitches

running stitch

As the name suggests, long and short stitch is worked with alternately long and short stitches. These interlock with the rows above and below, forming an all-over texture suitable for filling in motifs of all sizes and irregular shapes, particularly those too large to be filled by a row of ordinary satin stitch.

The beautiful 'painted' effect is achieved by using several different tones of one colour thread. The stitch is often used in crewel work, which is described in chapter 10, page 49. Padded satin stitch gives a lovely plump, glossy look to simple shapes – making it a good stitch for initials. By slanting the stitches on each motif in a different direction, you can make the same shades of thread look paler or darker.

Overcasting stitch is invaluable for working flower stems or raised, curved lines.

To work neatly, outline the motif to be stitched with running stitch. Work the first row, carefully following the outline of the shape with alternate long and short stitches lying very close together, as shown.

Work the next row of long stitches following the outline created by the first row. Place the stitches so that they butt up against those above, or even work slightly into the base of them. When you reach the lower edge of the motif, fill the last row with alternate long and short stitches as on the first.

Framing light fabrics

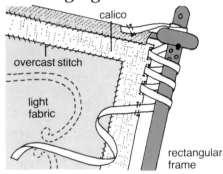

calico

overcast stitch

light fabric

rectangular frame

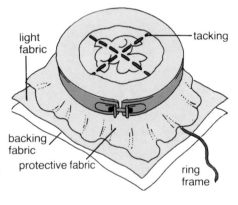

light fabric — tacking

backing fabric

protective fabric

ring frame

Fine embroidery deserves fine fabrics. When working embroidery on a light, flimsy fabric such as silk, it is best to back it with a firmer fabric such as calico or holland.

When using a rectangular frame Cut the calico larger than the main fabric and attach to the embroidery frame rollers.

Using cotton tape instead of twine, lash the side edges of the calico to the side stretchers, securing each loop of tape to the calico with two pins set in opposite directions, as shown. At this stage the calico should be slightly slack.

Centre the main fabric (marked with the design) on the calico, matching the grain. Pin along each edge from the centre outwards, stretching the fabric as you go, then overcast it all round the edge. Adjust the frame to make the fabric drum-tight. You can either cut away the calico backing fabric behind the main fabric before working the embroidery, or work through both layers to give extra body.

When using a ring frame Lay the main fabric over the backing fabric and tack together securely with two lines of tacking crossing at the centre. Bind the inner ring of the frame with cotton tape, then mount the two fabrics in the frame.

If the top fabric is liable to be marked by the ring (as in the case of silk, for instance), lay a third piece of spare, clean fabric over it before positioning the outer ring. Cut the protective fabric away over the area you wish to embroider.

Chinese-style bag

This exquisite little bag could well become a family heirloom. The range of colours used is astonishing – palest salmon pink shades to deep red for the flower petals, subtle shades of green for the leaves and touches of deep violet for contrast.

Work the embroidery before cutting out and making up the bag. It would look equally beautiful worked on ivory or cream silk.

If you only want to work a small amount of embroidery, trace off a part of the design – a single flower for instance – and bring a touch of oriental charm to a silk T-shirt, kimono or cushion cover.

You will need

1 skein each Twilleys Lystra stranded cotton in 532, 621, 530, 524, 724, 519, 520, 843, 544, 612, 628, 527
Crewel needles size 8
50cm/½yd black fabric – Honan silk, Antung, taffeta or other matt black silk or cotton fabric (any width)
40cm/½yd backing fabric – calico or firm cotton (any width)
Ring frame or rectangular frame
Snap fastener
2 sheets tracing or greaseproof paper

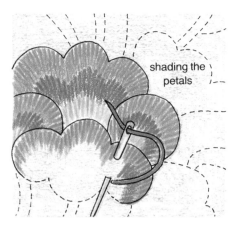

shading the petals

Overcast stitch

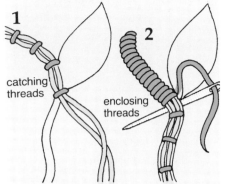

1 catching threads

2 enclosing threads

Padded satin stitch

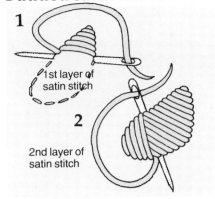

1 1st layer of satin stitch

2 2nd layer of satin stitch

Shading technique When you wish to shade gradually, such as on petals, leaves etc, change the colour of the thread. The progressively paler (or darker) tones will overlap, shading into one another.
Begin at the top of the motif and work downwards, stitching the lower petals and leaves first.
Be sure to keep all the stitches running in the same direction on each petal.

Sometimes called trailing, this is an effective way of giving stems in floral motifs an attractive, raised look.
1 Lay down a few threads on the fabric surface, along the stitching line, catching them at intervals with tiny stitches to hold the shape of the design.
2 Work neat, close, overcasting satin stitches over the top of the laid threads, to completely enclose them.

To give satin stitch more relief and add emphasis to parts of a design, work them in padded satin stitch.
1 Outline the motif in tiny chain or running stitches.
Work over the top in satin stitch, with each stitch running in the same direction, to enclose the outline.
2 Now work another layer of satin stitch over the top, running in the opposite direction to the first.

Black machine twist – same composition as main fabric
Purchased black tassel trim

Preparing the fabric
From the main fabric, cut two 30cm/11¾in squares and two straight crosswise strips, each 5.5cm/2¼in wide and 87cm/34in long.
Trace off the design on to tracing or greaseproof paper. Centre the tracing over one of the squares of main fabric and pin in position. Mount the fabric (and backing fabric) on whatever frame you are using, as described on the previous page. If using a rectangular frame, cut the backing fabric to 40cm/16in square. For a ring frame, cut both pieces of fabric to the same size. Stitch along the main design outlines in small running stitches through the tracing paper, using two strands of the appropriately coloured stranded cotton. This marks the design and also helps to hold the main and backing fabrics firmly together. Carefully tear away the tracing or greaseproof paper.

Right: The unusual shape of this pretty embroidered bag makes it extra special.

Working the design

Use three strands of stranded cotton throughout. Work all the petals and leaves in long and short stitch. You will find it easier to work the outer petal and leaf edges before filling in the inner areas. The secret of success is to work methodically and keep the outlines even. Work the stems and pink design outline in overcast stitch (lay down 4-8 threads underneath, depending on thickness of lines), and the remainder of the design in padded satin stitch.

Finish off each thread neatly and snip it off at the back before beginning the next colour. This prevents you from bringing up strands of the wrong colour on the front of the work.

Trace pattern and colour guide

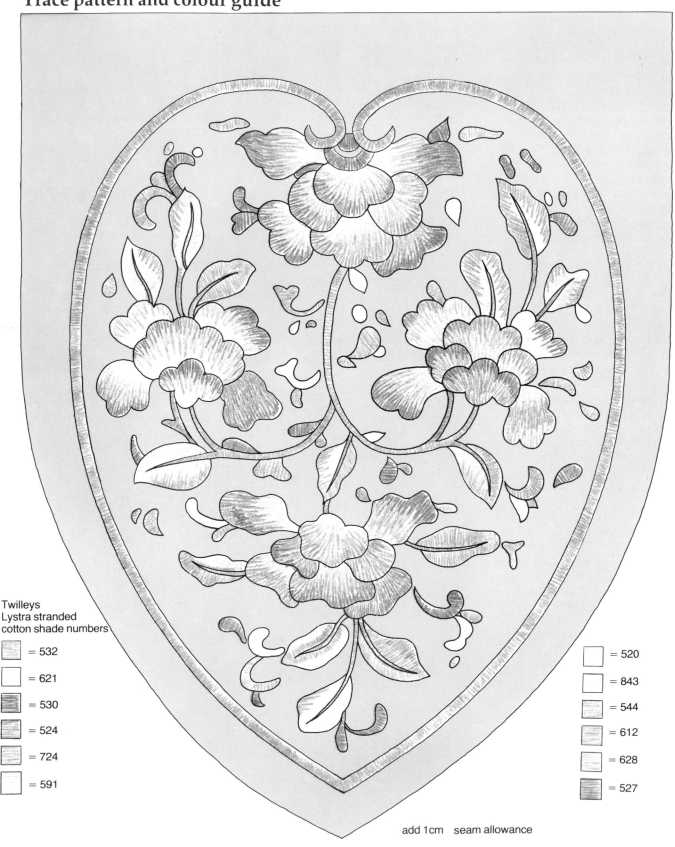

Twilleys
Lystra stranded
cotton shade numbers

☐ = 532

☐ = 621

☐ = 530

☐ = 524

☐ = 724

☐ = 591

☐ = 520

☐ = 843

☐ = 544

☐ = 612

☐ = 628

☐ = 527

add 1cm   seam allowance

Making up the bag

Remove main fabric and backing from the frame. Make a tracing paper pattern piece from the outline given and use it to cut out the bag front (embroidered) and back. When cutting out, add 1cm/½in seam allowance all round. Cut an extra piece in backing fabric for lining the back. Tack the bag back and back lining together along seamline (1cm/½in in from edges). Turn over 5mm/¼in on top edges of bag back and front; turn over a further 5mm/¼in and topstitch. Place the two long strips of fabric right sides together and join with a 1cm/½in seam. Then join the two remaining short ends with a 1cm/½in seam, to make a continuous band for the 2cm/¾in wide bag strap and gusset. Press seams open. With right sides together, and placing one strip seam at lower point of bag, pin and tack one long side strip to bag front, taking a

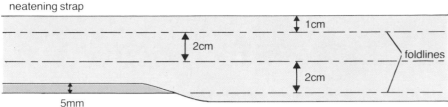

1cm/½in seam. Stitch, taking particular care around curves. Now pin other long side of strip to bag back, taking a 1cm/½in seam allowance on the bag side and a 2.5cm/1in seam on the strip. Stitch. On the strap, press under 5mm/¼in on deeper seam allowance; fold 1cm/½in allowance to middle on opposite side, lap over remaining 2cm/¾in allowance, tack and topstitch strap all round close to both edges. Inside bag, trim seams and overcast to prevent fraying. Attach tassel trim to bottom of bag and snap fastener at centre of top edges to close.

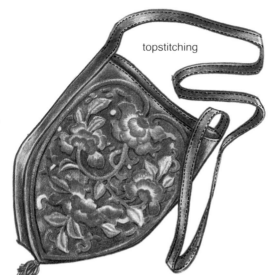

topstitching

— DESIGN EXTRA —

Exotic embroidery extras for your wardrobe

You don't have to work the whole design given for the Chinese-style bag. There are many ways in which you can pick out individual motifs and use them to add a luxurious touch to special garments. Remember to work the embroidery before making up the clothes – you'll find it much easier.

Make up a simple silk T-shirt from fabric on which you have first embroidered one of the beautiful blossoms and some of the leaves. Or position the same motif close to the front shoulder of a silky evening jacket. The centre top blossom, inverted, is a perfect motif for the front of a silk-covered cummerbund. It's not essential to stick to the colours shown here. Try working the entire design in cream and white – it would look stunning on coffee-coloured ground fabric.

pretty motif for a party dress collar

part of bag design added to a waistcoat

coffee and cream colour scheme

decorate the flap of an evening bag

trace motif from bag design

CHAPTER 8

Pattern darning for border designs

Pattern darning on evenweave fabrics allows you to create intricate patterns from simple running stitch. You can adapt all kinds of designs ranging from geometric borders for clothes and household linens to pictorial designs with varied fillings.

Darning stitches as decoration have a rich worldwide history. In Mexico and Guatemala, pattern darning decorates women's blouses with bold, geometric patterns. The blouses are

Below: Traditional pattern darned pieces show intricate geometric and stylized designs.

so covered with stitches that you have to look at the wrong side of the fabric to discover that they are not woven designs. In ancient Peru, people pattern darned geometric borders on the edges of large mantles, and the modern descendants of the Incas still decorate their ponchos with bands of these stitches. There is

also a strong European pattern darning tradition – stylized birds and flowers being popular subjects for embroidery particularly in Sweden where the technique dates back to mediaeval times and is still used today.

People in Southern Russia embroidered linen towels at either end using red silk thread. These were used to decorate the house and cover icons or ceremonial carts or sleighs. The decoration often consisted of double-headed eagles or men on horseback outlined in stem or chain stitches, filled with bands of pattern darning. The Ukraine, Greece and Northern Ethiopia also have a tradition of pattern darning.

English needlewomen this century have made pattern darning popular for decorative bands on table linen and cushions, often combining it with blackwork (see page 44).

Pattern darning techniques

By working rows of running stitch over and under the vertical or horizontal threads (warp or weft) of an evenweave fabric, you can produce patterns resembling woven brocade. Most of the thread in these patterns lies on the right side of the fabric, forming an effect of solid colour. Real woven brocade needs a more complicated loom and takes longer to weave than plain fabric, so pattern darning achieves a quicker result.

The range of geometric patterns that you can create is endless. By working over different numbers of threads, try stitching zigzags, triangles, stars, crosses, squares and stripes. As with all counted threadwork, you cannot make a true curve, so figurative designs become angular and stylized.

How to work the darning

Using a tapestry needle, work in running stitch only. It is very important to count the threads accurately to achieve a neat and accurate result. Work out your pattern on graph paper first, having the grid lines representing the horizontal and vertical threads. If the pattern is complicated, lay a ruler under each row being followed. The pattern can run across the width of the fabric so that each row is worked from left to right (or right to left) and the thread finished off on each row.

Otherwise, a simple motif can be used as a scattered design all over the fabric, or can be repeated vertically to form a multi-coloured band. The darning may be all in one colour, or worked in stripes of different colours.

Take care that none of the stitches are too long as they may catch in use. It is also more difficult to keep an even tension whilst working. To darn a narrow band or a single motif, work in the hand, turning the embroidery after each row so that you are always working in the same direction. Stretch larger pieces of work in a ring or slate frame to keep an even tension. Begin with a long end of thread and weave this into the reverse side of the stitches later. Use a length of thread long enough to complete a whole motif, or to darn across the full fabric width. Fasten it off on the wrong side by weaving the end through a few of the reverse side stitches.

Right: A variety of ground fabrics including hessian, Hardanger tape, evenweave linen and Huckaback.

Types of pattern darning

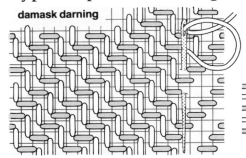

Pattern darning can take various forms according to the materials and stitches used.

Damask darning is a very striking technique which gives an effect closest to that of real damask or brocade. The darning is worked both horizontally and vertically, either in the same thread, or in two shades of one colour to give a 'shot' effect. The damask darning covers the whole surface of the fabric.

Huckaback darning is a traditional Scandinavian technique. Its

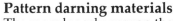

characteristic appearance comes from the fact that it is worked on special Huckaback linen towelling which has regularly-spaced, long floats of threads on the right side. The embroidery needle and thread pass under these floats, diagonally as well as horizontally and vertically. Huckaback can be difficult to obtain but it is possible to work similar patterns on ordinary evenweave fabric – there will not be quite so much thread showing on the right side.

Pattern darning materials

The more loosely-woven the fabric, the easier it is to weave the needle in and out. Evenweave linen and Hardanger can be used for table linen and cushions, and even hessian and loosely woven tweed can be quite effective. For clothing projects, work the embroidery on collars, cuffs, pockets, yokes or belts.

Suitable threads depend on your choice of fabric. Stranded cotton is best for linen, Hardanger or evenweave cotton if you want a dense, smooth finish. For a lighter effect, use pearl cotton or coton à broder which will let the ground fabric show between the rows of darning. On heavier woollen fabrics, use Persian yarn or knitting yarn.

Pattern darned hand towel border

What could make a prettier present than a fluffy hand towel with an embroidered pattern across one end. There's not too much stitching to do, and a length of convenient ready-to-use Hardanger tape makes the work light and easy to handle.

Choose colours of thread to tone or form an attractive contrast with the towel. The design used here includes four different shades but you can work in as many as you like, or in the same colour throughout.

You could also use the embroidered Hardanger tape to trim a matching facecloth or sponge-bag.

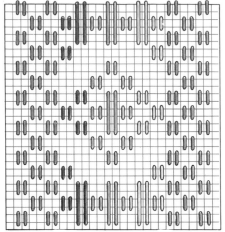

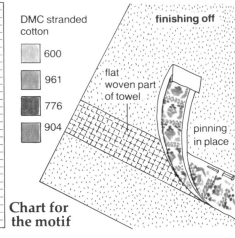

DMC stranded cotton

600
961
776
904

Chart for the motif

You will need

Hand towel about 40cm/16in wide
50cm/½yd of 6cm/2¼in wide white Hardanger tape (22 threads to 2.5cm/1in)
DMC stranded cotton, 1 skein each in four shades (red 600, pink 961, pale pink 776 and green 904 are used here)
Tapestry needle size 22
White sewing thread

Trimming the towel

Begin the pattern darning 2.5cm/1in away from one end of the length of tape and about 1cm/½in from top edge so the design is roughly centred.

Using the full six strands of stranded cotton and beginning with the green, follow the pattern as given on the chart working each row across the width of the tape. The horizontal and vertical lines represent the fabric threads. There is no need to finish off the thread after each colour section, just carry threads down the side of the work on the back. Repeat the pattern about 17 times (or to cover the width of the towel) – an extra six rows of green will finish off the design nicely.

Finishing off Steam press the embroidery on the wrong side. Turn under the excess tape down each long side of the work leaving 3mm/⅛in edge. Trim and turn under each end so the tape fits the towel width. Pin it in place on the flat, woven part of the towel and hem in place.

Left: Pattern darning trims a towel – try darning a name or initials, too.

Set of pattern darned table mats and napkins

A simple pattern darned border makes a most beautiful set of table linen. These mats and napkins are of evenweave Hardanger fabric, embroidered in brightly-coloured stranded cottons. The four-way heart motif which is repeated across each mat is used singly on the corner of each napkin.

You will need

To make four table mats
  41cm×30cm/16in×12in and four napkins 30cm/12in square
1m/1yd Hardanger fabric, with 150cm/60in (25 threads to 2.5cm/1in) in chosen shade
DMC stranded cotton, 2 skeins each in four shades (red 817, yellow 743, brown 433, blue 995 used here)
Tapestry needle size 22
Sewing thread to match fabric

Working the mats and napkins

From the Hardanger fabric, cut out four mats 34cm×45cm/13½in×17½in and four napkins 34cm/13½in square. This allows for turnings of 2cm/¾in.
To begin the pattern darning on a mat, place the first motif 7cm/2¾in down from the top and 2cm/¾in from the left-hand side. Follow the motif pattern given on the chart,

and using the full six strands of embroidery thread, work the motifs in the colour sequence you have chosen. Cut a 75cm/30in length of thread for each motif.
Follow the pattern for each row with a ruler to help yourself work accurately. If you find the work difficult to see, use a magnifier which hangs around the neck.
On each napkin, embroider a single motif (one in each colour), placing it 6cm/2¼in from two adjoining edges. Steam press the embroidery on the wrong side and turn in a 2cm/¾in double hem all round each mat and napkin, mitring the corners neatly. Pin, tack and hem in place. Press thoroughly.

Above: Bright, homely table settings.

Chart for motif

start here

CHAPTER 9

Blackwork: block designs in geometric patterns

These intricate-looking geometric patterns are derived from Moorish designs but are worked using simple straight stitches on an evenweave fabric. Try the technique using gingham to help keep the patterns even and embroider a bright kitchen set.

Blackwork is a counted thread technique and was originally used to make beautifully embroidered clothes. Black stitches were worked on white linen and sometimes a little gold thread was included for added richness. The little geometric motifs, worked as all-over patterns, give varying densities according to the thickness of the thread and the pattern being worked.

The other traditional role for blackwork was as fillings for pictorial motifs. Designs of fruit, leaves, flow-

ers and animals, outlined in backstitch or Holbein stitch, were filled in with different patterns forming areas of solid texture.

Blackwork is normally worked on an evenweave fabric in stranded or pearl cotton using a tapestry needle. It is not essential to stick to black and white – other colour combinations can look just as striking.

Blackwork patterns

The simplest use of blackwork is in block patterns to decorate table linen or cushions as shown opposite and on page 46. Blackwork can be used for pictorial designs but more care is needed in the choice and placing of these patterns.

Many blackwork patterns look far more complicated than they actually are. Most are built up using backstitch or Holbein stitch combined with other straight stitches. It is the way the stitches are arranged that makes the pattern easy or complicated but the range of patterns is limitless and it is easy to make up your own. Samplers of different blackwork patterns can look attractive and if you make your own it can be used for future reference.

Basic blackwork stitches

Small, straight stitches make up the majority of blackwork patterns. Backstitch is useful for outlining and chain stitch, coral stitch and stem stitch are occasionally used (see pages 10 and 30). Two new stitches are Holbein stitch and double cross stitch given below.

Two new stitches for blackwork

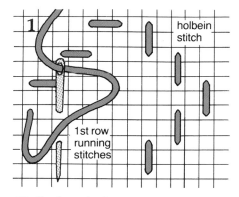

Holbein stitch

This is sometimes known as double running stitch because it combines two rows of running stitches.

1 Work a row of running stitches – passing the needle over and under the required number of threads – following the outline of your pattern.

2 Working in the opposite direction, a second row of running stitches fills in the gaps left by the first row. Try to bring the needle up very slightly to one side of the last stitch and go down slightly to the other side, for neatness.

Double cross stitch

This forms a series of star-like motifs on the fabric. First work a regular cross stitch, then work an upright cross stitch over the top with the horizontal crossing thread as the final part of the stitch. Make sure you work the stitches in the same order for each star.

Gingham kitchen set with blackwork embroidery

This set consisting of tablecloth, cushion and potholder is unusual in using gingham as a background fabric for blackwork. The stitches are placed using the checks as a guide instead of the more usual evenweave fabric and the brown and white colour scheme adds originality to the contemporary use of this traditional technique. Use the stitch pattern guide overleaf to help you form the stitches and work from the pattern block charts which follow. The arrangement of the light, medium and dark pattern blocks gives a patchwork effect. The brown and

Left: This tablecloth is simple to embroider. Choose coloured gingham and matching thread or pick the traditional black stitching on a white background.

white gingham has square checks but it will not matter if you use a fabric with slightly rectangular checks as is the case with many ginghams.

Tablecloth

This cloth can be made for any shape of table – square, round or rectangular. Measure the table first to determine how much fabric you need. For a rectangular cloth such as the one shown here, follow the positioning guide overleaf for the placing of the pattern blocks. For square and round cloths, work 13 pattern blocks as given overleaf for the cushion.

You will need

For a rectangular cloth with 23 pattern blocks

Enough gingham to cover the table and give a good drop at the sides (you may have to join two widths)
8 skeins stranded cotton to match
Bias binding for edging (optional)

Working the embroidery

Find the centre of the piece of gingham by folding in quarters. In the centre check of the fabric, work the centre motif of pattern block five. (If the cloth is square or round, work the centre motif of pattern block seven.)

Keeping a row of checks between each block, work the various pattern blocks following the positioning guide, progressing outwards from the centre.

Neaten the four edges by binding with the toning bias binding, or with a double hem if you prefer.

Cushion

If your gingham has square checks the unstitched border all round the embroidery will be the same number of checks deep. If the checks are rectangular, make sure you trim the finished work so that it is square and will fit the cushion pad when seamed and bound.

You can back the cushion in a plain matching fabric as shown here but it would be more economical to use gingham as given below.

You will need

for a 50cm/20in square cushion
5 skeins stranded cotton
6mm/¼in-check gingham in chosen
  shade – 60cm/⅝yd of width
  112cm/44in or 1.20m/1¼yd of
  width 90cm/36in
1 pack matching bias binding

Left: These patterns are extremely adaptable – here they are used to smarten up a gingham cushion cover.

Crewel needle, size 6
Cushion pad, 50cm/20in square
15cm/6in diameter ring frame
  (optional)

Working the embroidery

Cut the piece of gingham in half – lengthwise for the wider fabric, widthwise for the narrower – and set aside one of the pieces for the cushion back.

Find the centre white check of the cushion front by folding the fabric in quarters and pressing. If you have one, mount the fabric in a ring frame with this check in the centre. Begin by working a French knot in the middle of the central check, using the full six strands of stranded cotton.

Complete the rest of pattern block 7, placing knots in the white squares only. Leave a row of checks all round the block before working the next block diagonally from the first and continue adding pattern

Stitch pattern guide

Each pattern is worked on an area of 13 checks by 13 checks. The stitch patterns show up well because they are worked mainly in the white checks.

For a slightly lighter effect, use only three or four strands of the embroidery thread. Remember not to pull the needle too tightly.

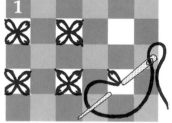

1 Work four detached chain stitches in the white checks only. The stitches are caught down at the four corners.

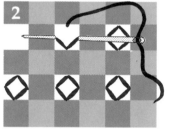

2 Using backstitch, make a diamond in each of the white checks in the block as shown.

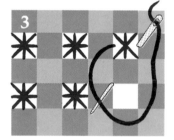

3 Work a double cross stitch in each of the white checks.

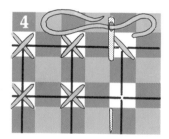

4 Work Holbein stitch between the centres of each white check until you have stitched a framework over the whole block. Now work a regular cross stitch in each white check, covering the ends of the Holbein stitches.

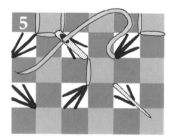

5 Stitch a bird's foot motif in each white check using straight stitches. Each bird's foot has three stitches, all beginning in one corner of the check and running to the opposite corner, and the centres of the two opposite sides. Follow the pattern chart to see

the angle of each bird's foot.
Now outline every other central dark check with a backstitch square, again following the chart.
6 Work a cross stitch in each white check. Now run a thread in and out between each vertical line of crosses without

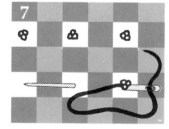

piercing the fabric as shown, starting at the bottom right of the edge cross stitch. Run a second thread down the other side of the row starting bottom left of first stitch.
7 Work a French knot in the centre of each white check.

blocks until you have a chequerboard effect of alternately embroidered and free blocks. Do not pull any of the stitches up so tightly that the fabric puckers.

Making up the cushion

When all the pattern blocks have been stitched, trim the sides of the fabric outside the embroidery to make a 50cm/20in square making sure the pattern is placed centrally. With right sides together stitch bias binding round the edge of the cushion front. Place the fold of the binding on the line between the first and second rows of checks and sew along this line.

Cut the cushion back to the same size as the front and stitch front to back, wrong sides together. Leave a 28cm/11in gap along one side for inserting the cushion pad. Insert the pad, fold the bias binding to the back and hem in place over seam, closing opening at the same time.

Matching potholder

Make one or two of these quick and easy potholders and work embroidery on both sides. Double the fabric and wadding requirements for two potholders.

You will need

For one 22cm/8¾in square potholder
25cm/¼yd of 6mm/¼in square gingham
1 skein stranded cotton
1 pack matching bias binding
25cm/¼yd cotton wadding

Working the embroidery

Cut two 22cm/8¾in gingham squares. Embroider two blackwork pattern blocks on each fabric square, making sure that the corners where the blocks meet are at the centre of the square. Choose whichever patterns you like – up to four different ones.
Cut four 22cm/8¾in squares of

wadding and stitch a double layer to the back of each square. Add bias binding and join the squares in the same way as for the cushion but without an opening. Make a hanging loop from binding and sew to one corner.

Below: A quickly embroidered potholder makes an ideal small present.

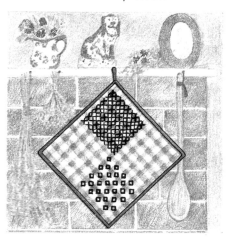

Pattern block charts for blackwork

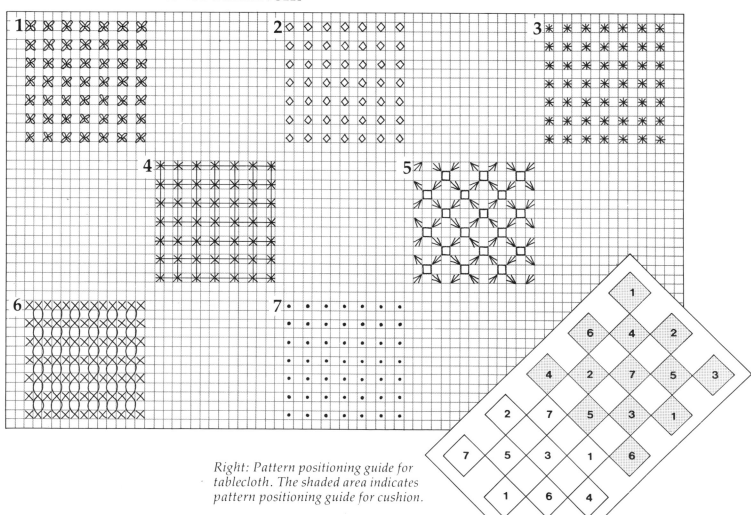

Right: Pattern positioning guide for tablecloth. The shaded area indicates pattern positioning guide for cushion.

47

Trace pattern for embroidery

Here is a pretty motif which would be ideal for crewel embroidery. Use it for a picture or a cushion cover. Transfer it onto your fabric and work with crewel wools or stranded cotton, either in outline stitches or by filling in the shapes.

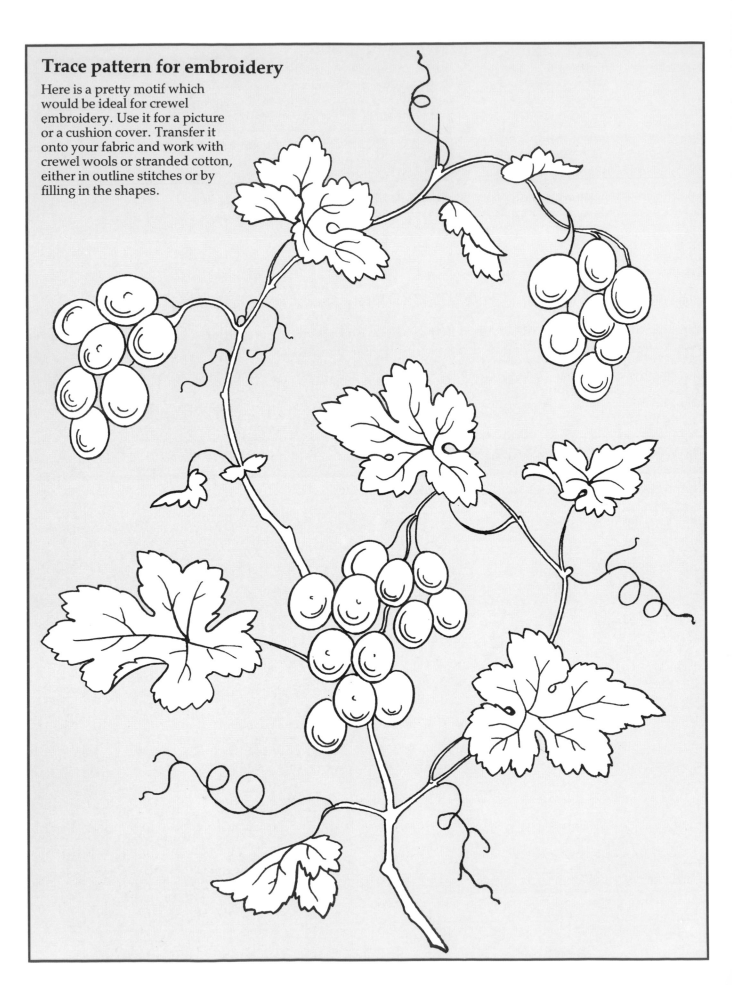

CHAPTER 10

Traditional crewel work

*Crewel embroidery is traditionally English, inspired by designs
on 17th and 18th century Indian chintzes.
Its rich colours and shaded effects make it ideal for this
lovely cushion – learn some typical crewel
stitches and use some old favourites too.*

Crewel designs are usually flowing abstract floral patterns, sometimes with birds, animals and trees included.

Like many traditional crewel designs, this one is worked in wool – a twisted Persian yarn – with stranded cotton used for smaller details. See design on pages 52-53.

Stitch techniques show a combination of filling and outlining with some couching (laid work). All the new stitches you need are shown on pages 50-51. Given in earlier chapters are long and short stitch and padded satin stitch (pages 36 and 37), chain stitch, backstitch and straight stitch (page 10), French knots (page 19), fly stitch and coral stitch (page 30).

Cover design lines with your stitches, carefully following motif contours and directions with stitches such as long and short and fly stitch.

*Below: Pick out separate motifs from
the cushion design to use individually.*

Trellis stitches

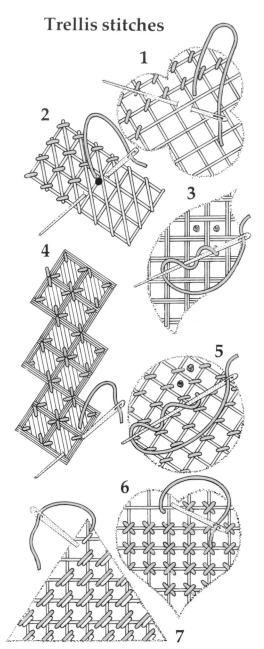

Stitches you will need

These attractive stitches are characteristic of crewel patterns. It is essential to work on a frame.

Trellis stitches

Trellis 1 Begin by laying evenly spaced threads across the area to be filled with all threads parallel. Next lay a second group of threads, across the first ones, forming squares. These long stitches only show on the reverse of the fabric. Tie each intersection of the crossing threads with a small couching stitch as shown. These stitches are often worked in a contrasting colour.
Trellis 2 Work as for trellis 1, but before couching the threads, add a third set, laid diagonally.
Trellis 3 Lay a set of double threads vertically, then weave two threads across them, close together and finish with a French knot in the centre of each square.
Trellis 4 Lay a set of double parallel threads, then lay another set across them, making exact squares between them. Fill these squares with satin stitch as shown and finish with four tiny straight stitches at each intersection of laid threads. These stitches do not quite meet.
Trellis 5 Work as for trellis 1, adding a French knot in each square.
Trellis 6 Work as for trellis 1, but tie intersections with cross stitch.
Trellis 7 Work as for trellis 1, working two straight stitches at intersections, one slightly longer than the other.

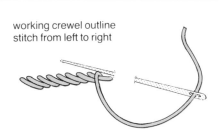

working crewel outline stitch from left to right

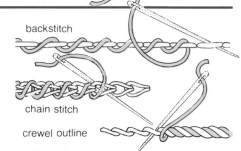

backstitch

chain stitch

crewel outline

Crewel outline stitch

This stitch is widely used in crewel designs, both as an outline or, in several rows, as a filling. It is very similar to stem stitch.
Work from left to right with the thread towards you, bringing the needle up along the design line each time, at the end of the previous stitch.

Whipped stitches

Whipping is the technique of emphasizing a line stitch by threading it with a new length of yarn, sometimes in a new shade. Use a tapestry needle and pass it once through each stitch along the line, in the same direction each time, to give a raised, corded effect. Do not catch any of the ground fabric.

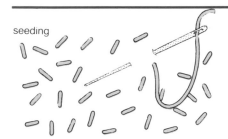

seeding

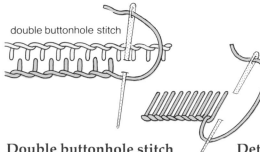

double buttonhole stitch

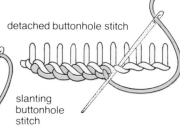

detached buttonhole stitch

slanting buttonhole stitch

Seeding

Make a series of tiny backstitches to fill an open area, placing them an even distance apart and at different angles, scattered over the fabric.

Double buttonhole stitch

Work two interlocking rows of buttonhole stitch, as shown.
Slanting buttonhole stitch A row of regular buttonhole stitches, close together, with the long parts sloping sideways in the direction you are working.

Detached buttonhole stitch

Add an extra row of stitching to the looped edge of buttonhole stitch to make a raised frill. Using a tapestry needle, work one stitch into each loop, being careful not to catch the fabric. Do not pull stitches too tightly.

Twisted chain stitch

A chain stitch variation which produces a textured line – the stitches can twist either way. It looks most effective when the loops are worked close together.

1 After bringing the needle up and looping the thread round it, re-insert it slightly above (or below) where it came up before, bringing it up along the stitching line and

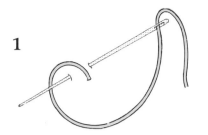

starting a row of twisted chain

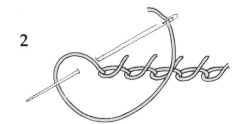

stitches twisting to the left

catching the loop.
2 Repeat for subsequent stitches,

remembering to re-insert the needle outside the loop, not inside.

A crewel embroidered cushion

To avoid confusing subtle colours, make yourself a colour guide by attaching small pieces of yarn to a card and marking the appropriate shade numbers against them.

You will need
½m/½yd ivory embroidery satin
2 crewel needles
1 tapestry needle
Paterna Persian yarn, 1 skein each in 583, 513, 269, 274, 287, 145, 492, 380, 381 and 382
2 skeins each in 573, 563, 280, 286, 462 and 466
DMC stranded cotton, 1 skein each in 3052, 932, 931, 758 and 356
Water erasable marker
½m/½yd furnishing fabric, for backing
35cm/14in zip
Piping cord (optional)
45cm/17½in cushion pad

Preparing to work the design
Enlarge the design so that 1 square equals 5cm/2in. Transfer it to the fabric using the window method (see page 12). Use one strand Persian yarn or three strands stranded cotton. Practise any new stitches first, on spare fabric. Mount the fabric in a taped ring frame (remove it when not working) or a rectangular frame, and make sure it is 'drum tight'.
Follow the working order carefully – it starts with the easier motifs and progresses to more difficult ones.

Motif A
Outer petals: lay trellis 1 (145) and tie intersections (381)
Outer edges: crewel outline (145)
Petal centres: long and short stitch (492, shading to 466 at base).
Crewel outline (274)
Leaves: outline with chain stitch

(573), line with another row (563), fill centres with crewel outline (583)

Motif B
Centre: fill with French knots (462), surrounding with slanted satin stitch (573), outer edge in twisted chain stitch (563)
Remaining space: seeding (492)

Motif C
Leaves: fly stitch (573)
Flower centres: lay trellis 1 (462) and tie intersections (145)
Flower petals: long and short stitch (shade some 287 to 286, others 286 to 280 or 280 to 274)
Centres: crewel outline (145)

Motif D
Long and short stitch, starting at turned-over tip (573 shading to 563, shade lower part similarly with 513 and 563)

Motif E
Centre petal: lay trellis 2 (280, then 274) and tie at intersections (381)
Circle: padded satin stitch (382) and crewel outline (274)
Outer petals: long and short stitch (492 shading to 466, a little 462)
Crewel outline trellis (274)
Leaves: crewel outline (573) and whip (563)
Centre vein: crewel outline (573) and whip (583)
Leaf centres: fly stitch (513)

Motif F
Lower part edges: twisted chain stitch (573 lower side, 563 upper side). Add small straight stitches inside (462 lower, 466 upper)
Flowers and stems: using stranded cotton, detached chain stitch (some 932 and some 931, with French knot centres (758 and 356)

Crewel outline their stems and work tiny detached chain stitch leaves (3052). Add two extra French knots (356) on stems (3052)
Leaf tip: slanting satin stitch (513 upper part, 563 lower)

Motif G
Three small leaves: fly stitch (563 outer two, 573 centre)
Each side of centre: three rows of whipped crewel outline (269, then 274, then 280)
Centre: padded satin stitch (466) long straight stitches lengthwise over the satin stitch (462)
Outer area: slanting satin stitch (286)
Larger leaf, beginning at the top: chain stitch (513) with French knots in centre of each chain (466). Repeat twice more, (563 with 462 knots, 573 with 145 knots)
Between these three rows, work crewel outline (466, 492, 466 between the first two, 462 between the next two, outlining lower edge with 145)
Smaller leaf: crewel outline filling (563 outer, 466, 462, 573 in centre)

Motif H
Centre part: lay trellis 3 (380 and 381 close up, French knots in 145)
Double buttonhole area round trellis (466 outer, 462 inner)
Upper part of large leaf: long and short stitch (563 shading to 573)
Upper edge: crewel outline (573 and 583)
Lower edge: crewel outline (573, whip with 583), fill with slanted satin stitch (274)
Between the long and short stitch and the satin stitch: crewel outline (583). Fit a line of crewel outline (563) below the satin stitch
Smaller leaf: fill outer section with

Graph for embroidered cushion

1 square = 5cm

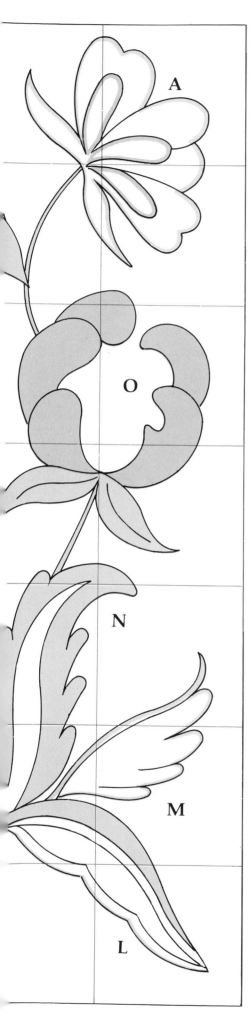

slanting satin stitch (563)
Centre vein: chain stitch (462), work over with backstitch (269), crewel outline round base of satin stitch (466)

Motif I
Lower part: lay trellis 4 (573), satin stitch filling (shades 492 to 466 to 462), tie (280)
Upper part: slanted satin stitch (563)
All lines: crewel outline (573) with upper vein (583)

Motif J
Outer edge: twisted chain stitch (563) another row inside it (573)
Centre area: long and short stitch . (shade from 563 outer to 573 inner)
Remaining area: French knots, widely spaced (583)

Motif K
Flower centre: trellis 5 (lay in 381), tie (380), French knots (462)
Petals: long and short stitch (shade two petals 287 to 280, two 286 to 274, and one 280 to 269)
Crewel outline round trellis (380)

Motif L
Upper side: slanting satin stitch (563)
Lower section: trellis 1 (lay in 573), tie (462)
Between satin stitch and trellis: one row crewel outline, (573) continue to form stem, one row chain stitch (145), and one row crewel outline (583), continue down stem
Below trellis: crewel outline (583), chain stitch (466), crewel outline (462) on outer lower edge

Motif M
Upper edge: chain stitch (462) with a French knot in each chain (274), next row repeat (145 with 269)
Lower edge: slanting buttonhole begin at tip (466, then 462 and repeat), knots on outside
Centre: detached chain stitch (381) with a French knot in each (462)

Motif N
Outer sections: long and short stitch (513 shading through 563 to 573)
Centre vein: chain stitch (583), whipped (462).
Rest of centre area: crewel outline (583)

Motif O
Central area: lay trellis 6 (380 and

381 close up, lay 381 and 380 across), cross stitch (462)
Petals: Long and short stitch – crewel outline overlapping petals first and work over the top (269, 274, 280, 286, a little 287)
Leaves: whipped crewel outline filling (583, 573, 563 alternating)

Motif P
Lower part: lay trellis 7 (563), tie with (563), longer stitch (466). Outline with chain stitch (573), cover this with backstitch (583) continuing to tip and fill tip with coral stitch (513 and 563), alternating knots on adjoining rows

Motif Q
Lay trellis 7 (563), tie (462), use chain stitch (573) and backstitch (145) as leaf P.
Tip: round off in slanted satin stitch (563)

Motif R
Trellis as leaves P and Q tied (145). Chain stitch and backstitch as P and Q, tip as Q

Motif S
Centre circle: padded satin stitch (492)
Inner petals: buttonhole stitch and detached buttonhole (280)
Crewel outline centre circle (466)
Middle petals: blocks of buttonhole and detached buttonhole (alternating 462, 466 and 513)
Outer petals: same as inner and middle (286 and 280).

Stems
Work all stems and remaining leaf veins in crewel outline using a combination of 583, 573 and 563.

Making up the cushion
Remove fabric from frame and trim to a 48cm/19in square. Cut backing fabric to the same size and join with right sides together, inserting zip along one edge and inserting piping if desired. Take 1.5cm/⅝in seams. Turn, and insert cushion pad.

CHAPTER 11

Mountmellick embroidery: a form of whitework

White stitchery on white fabric is a traditional choice for some of the prettiest and most prized embroideries. Here are five new stitches you'll need for the typical Mountmellick work tablecloth with its lovely raised and embossed look.

Whitework is the name generally given to white embroidery on a white background, of which one of the most distinctive types is Mountmellick work. This traditional technique from Ireland was introduced in about 1825 by a lady of the Society of Friends, Johanna Carter, to provide work for the poor people of the town of Mountmellick.

It was originally worked on white satin jean (a strong cotton fabric) with the stitchery in varying thicknesses of knitting cotton. This was used to make household articles such as bedspreads and pillow cases. A finer version for pinafores and dresses was worked on linen, sateen or cashmere, sometimes with silk thread. Designs were usually naturalistic – blackberries, passion-flowers, oak leaves, acorns, ferns and wheat being the most popular. Highly padded satin stitch was used for flowers with French knots being another distinctive feature.

Its popularity was influenced by fashion. Later revivals, in the 1880's and 1930's, added new stitches, and today any suitable surface stitch can be seen in Mountmellick work.

Right: A classic example of Mountmellick work. Most forms of whitework have open spaces, this does not. Threads and fabrics are comparatively heavy.

Useful stitches for Mountmellick embroidery

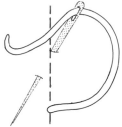
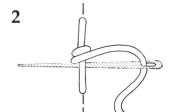

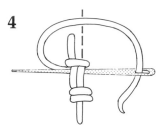

Portuguese knotted stem stitch
It is easiest to start this stitch by working away from you, but you can continue in any direction.
1 Make the first stem stitch in the usual way.

2 Pass the needle from right to left under this stitch, but without piercing the fabric. Repeat, making two little coils round the stitch.

3 Now make another regular stem stitch, along the stitching line with the needle coming up close to the two little coils.

4 Pass the needle under both stem stitches, twice, as before.
Continue repeating steps 3 and 4.

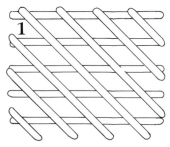
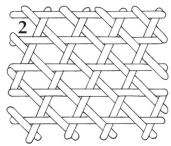
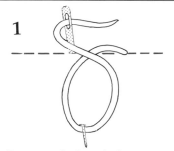
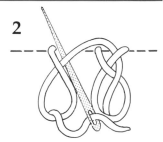

Honeycomb filling
1 Lay a set of threads horizontally across the space to be filled, taking care to space them evenly, then lay a set of threads diagonally across the first.

2 Weave a third set of threads under the horizontal and over the diagonal threads as shown, locking the pattern in place.

Rosette chain stitch
Work from right to left.
1 Bring the needle out at the start of the stitching line. Make a thread loop and take the needle through the fabric, behind the thread and through the loop. Do not pull too tightly.

2 Pass the needle up and under the thread to the right of the loop. Do not pierce the fabric. You are now ready to make the next stitch.

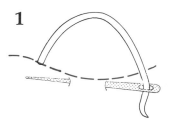

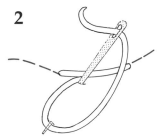

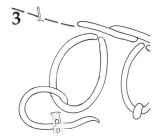

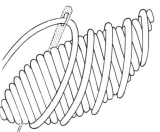

1 **2** **3**

Petal stitch
This stitch creates an
effect of detached chain
stitches hanging from a
stem stitch line. Work
from right to left.
1 Bring the thread out
close to the beginning of
the line. Insert the needle
at the beginning and

bring it out again
halfway along the stitch
formed.
2 Make an oblique chain
stitch as shown, slanting
it in the direction of the
stitching line.
3 Take a stitch over the
loop to secure it and
bring the needle out

along the line to be
stitched. Then insert the
needle at the top of the
chain stitch just worked.
Bring it out at the end of
the first stem stitch,
ready to work the next
chain.

Whipped satin stitch
This makes a good ribbed
effect for stalks and
leaves. Fill the space to
be covered with regular
satin stitch. Lay a set of
stitches across the satin
stitches, approximately
at right angles and a
short distance apart.

55

Circular tablecloth with Mountmellick embroidery

There are four identical passion flower motifs in the centre of this pretty tablecloth. Stitch the design first and make up the cloth afterwards, choosing a square or circular edge.

You will need
For a 114cm/45in cloth
Piece of medium-weight embroidery linen or similar, 122cm/48in square
12 skeins DMC Retors à broder (white)
2 skeins DMC pearl cotton No 5 (white)
Crewel needles size 6
Rectangular frame, at least 45cm/ 18in wide
Tracing paper and dressmaker's carbon paper
A fine, coloured pencil

Marking the design
Fold the fabric in four and mark with tacking along the straight grain of the folds. Trace off the motif outlines and the red dotted lines. Place the tracing in position on the fabric, matching tacking and dotted lines and transfer the motif using dressmaker's carbon paper. Repeat for each quarter of the design.

Framing up the design
The embroidery is quite thick and chunky, so mount the fabric on a frame if possible. If the frame is 90cm/36in or wider, mount the fabric on top and bottom rollers as usual, folding in excess fabric at the sides. Tack pieces of tape or spare fabric down the folded sides and lash these to the stretchers. With a smaller frame, mount a piece of calico on it. Stretch the embroidery fabric over this and pin and tack in place. Cut away the calico behind the part to be embroidered, then tighten up the tension on the frame.

Trace pattern for passion flower motif

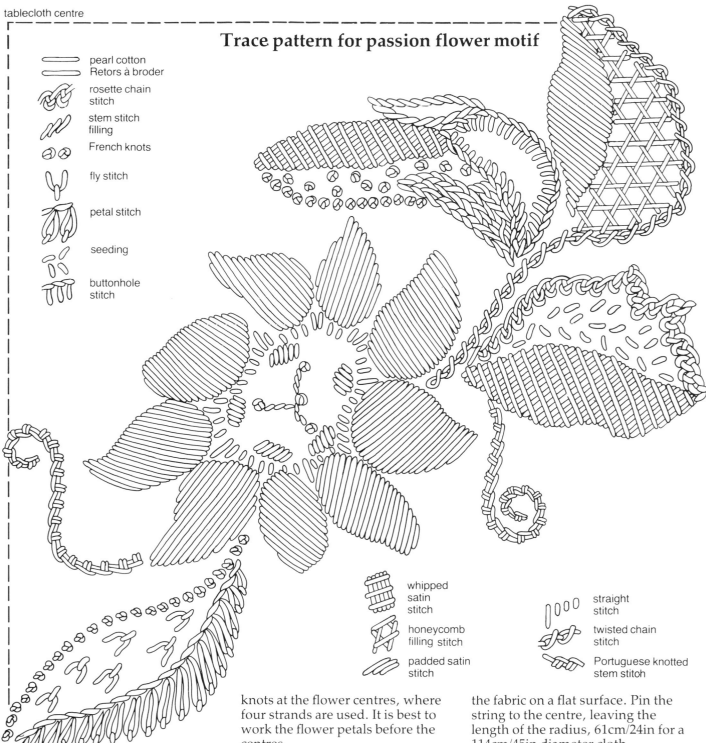

pearl cotton
Retors à broder

rosette chain stitch

stem stitch filling

French knots

fly stitch

petal stitch

seeding

buttonhole stitch

whipped satin stitch

honeycomb filling stitch

padded satin stitch

straight stitch

twisted chain stitch

Portuguese knotted stem stitch

Working the embroidery

Follow the stitch key throughout, and note which parts of the design are worked in pearl cotton and which in matt cotton.

For the padded satin stitch petals (page 37), work over two layers of padding.

Use two strands of pearl cotton throughout, except for the French knots at the flower centres, where four strands are used. It is best to work the flower petals before the centres.

Where there is honeycomb filling, work this first, then outline.

Finishing off

Take the work off the frame and press lightly on the back. Any stitch marks left from framing the work can be removed by scraping gently along the weave in both directions with a finger nail.

To make a circular table cloth, use a piece of string or a tape measure with a pencil tied to the end. Lay the fabric on a flat surface. Pin the string to the centre, leaving the length of the radius, 61cm/24in for a 114cm/45in diameter cloth.

Mark out the circumference with short strokes of the pencil. Trim away excess fabric leaving an even amount all round for hem. To prevent a wavy edge, run a line of machine staystitching around marked hemline, taking care not to stretch the fabric.

Turn under the hem to staystitching, pin, tack and press. Hem by hand or machine, then remove all tacking before the final pressing.

CHAPTER 12

Cutwork motifs for a delicate openwork tracery

Cutwork embroidery is one of the prettiest ways of decorating household linens or even clothes. The design is worked in simple buttonhole stitch and then parts of the fabric are cut away from the finished embroidery to give a delicate lacy look.

There are several types of embroidery which come under the heading of openwork. One of these techniques is cutwork where the open spaces create part of the design or outline it. Cutwork edgings, where a decorative edge is worked in buttonhole stitch and the fabric cut away beneath, add a pretty finish. Running stitch is used for outlining motifs before edging them in a close neat buttonhole stitch.

In cutwork, the stitched design is worked first and the areas of fabric to be removed are then cut away. If comparatively large areas of fabric are cut away, the open spaces are made stronger and prettier by the addition of buttonhole bars, which run between two solid areas of fabric. The stitchery is then known as Renaissance work.

Stitch the butterfly on a tablecloth or traycloth or use the alternative design as a decorative motif.

Materials Choose a firm fabric which does not fray easily, such as lawn or closely-woven linen. Stranded or pearl cotton and crewels are probably the best choice of thread and needles. You will need a small, sharp pair of pointed embroidery scissors for cutting away the fabric when the stitching is completed. For best results, work in a ring frame, although this is not essential.

Right: Pale pastels or white are the best colours for this butterfly cloth.

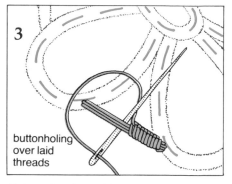

The technique of cutwork

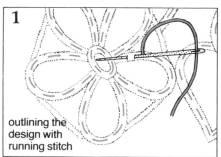

1 outlining the design with running stitch

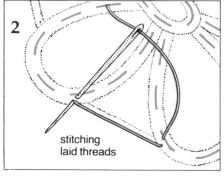

2 stitching laid threads

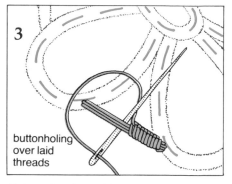

3 buttonholing over laid threads

Mark the design lightly on the fabric. Designs are sometimes printed with double lines. This shows the width of the buttonhole stitches to be worked along the outline.

1 Secure the thread with a backstitch and outline the design in neat running stitches about 3mm/⅛in long. Stitch between the double lines or close to the cutting edge. This helps to strengthen the cut edges of the design.

2 Buttonhole bars If the design you are working includes any buttonhole bars, stitch these next. Insert the needle at one side and take the thread across to the far side of the area to be spanned by the bar, and catch it securely into the fabric.

Bring the thread back to where it started and again catch it securely. Repeat once more so that you have three threads laid over the fabric surface.

3 The bar is worked by buttonholing over the laid threads from one end to the other without catching in any of the fabric underneath. Keep the knotted ends of the stitches in line.

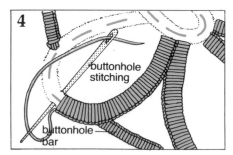

4 buttonhole stitching
buttonhole bar

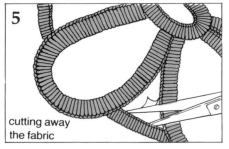

5 cutting away the fabric

4 When all the bars are complete, work the rest of the buttonhole stitch along the outlines of the areas to be cut out. In this way, the ends of each bar are neatly covered. Make sure that the knotted side of the buttonhole stitch lies along the side to be cut to reinforce it and give a neater finish. Anchor all threads securely, and clip off any ends. When all the embroidery is complete, take the work out of the frame if you have used one.

5 Using very sharp embroidery scissors, cut away the fabric in the appropriate areas. Cut as close as you can to the buttonhole stitches. The knots of the buttonhole should hide any fluffiness left by the ends of the fabric threads. Take care not to cut the bars as you work.

A butterfly tablecloth in Renaissance work

Once you have learnt the basics of simple cutwork, you can make this beautiful tablecloth, adorned with butterfly motifs stitched in the same colour as the fabric. The one shown here has four butterflies on it, but even just one would make a charming and delicate cloth.

Apart from the running and buttonhole stitches, chain stitch has been used to give additional padding to the stitching and some interlaced backstitch adds a pretty touch to the head and wings.

You will need
For a cloth 115cm/45in square:
1.20m/1⅜yd cotton (heavy poplin) or linen fabric 115cm/44in wide
or a ready-made cloth in a firmly woven fabric

1 skein matching stranded cotton for each butterfly motif
1 skein coton à broder No 16
1 crewel needle size 8
1 tapestry needle size 24
Tracing paper and dressmaker's carbon paper
Ring frame large enough to hold the motif comfortably (optional)

Stitching the motif for cutwork

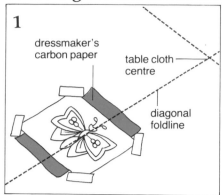

1

dressmaker's carbon paper

table cloth centre

diagonal foldline

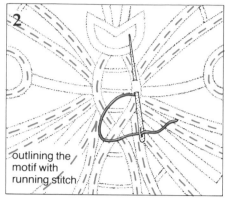

2

outlining the motif with running stitch

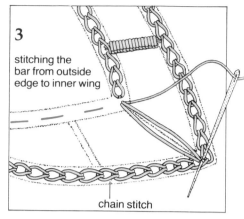

3

stitching the bar from outside edge to inner wing

chain stitch

Preparing the fabric First trim the piece of fabric so that it is square. To transfer the butterflies to the fabric, trace the required number on to tracing paper and arrange them on the fabric. To make sure you place the butterfly motifs accurately at the corners of the square, fold it in two diagonally and position the body of the butterfly along one of these diagonal lines. Leave about 20cm/8in between the motif and the edge of the fabric or cloth. Secure the tracings with small pieces of adhesive tape.

1 Place the fabric on a firm, smooth surface such as a table. Slip a piece of dressmaker's carbon paper between the tracing paper and the fabric, and trace the outlines so that

a clear, but faint line is produced on the fabric.
Remove all the papers and tape and mount one motif in a ring frame, if you have one.
Outlining the motifs The areas to be cut away are shaded on the trace pattern. As this cutting will weaken the fabric, the edges to be cut must be strengthened.
Thread a crewel needle with coton à broder and, starting at the body, secure the thread with a backstitch and stitch around the outer and inner edges of each wing, outlining the shaded areas with neat running stitches about 3mm/⅛in long. The stitches should run midway between the two lines which indicate the width of final stitching.

2 Stitch round the spots on the wing in the same way and finally stitch round the body working in a figure of eight. The weakest point in the design will be strengthened where the stitches cross.
3 With coton à broder in the needle, and starting at the body, work over the running stitch with fine chain stitch, along the *outside* edges of the wings. On the inside line, work along until you reach the first bar. Secure the chain stitch by catching down the last loop and coming up again in that stitch.
Working the bars Take the thread across to the far side of the chain stitch on the outside edge and catch the thread securely in the fabric, coming up close to the inside edge

Trace pattern for butterfly

inner wing edge

outer wing edge

shaded areas to be cut away

buttonhole bars

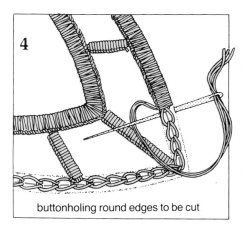

buttonholing round edges to be cut

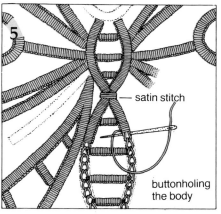

satin stitch

buttonholing the body

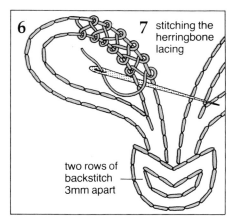

stitching the herringbone lacing

two rows of backstitch 3mm apart

of the chain stitch.

Bring the thread back to the side you are working, catch it securely in the fabric, then repeat.

There are now three threads across the shaded area, and the thread is on the outside edge of the wing. Now work a buttonhole bar from the outside edge to the inside edge. Remember not to catch in any of the fabric.

4 When the first bar is finished, work along to the second in chain stitch, and so on. Continue working in chain stitch along the inner wing edge until the second bar is reached and repeat for a buttonhole bar. When the wings have been outlined and all the bars worked, you can, if you prefer, remove the ring frame

although it is better to retain it if possible.

Working the embroidery Thread the needle with three strands of stranded cotton and work buttonhole stitches all round the areas to be cut.

5 When working the body, buttonhole round one half until you reach the crossover point. Fill the crossed area with satin stitch, making sure when you start to buttonhole again that the knots are on the edge to be cut.

The wing spots are worked in the same way – outlined in running stitch, then chain stitch, and finally buttonholing with the knots at the inside of the shape.

6 The head, wing stripes and

antennae are worked in interlaced backstitch. First work two rows of backstitch about 3mm/⅛in apart, using the coton à broder. The stitches must be small and regular and staggered across the parallel rows.

7 Thread the tapestry needle with two strands of stranded cotton and work herringbone stitch between the two rows of backstitch. The needle passes under the stitches without piercing the fabric at all. Anchor all threads securely and trim any ends.

Take the work out of the frame if you have used one and carefully cut away the fabric in the shaded areas. Hem the edges of the tablecloth by hand.

Alternative trace patterns

motif suitable for corner decoration and edges: repeat pattern as required

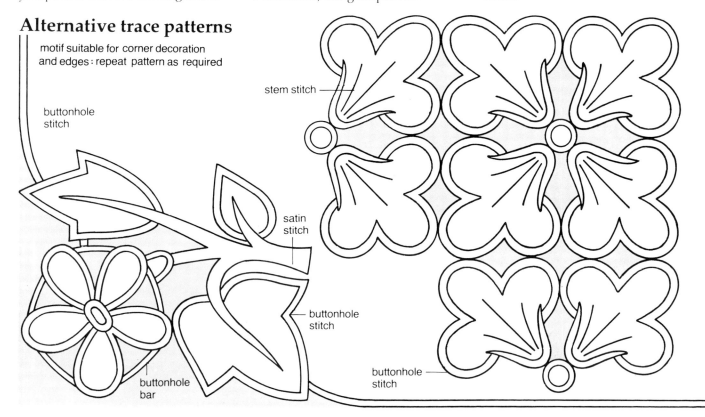

buttonhole stitch

stem stitch

satin stitch

buttonhole stitch

buttonhole bar

buttonhole stitch

buttonhole stitch

CHAPTER 13

Decorative borders in drawn thread work

Use this openwork technique to form decorative borders on household furnishings or to add a panel to a shirt front or a band round the hem of a skirt. The linen mats given in this chapter are laced with narrow satin ribbon and are ideal for a dressing table.

Drawn thread work is a type of counted-thread embroidery which can also be looked on as openwork. You first remove the warp or weft threads from an evenweave embroidery fabric leaving a series of threads running in one direction only. You then work embroidery stitches over these threads, forming decorative bands and borders. The technique is ideal for adorning table linen and, occasionally, panels on clothing – add extra embroidery to the work to create a harmonious piece.

Drawn thread stitches

The most useful basic stitch for drawn thread work is hemstitch. As the name suggests, it makes a neat, pretty hem on evenweave fabric, or you can simply use it for decorating the edges of a border cut within an area of fabric.

You must work each stitch over a fixed number of vertical fabric threads, usually between two and five. The stitches bunch these threads into groups. It is important to plan the work so that the length of border to be worked has a number of vertical threads exactly divisible by the number covered in each stitch.

Apart from simple hemstitch, there are variations such as ladder hemstitch, where both sides of a border are hemstitched over the same vertical threads, and interlaced hemstitch, where a thread is passed through the loose centre threads so they twist round each other in pairs.

Below: Drawn thread borders are much simpler to work than they look, and create beautiful, delicate designs on items like these matching dressing table mats in yellow and white.

Cutting and withdrawing the threads

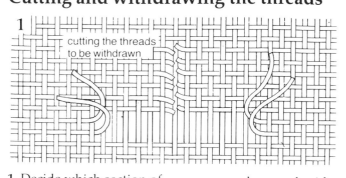

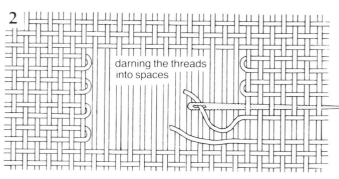

1 Decide which section of horizontal threads is to be withdrawn from the fabric and cut through them carefully at the centre of the open area using a pair of

sharp embroidery scissors. Unpick cut threads using a tapestry needle.
2 You can either fasten the ends with neat backstitches on the wrong side, or you can remove alternate

threads completely and darn the remaining threads back into the spaces in the fabric for at least 2.5cm/1in before trimming. This gives a secure, invisible finish.

Hemstitch

Prepare an open border by withdrawing the chosen number of horizontal threads and finishing off. Work from the wrong or right side, depending on which effect you prefer. This stitch can be worked from left to right as well as from right to left. This is how to work from right to left.
1 Secure the thread neatly and bring the needle up at the right-hand end of the border, two threads down from the edge. Pass the needle behind two or however many vertical threads you are

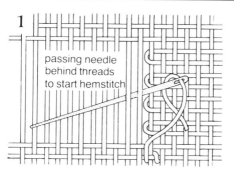

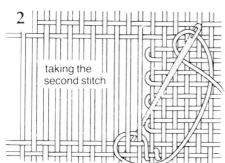

grouping in each stitch.
2 Pass the needle back across these vertical threads, round to the back of the fabric, emerging two threads (or three, four etc) to left of where it

first came up through the fabric. Repeat along the row. When you reach the end of the border, finish off the thread by passing it through last few stitches and snipping off.

Ladder hemstitch

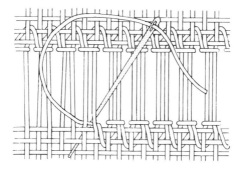

Prepare an open border by withdrawing the chosen number of horizontal threads and finishing off. Work a row of hemstitch, gathering the vertical threads into groups of two, three, or however many you wish. Now work along the opposite side of the border, stitching over the same groups of threads as on the opposite row.
Drawing the threads together on both sides makes them look like ladder rungs.

Interlaced hemstitch

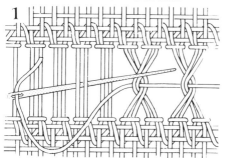

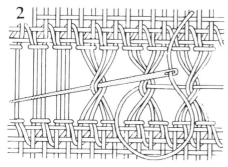

Having worked a border of ladder hemstitch, there are several ways of adding knotted or twisted patterns to the vertical threads in the centre. One of the commonest is interlaced hemstitch – a pretty variation which is simple and quick to work. Working from right to left, adjoining groups of threads are twisted around each other in pairs and held in place by a central thread.
1 Secure the thread halfway up the right-hand end of the open border. With the needle pointing from left

to right, pass it under the second group of threads, and over the first.
2 Bring the needle eye up and over so that the needle now points from right to left, and the first group of threads has been brought under the second one. Pull the thread through tightly to hold the twisted fabric threads in place. Treat the next two groups of threads in the same way and continue along the row, making sure you keep the central thread straight and taut. Secure it neatly at the end of the border.

Drawn thread work mats

This delightful set of three mats has drawn thread work borders, satin stitch embroidery and a ribbon trim. Practical as well as pretty, when the mats are used on a highly-polished wood surface they will prevent your trinkets, vases and cosmetics from scratching the surface while the dark grain of the wood shows off the delicate twisted thread pattern.

Although the decorative hemstitches given on pages 63 and 65 are worked using stranded cotton which matches the evenweave linen of the mats, you may prefer to experiment with different coloured cottons which contrast with the background fabric you are using. Work with three or more strands in the needle to obtain a colourful effect.

You will need
Coats Anchor stranded cotton,
  2 skeins each gorse yellow 0301,
  buttercup 0293, cream 0386 and
  white 0402
30cm/⅜yd white evenweave fabric,
  21 threads to 2.5cm/1in (width
  150cm/60in)
4.80m/5¼yd Offray white double-
  face satin ribbon width 3mm/⅛in
Tapestry needles size 20 and 24

Preparing the fabric
The width of the large mat is equal to each of the sides of the square mats. It is well worth taking the trouble to prepare the pieces of fabric carefully and count the threads accurately.

Cut one piece 43cm×24cm/ 17in×9½in and two pieces 24cm×24cm/9½in×9½in. Mark the centre line of each piece of fabric in both directions with a row of tacking stitches. The position of the drawn thread borders is determined by counting threads outwards from the centre. The layout diagram shows the lower left-hand quarter of both the oblong and square mats and gives the numbers of fabric threads between the centres and the borders. The broken lines YY indicate the centre lines of the oblong mat, and YZ are the centre lines of the square mats. All numerals denote numbers of threads and the bracketed numerals show the number of threads which have been withdrawn.

Working the oblong mat
With one long side of the fabric facing, and following the layout diagram, cut through twelve horizontal threads at the centre. Prepare the left-hand half of the border first. Withdraw every *alternate* cut thread completely. Now withdraw the remaining threads back 128 threads to the left, darn the loose ends invisibly into the spaces left by the threads removed and trim. Complete the right-hand side of the border in the same way.

Repeat the procedure on the other three sides of the mat, following the layout diagram, until you have cut and finished off the four borders.

Begin hemstitching at the centre tacking line on one long side. Using three strands of white stranded cotton and size 24 needle, work ladder hemstitch on the right side over groups of two threads on all long edges of the open borders. The two long borders should have 128 pairs of threads, the two short borders 48 pairs. The arrangement of stitches at each corner is shown in the diagram.

Satin stitch Using the full six strands of thread and size 20

Below: Tie neat ribbon bows at the corners and snip diagonally across the ends.

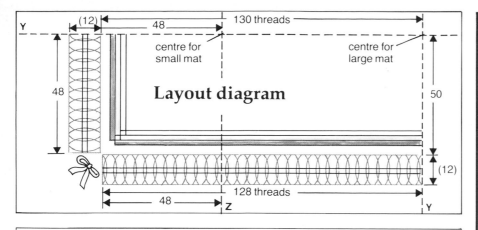

Layout diagram

Y · (12) · 48 · 130 threads · centre for small mat · centre for large mat · 48 · 50 · 128 threads · 48 · Z · Y · (12)

Stitching guide

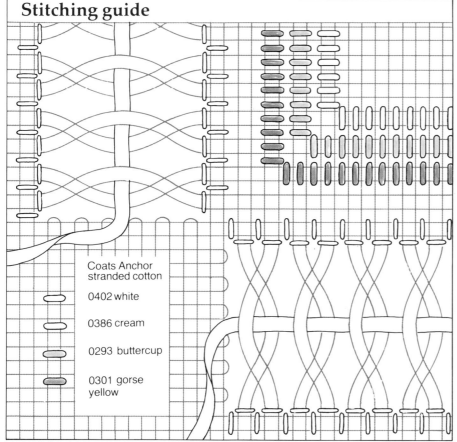

Coats Anchor
stranded cotton

0402 white

0386 cream

0293 buttercup

0301 gorse
yellow

needle, work three bands of satin stitch – each band over two fabric threads – in the colours shown. The dark yellow is on the outside, then paler yellow, then cream – leave two free threads between the hemstitching and the satin stitch as shown in the diagram.

Working the square mats
Following the layout diagram, cut, withdraw and darn in loose ends of the borders. Work ladder hemstitch in the same way as for the oblong mat, beginning at the centre of each border. Add the same satin stitch embroidery within the borders.

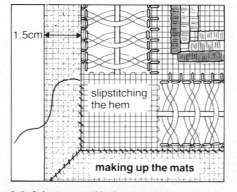

1.5cm

slipstitching the hem

making up the mats

Making up all the mats
Allow a 1.5cm/⅝in border between the drawn threadwork and the folded edge of each mat. Turn over

Hemstitch variation
Here is another decorative variation on basic hemstitch which can be substituted for the borders used on the mats.

Working Italian hemstitch
Withdraw threads from the fabric for the required width, miss the required number of threads and withdraw another band of the same number of threads as first.
1 Bring the needle out two vertical threads to the left (or the required number) in the upper band of drawn threads; pass the needle round and behind these two threads, bringing it out where the needle first emerged.
2 Pass the needle diagonally across the fabric and behind and round the next two threads in the lower band, emerging two threads up and two threads to the left in the upper band, ready for next stitch. Repeat steps.

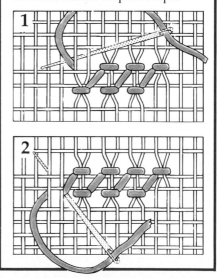

a double hem on the wrong side to the edge of the ladder hemstitch and slipstitch in place, mitring the corners.
Adding the ribbon trim Cut ten lengths of ribbon 36cm/14in long and two lengths 58cm/23in long. Thread each length of ribbon on to a needle and work interlaced hemstitch between all the hemstitched edges. Leave equal lengths of ribbon loose at each end to tie together in bows at the corners. The interlaced ribbon should be pulled firmly to lie in position through the centre of the twisted groups of threads.

CHAPTER 14

Lacy pulled thread stitches

*Pulled thread work is a form of counted thread embroidery
where the stitches are pulled tight, making
pretty, open patterns on the ground fabric. There's no need
to withdraw any threads and if you work
the stitches as fillings, the effect is beautiful.*

Some of the earliest existing pulled thread work comes from seventeenth century Italy. Decorative bands, probably from church linen, are worked in red or green silk threads on linen fabrics, using backgrounds of pulled thread stitches to surround plain motifs.

Eighteenth century pulled thread is lighter and more delicate and often worked in imitation of expensive lace. Satin stitch, shadow work and pulled work filling combined in pretty flower patterns adorn ladies' fichus, aprons and sleeve ruffles. Pulled work is also seen accompanied by English and trapunto quilting.

During the nineteenth century, the fine work develops into Ayrshire work but with more emphasis on the satin stitch motifs, and only a little filling. Pulled work is seen on European folk costume and household linens rather than on fashionable dress. Most of the work is bold and geometric on white or cream linens using matching thread.

The Scandinavian countries have carried on their peasant traditions today and use pulled work in both pictorial and geometric designs on their table linens and furnishings.

Choosing suitable materials

You can work pulled thread on any loosely-woven evenweave fabric using a matching or toning thread. Evenweave linen is best for table wear which needs to be washed regularly. For clothes or furnishings, you could use openly woven cotton or evenweave wool. The more open the weave, the lacier the finish. Some furnishing fabrics with a loose, open weave, or even hessian, can be suitable for pulled thread work.

Thread It's best to use a matching thread, or, if adding colours, be sure that they are not too bright and tone with the fabric. As each stitch has to

Framed cross filling

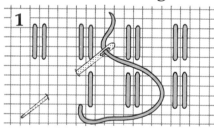

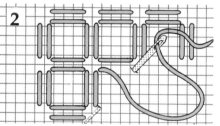

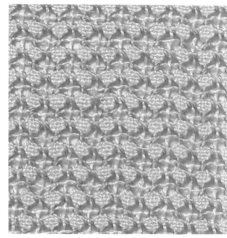

1 Work in pairs of satin stitches over four threads, leaving four threads between each pair. Pull all stitches tightly and leave one horizontal thread free between each row.

2 Now work horizontal rows of pairs of satin stitches (the other direction), again over four threads. As the stitches are pulled tightly, a cross appears in each hole.

Satin stitch filling

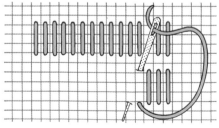

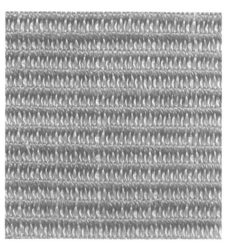

Work along the row in vertical satin stitch, each stitch over four horizontal threads. Pull each stitch tightly to draw the horizontal threads together, creating an open effect.

Honeycomb filling

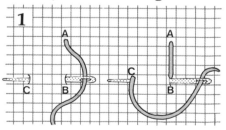

1 Working all stitches over four threads, bring the needle up at A, insert it at B and bring it out at C. Re-insert it at B, coming up at C to make a backstitch.

be pulled tight, the thread must be strong enough to stand the strain. Choose a thread of the same thickness as the fabric threads. Coton à broder, buttonhole twist, crochet cotton and pearl cotton are all good for pulled work. When using a coarse evenweave fabric, the unravelled warp threads can be used for the pulled work.

Always stretch the work in an embroidery hoop or frame. This makes it much easier to count threads when stitching and keep tension even. Darn all thread ends into the back of the work.

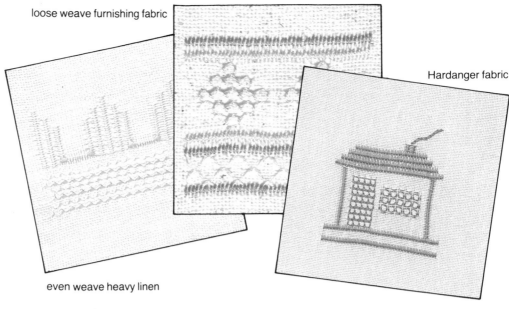

loose weave furnishing fabric

Hardanger fabric

even weave heavy linen

Designs

Geometric or pictorial designs are equally suitable for pulled thread work which is often used as a filling for motifs. Work the outline first in stem stitch, chain stitch or whipped chain stitch and fill in with the chosen pulled thread stitch.

Filling stitches

Most pulled thread stitches are worked from right to left, turning the work at the end of each row.

Begin the first row of the filling at the widest part of the motif, filling the motif on first one side of the first row, then the other. At the beginning and end of each row make part stitches against the outline to add strength. If the first stitch on the next row begins in the same hole as the last stitch of the previous row, take a small stitch through the back of the outline stitches on the wrong side of the work between the two stitches.

Four-sided filling

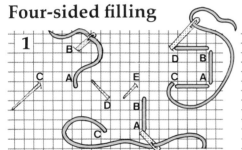

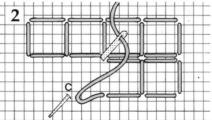

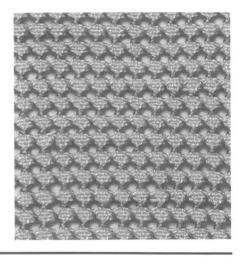

1 Working over four threads, bring the needle up at A, insert it at B and bring it out at C. Insert it again at A, bring out again at D. Next insert at B, bring out at C, and finally insert at D, bringing out at E ready for the next square.

2 Work in rows from right to left, turning the work at the end of each row. Pull all the stitches tight as you work. Notice how horizontal stitches share holes with adjacent stitches in the rows above and below.

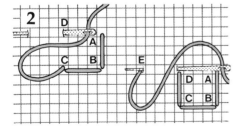

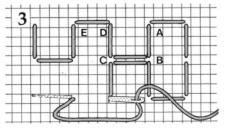

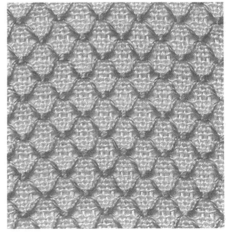

2 Insert the needle at D, bringing it out at E. Finally, insert it again at D, coming out at E to make the backstitch.

3 Work from right to left turning at the end of each row. As each stitch is pulled tight during working, the vertical stitches become slanted. The backstitches share holes with stitches in the rows above and below.

Café curtain with green leaf border

Above: Pulled thread filling stitches give a light, lacy look to simple motifs.

Fresh green leaf motifs in pulled thread work are the ideal decoration for a café curtain. An embroidered curtain like this one is the perfect answer when you need a half curtain, yet wish to add interest to a window The curtain shown here is made up in pure evenweave linen, but you could use an open-weave furnishing fabric.

You will need

For a curtain measuring 90cm/36in wide and up to 89cm/35in deep
1m/1yd white evenweave linen, width 140cm/54in, 20 threads to 2.5cm/1in
DMC pearl cotton No 5, 2 skeins each in 704 (mid green) and 966 (pale green) and 1 skein in 369

(very pale green)
Sewing thread to match fabric
20cm/8in diameter embroidery ring frame
Tapestry needle size 22
Dressmaker's carbon paper
Tracing paper
Plain paper
Hanging rod or wire

Preparing the fabric and working the embroidery

Trim the piece of fabric to 110cm/
43in width and mark 10cm/4in in
from each side edge with a row of
contrasting tacking along the
straight grain. (These form the
finished curtain edges).
Tack a line across the fabric 15cm/
6in up from the bottom edge then
tack a line up the centre of the
fabric.
Enlarge the leaf shape from the
pattern below (1 square = 3cm/
1¼in).
Using dressmaker's carbon paper,
trace five leaf shapes across the
lower edge of the fabric, spacing
them evenly between the two outer
lines of tacking and having the
lower tip of each leaf two fabric
threads above the lower line.

Working the embroidery

First outline each leaf motif in
whipped chain stitch (page 50)
using shade 704. (The central ribs
are added after the pulled work
fillings have been worked.)
Following the stitch scheme and
with fabric stretched tightly, work
the appropriate filling in each leaf

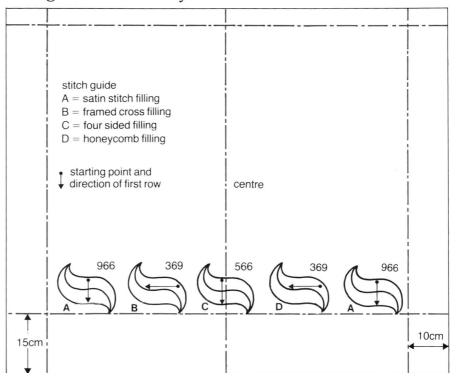

stitch guide
A = satin stitch filling
B = framed cross filling
C = four sided filling
D = honeycomb filling

• starting point and
↓ direction of first row

centre

966   369   566   369   966

A   B   C   D   A

15cm   10cm

shape. Begin the first row of the
pattern across the widest part of
each leaf as indicated.
When all the leaves are completed,

work the central rib of each in
whipped chain stitch in shade 704.
Steam-press the work on the wrong
side.

Finishing off the curtain

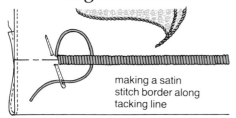

making a satin
stitch border along
tacking line

Remove central vertical tacking
thread. Cut down each side of the
curtain 2cm/¾in outside the tacked
lines and press along tacked lines.
Make narrow double hems along
sides. Pin, tack and catch into place
with the matching sewing thread.
Remove tacking threads.
Fold lower hem to wrong side
6cm/2¼in below lower tacking line,
pin and tack turning in place.
Using shade 704, make a counted
satin stitch border over five threads
along tacking line, making sure that
each stitch passes through both
layers of fabric. Trim away excess
fabric on reverse, close to stitches.
Trim and fold over fabric across the
top of the curtain to make a casing
at required position, for hanging.
Pin, tack and hem in place. Press.

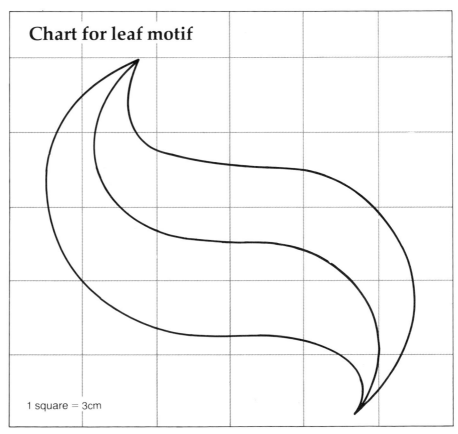

Chart for leaf motif

1 square = 3cm

69

CHAPTER 15

Mock smocking adds a special touch

Smocking is not just a decoration for babies and children's clothes – give a unique designer touch to your own blouse or shirtdress with bands of elegant smocking. Using a quick technique called mock smocking you can smock pretty collars and cuffs in no time.

Smocking is the technique of gathering fabric with rows of decorative stitching, giving it elasticity and fullness.

The earliest existing English examples are the wonderful country smocks of the 19th century on which intricate smocking incorporates extra embroidery stitches – chain stitch, feather stitch and buttonhole.

Smocked dresses were introduced in the 1880's and have remained firm favourites in babies' and childrens' wardrobes ever since.

Fabrics and threads

Any fabric which can be gathered satisfactorily can be smocked. Among the most suitable are cotton lawn, voile, fine wool, and cotton/wool mixtures.

Some fabrics have built-in smocking guides in their construction or design – a regular marking which enables them to be gathered up evenly. Needlecord, checked, striped or spotted fabrics and obvious even-weaves like hessian all fall in to this category.

Plain fabrics need extra preparation – the addition of smocking dots as a guide.

When smocking a printed fabric, make sure that the print and the smocking stitches enhance each other. Match the smocking thread to the weight of the fabric; single twisted threads such as pearl cotton, coton à broder, silk twist, linen thread, or even crochet cotton are best. Choose a thread which tones with the ground fabric, or picks out a colour from a striped or printed fabric.

Use crewel needles in fine sizes.

Marking fabric for smocking

Smocking is always worked on the fabric before cutting out and making up the garment.

Real smocking is worked on fabric which has first been gathered up evenly into tubes and requires about three times the finished width of fabric. In mock smocking (see below) the fabric is gathered as it is being smocked. In either case, the fabric needs to be marked with regularly spaced dots (unless it has a built-in guide – such as stripes) so that the gathers are neat and even.

Printed transfers of smocking dots in various sizes, obtainable from needlework shops, are transferred by ironing them on to the wrong side of the work.

Mock smocking

This type of smocking is not as strong as real smocking, so it should only be used as decoration.

However, it looks like real smocking and is quicker to work – smocking and gathering are done in one step. The smocking dots are transferred on to the *right* side of the fabric.

To do mock smocking you need only twice the finished width of fabric so it does not produce the fullness of real smocking. It is therefore often used for thicker fabrics such as corduroy. Even knitting, which would become very bulky if smocked by the traditional method, can be mock smocked successfully.

All the smocking stitches can be worked in the usual way, picking up dots (instead of tubes of fabric as on real smocking), and pulling each stitch tight, to gather up the fabric.

Two basic mock smocking stitches are shown here – cable stitch and surface honeycomb stitch.

Any edges not to be enclosed in a seam need to be neatened before you begin the smocking.

Mock cable stitch

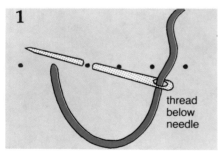

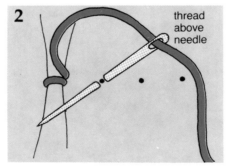

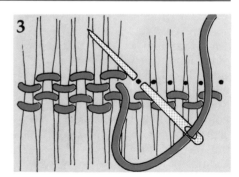

This pretty stitch is worked along a single row of dots.
Bring the needle out at the first dot, on the left-hand side of the row.
1 With the thread lying below the needle, pick up the next dot with the needle running from right to left. Pull thread to gather the fabric.

2 Now pick up the next dot with the thread lying above the needle. Continue along the row, placing the thread alternately below and above the needle. Make sure that all your gathers are even – giving the work the occasional pull from top to bottom to regulate the gathers.

3 Work the next row along the row of dots immediately below, turning the work so that you are still working from left to right and the worked row is beneath the dots you are stitching over.

70

Mock surface honeycomb stitch

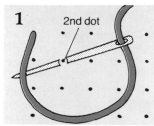

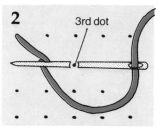

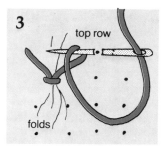

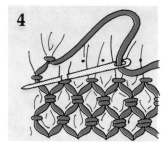

1 Working from left to right, bring the needle out at the first dot on the top row and make a small backstitch.
Now pick up the dot diagonally below to the right, with the needle running from right to left, and pull through. Pull these up and down stitches only slightly.

2 With your next stitch, pick up the next right-hand dot. The needle should still run from right to left. Pull tight to draw up the fabric, which forms two small folds.
Make sure you use every dot, taking the thread vertically up and down.

3 Now pick up the next dot on the top row so that the thread is taken round the right-hand fold. Join this dot to its right-hand neighbour with another stitch in the same way. Give the smocking the occasional pull from top to bottom to regulate the gathers.

4 On the next and other second rows, turn the work so you are still smocking from left to right. Treat the dots in the upper row as normal. On the lower (already gathered) row, pick up each left-hand fold, then make a small stitch over both folds close to the one below.
Bring the needle out between the two folds before picking up the next upper row dot.

Below: A fresh look for a pair of blouses – choose a matching embroidery thread for mock smocking on collars and cuffs.

Crisply smocked collars and cuffs

Give a touch of originality to a blouse already in your wardrobe or adapt a classical blouse pattern with the addition of a fresh white lawn smocked collar and cuffs.

The quick mock smocking technique is ideal for both these projects because it produces a neat frill.

Changing a plain collar

Here's how to transform a plain ready-made blouse into something special. Just remove the original collar and replace it with a smocked frill.

You will need

Blouse with regular or tab collar
10cm/⅛yd white cotton lawn (width 90cm/36in)
1 skein Coats Anchor coton à broder or stranded cotton to match blouse
5cm/2in-wide light iron-on Vilene
White sewing thread
Smocking dots size G transfer or one sheet each of tracing paper and dressmaker's carbon paper
Press stud

Preparing the collar

Remove collar and collar band from blouse and measure neck edge from centre front to centre front. Cut a strip of lawn 6cm/2¼in wide and twice neck measurement plus 2cm/¾in.

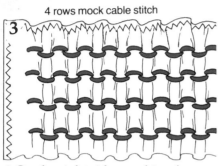

4 rows mock cable stitch

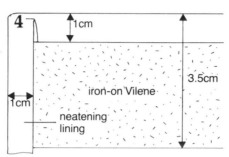

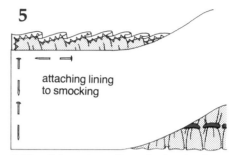

attaching lining to smocking

3 On the right side, working from left to right, smock four rows of mock cable stitch. Use one strand of coton à broder or three of stranded cotton. Check that collar fits neck edge.

4 Cut another strip of white lawn 4.5cm/1¾in wide and the same length as the first strip. Interface with iron-on Vilene. Press under a 1cm/½in hem on one long edge and both short edges.

5 Use this strip to line the back of the smocked frill. Pin it in place with top edge level with top row of smocking and short edges flush. Machine round close to folded edges of lining strip with white thread.

Adding a smocked collar and cuffs to a classic blouse

The smart red blouse shown on the previous page is made up from a commercial paper pattern; choose one with a collar band and cuffs up to 5cm/2in wide.

You will need

Blouse pattern and fabric
40cm/½yd white cotton lawn (width 90cm/36in)
1 skein Coats Anchor coton à broder or standed cotton to match blouse
10cm/⅛yd light iron-on Vilene
White sewing thread
Smocking dots size G transfer or one sheet each of tracing paper and dressmaker's carbon paper

cuffs smocked with mock surface honeycomb stitch

Collar

Cut out blouse, omitting collar, collar band and cuff pieces. Make up the blouse to the point where the collar is to be attached. Prepare the collar as for the ready-made blouse up to, and including, step 2.
On the right side, working from left to right, smock four rows of mock surface honeycomb stitch.
Make the collar band paper pattern piece smaller by pinning a fold in the centre so that finished collar band will meet at centre front and not overlap. Cut one collar band in white lawn and interface with iron-on Vilene. Press seam allowance under all round and trim to 8mm/⅜in. Complete collar as for ready-made blouse from step 4 to end, again setting collar on to neck edge so that only three rows of smocking show.
Adjust button positions so that top one lies just below upper neck edge.

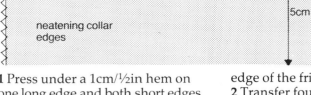

1
neatening collar
edges

|5cm

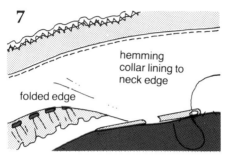

2 |1.5cm   transferring the dots

1 Press under a 1cm/½in hem on
one long edge and both short edges.
Neaten folded edges with a tiny
zigzag machine stitch and trim off
excess hem – this is the finished

edge of the frill.
2 Transfer four rows of smocking
dots to the right side of the lawn,
either by pressing them on from a
transfer or by tracing off the ones

given below and transferring them
with dressmaker's carbon paper.
Place top row of dots 1.5cm/⅝in
from the finished frill edge.

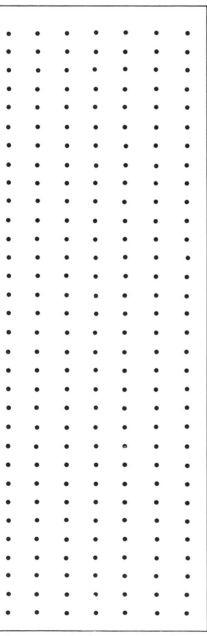

6
attaching collar
to neck edge

collar lining

7
hemming
collar lining to
neck edge

folded edge

Attaching the collar
Pin collar to blouse neck edge, right
sides together, taking care not to
catch in collar lining strip and
positioning collar so that its raw
edge is flush with neck edge of
blouse.
6 Tack and stitch all round between
first and second rows of smocking

so that only three rows show on
right side.
7 Turn under raw edge of collar
lining. Secure inside neck edge by
hemming. Add a press stud to top
of blouse opening to close (top
button may have been removed
with old collar).

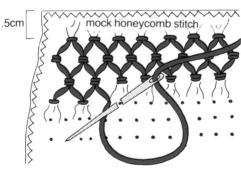

.5cm   mock honeycomb stitch

Cuffs
Using the cuff pattern piece as a
guide, measure finished length and
width of cuff. Cut two strips of lawn
measuring this width plus 4cm/1½in
by twice finished length plus 2cm/
¾in. Press under a 1cm/½in hem on
one long edge and both short edges.
Neaten these pressed edges with a
tiny zigzag and trim off excess hem
– these are the finished cuff edges.
On the right side, transfer the
smocking dots, placing top row
1.5cm/⅝in from frill edge and bottom
row not less than 1cm/½in from

unfrilled edge. The number of
smocking rows will depend on the
cuff width.
Smock the cuff with mock surface
honeycomb stitch, working from
left to right. Check that smocked
cuff will fit nicely round wrist with
overlap for button and buttonhole.
Cut two more cuff pieces in lawn.
Interface with light iron-on Vilene,
turn in seam allowances and trim to
8mm/⅜in. Use these to line the back
of smocked cuffs. Pin in place with
outer edges flush with top row of
smocking. Tack and machine along
short edges and outer edge.
Sew cuffs to gathered sleeve edges
with right sides together,
positioning cuff so that one row of
smocking is caught inside the seam.
Do not catch in cuff lining. Trim
seam, turn in raw edge of cuff lining
and slipstitch to inside of cuff.
Complete blouse as given in the
pattern instructions, making
buttonholes as normal.

*Above: Transfer these smocking dots to
the fabric with dressmaker's carbon
paper. Trace them off as many times
as you need to cover the length of the
collar piece.*

transfer dots this way up for collar and cuffs

73

CHAPTER 16

Traditional smocking

Today's new interest in smocking means that the range of traditional patterns is expanding. Items ranging from cushions and mobiles to pretty childrens' clothes are smocked with motifs such as bears, rabbits and flower baskets, using easy stitches.

This party dress is made even prettier with smocking decoration in pastel shades of stranded cotton and three flower baskets on the front.

With real smocking, unlike mock smocking, you need to pleat (gather) the fabric before working the embroidery. Preparing pleats takes time, but it is worth doing well.

Pleating machines It is possible to obtain small machines which can automatically pleat 16 rows at the same time in 15 minutes, although these are rather expensive.

Pleating by hand

You'll need transfer dots size K for cottons and size Q for wools, strong sewing thread and a steam iron if possible. Remember to allow three times as much fabric as the width of smocking you need.

Wash and press fabric. Straighten it by tearing across the grain or pulling a thread and trimming.

Cut the dots transfer to the required size – two more rows than you plan

Basic smocking stitches

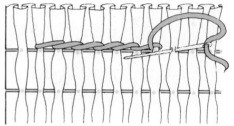

Outline stitch

Pick up a pleat just above the line of the gathering thread. Keeping the thread above the needle, make the stitch from right to left. Stitch into each successive pleat.

Deeper smocking stitches

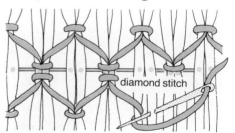

diamond stitch

Wave stitch

Work one downward cable. Keeping the thread below, move up halfway to the next gathering thread (one half space) and pick up the next pleat. Work one upward cable.

Diamond stitch Work two rows of half-space waves one above the other.

Some basic guidelines
Refer to page 70 for basic know-how and materials. Use three strands of stranded cotton on cotton fabrics and four strands of No 8 pearl cotton on wool or Viyella.
Never smock the first three and last three pleats – they serve as your seam allowance. Most stitches are worked from left to right (if right-handed).

Left handers should hold the work vertically rather than horizontally and turn stitch diagrams upside down. To begin a smocking thread, knot one end firmly. Pick up one pleat on the back of the work and come to the front through the left hand side of a pleat. To finish off, go through to the back on the right side of a pleat, then make two backstitches.

Pick up no more than a third of the depth of a pleat and always keep the needle parallel to the pleating threads. Make sure all the threads lie flat – control stranded cottons by running them over a block of beeswax. **The basic smocking stitches** are worked from left to right. None of them is very elastic. Always begin your smocking with one of these.

to smock – and transfer as described in the last chapter.
Picking up the dots Using a contrasting colour of strong thread, with a knot at one end, about 15cm/6in longer than the width of the fabric, begin picking up the dots from right to left. These threads are removed later.
When all the dots are picked up, slowly pull up the threads to form

pleats. Pull the fabric lengthwise, to make the pleats sit correctly, and steam it to set them.
Tie off the threads in pairs with an overhand knot, having all the knots in a straight line and the pleats evenly distributed. In general, the pleated fabric should be about 2.5 to 3cm/1 to 1½in narrower than the desired size, because of the elasticity of the finished smocking

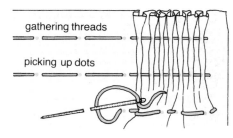

after the gathering threads have been released.

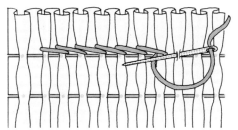

Stem stitch
Work as for outline stitch, but with the thread below the needle.

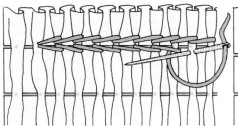

Wheat stitch
Work row of outline stitch with a row of stem stitch directly underneath. This gives a pretty effect like continuing ears of wheat.

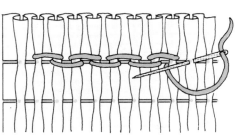

Cable stitch
Use this stitch on the back of the work where extra hold is needed. Pick up a pleat with the thread above the needle (upward cable), then pick up the next pleat with the thread below (downward cable).

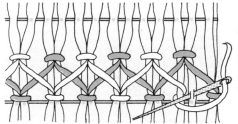

Crossed diamond stitch
Work one downward cable. Now work a half-space wave upwards and continue in wave stitch along the row. Change the colour of thread and work another row crossing the first, on the free pairs of pleats.

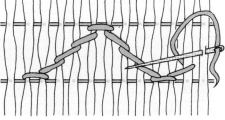

Trellis stitch
This combination of cable stitch and outline stitch is worked over the space between two pleating threads – divide the area roughly into three, by eye.
Begin with a downward cable at the

pleating thread, then work outline stitches at ⅓ the way up, ⅔ the way up, and the whole way up (just below the pleating thread).
Work an upward cable just above the pleating thread – this is the centre top stitch. Work the second to fourth stitches in reverse, with the thread above the needle to return to the bottom pleating thread. Work a downward cable stitch to match the first one.

Party dress with smocking

Smocked dresses are traditional for little girls, but here's a delightfully pretty one with flower basket motifs instead of the usual rows of cable and wave stitches.

The top and bottom border design from the front of the dress is used over the whole back yoke. If your pattern's smocked area is deeper, add extra rows of this border.

You will need

Commercial paper pattern for smock-yoked dress (the one shown here has a smocked back yoke too. If your pattern has a plain back, allow extra fabric for smocking)

Fabric and notion requirements as given on pattern envelope

Strong thread for pleating

DMC stranded cotton in greens 369 and 955, yellows 743 and 745, lilac 211, pink 899, blue 813, plus 1 skein to match fabric

Preparing to smock

When smocking a dress yoke or bodice like this one, treat the back as one piece of fabric until after working the smocking. Mark the centre back (position of back opening) and do not smock the six centre pleats. This allows space for a centre back opening and seam. Pleat 16 rows on the rectangular pieces for the front and back. Do not cut out the armholes until the smocking is completed. Pull up pleating threads to desired size.

Smocking the front

Row 1: Begin at the top with one row of wheat stitch (369).

Rows 2 to 3½: Beginning on row 2, work five cables (starting upward), one half-space wave, three cables (starting downward), one half-space wave, continue along the line (955).

Between each group of five cables and level with them, work three cables in alternating colours (745, 899 and 813). Repeat on row 3, reversing the pattern.

Rows 13½ to 15: Repeat as above, but only add the three cables on the top row of cables and waves.

Rows 9½ to 12: Work three baskets,

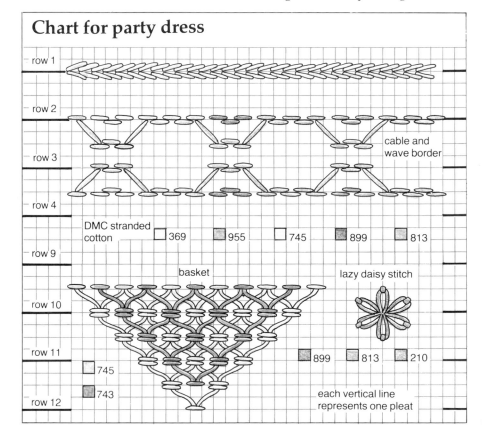

Chart for party dress

row 1

row 2

row 3

row 4

cable and wave border

row 9

DMC stranded cotton

☐ 369 ◧ 955 ☐ 745 ◼ 899 ◧ 813

row 10

basket

lazy daisy stitch

row 11

◧ 899 ☐ 813 ☐ 210

☐ 745

◧ 743

row 12

each vertical line represents one pleat

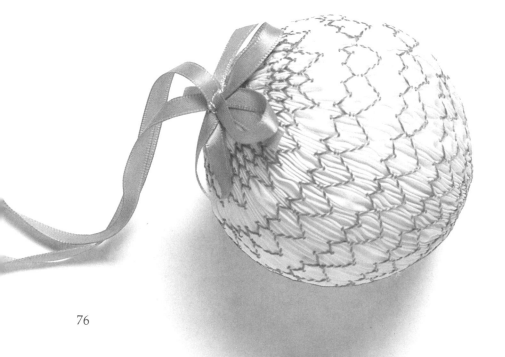

Smocked ball

This original plaything for a baby's cot is exquisitely pretty yet inexpensive to make. All you have to do is smock a length of fabric, join it into a tube, and use it to cover a child's lightweight ball.

You will need

18cm×70cm/7in×28in white cotton poplin

1.50m/1⅝yd 6mm/¼in ribbon

1 skein stranded cotton

1 foam playball

Left: Cover a lightweight ball with smocked fabric to make a delightful gift for a new baby. Stitch it in pink, as shown here, or blue.

centring them by counting pleats. The top row of each basket is five crossed diamonds in 745 and 743. Reduce by one wave stitch each time, turning work upside down after each row, until you have just one stitch at the base of the basket.

Flowers Using lazy daisy (detached chain) stitch (page 11), embroider five flowers above each of the basket – two pink, two blue and one lilac. Work the petal catching stitches through the peaks of the pleats.

Rows 6 to 13: Smock on the reverse side with cable stitch to match fabric.

Smocking the back
Remember to leave the six centre pleats empty.
Rows 2 to 14½: Work as for front borders (form double rows).
On back, smock one row of cable stitch at row 2½.

Making up
Oversew (or machine zigzag) along top and bottom edges of smocked rectangles. Follow pattern instructions for remainder of cutting out and making up. Remove pleating threads.

Right: You don't have to smock the back of the dress as well, but it does look enchanting. The cable and wave border design is used throughout.

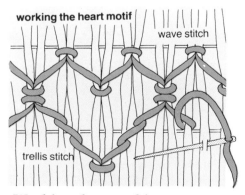

Working the smocking
Pleat 16 rows. Rows 1 and 16 are not smocked, these threads are used to pull the ends together for mounting and making up. Work in heart motif on rows two to 14.
To form heart motif, work one row

of half-space wave stitch. Beneath the downward cables of this row, work a full-space row of trellis stitch, so that every upward point of the trellis lies close to every alternate downward cable of the wave stitch.

On row 15, work cable stitch. When the smocking is completed, pull out all the gathering threads except the first and last. Slipstitch ends of fabric together to form a tube, and insert the foam ball.

Making up
Pull the two gathering threads to enclose the ball and trim fabric edges so they do not overlap. Work white tacking stitches over both ends to make fabric lie as flat as

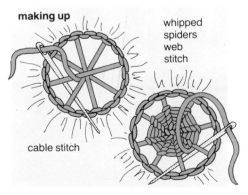

possible.
Cover these raw ends with a whipped spider's web embroidery stitch (see diagram).
Make a rosette bow with the ribbon; make a large loop and stitch to one end of ball.

CHAPTER 17

Tambour beadwork

Try this method of attaching decorative beads to fabric using a hook instead of a sewing needle. With practice, it soon becomes a quick technique, suitable for adding glamour to evening wear and accessories, like the silk scarf shown in this chapter.

Tambour embroidery (threadwork without beads) originated in the Orient and was used a lot in Europe between 1780 and 1850 when many dresses and accessories were tamboured. The fabric was stretched in a circular tambour frame (so called because it resembled a drum), so tambour embroidery got its name from the frame it was worked in. Tambour beading appears to have originated in Luneville, France in 1878.

Equipment for tambouring

Apart from the beads themselves and the thread to secure them, the two main pieces of equipment you need are a frame and a special hook.

Frame The fabric must be stretched taut in a supported frame, leaving both hands free for working. A ring frame with a table clamp is suitable if the whole design to be beaded will fit inside it, leaving a margin all round for ease of working. If the design is larger, use a supported rectangular (slate) frame.

Tambour hook The tambour hook is like a very fine crochet hook. It is held in a wooden holder by means of a screw. The hook is inserted into the

Tambouring techniques

Work with the design marked on the wrong side of the fabric, which is mounted in the frame with the wrong side uppermost.

When working the tambour stitch, a chain stitch forms on the upper surface and a backstitch forms on the underside holding each bead.

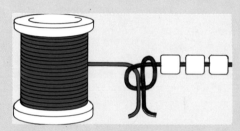

Threading the beads

First thread the beads you need on to the reel of working thread. If the beads are pre-strung, make a weaver's knot with the beads' thread and the working thread and slide the beads across on to the working thread.

Basic stitching technique

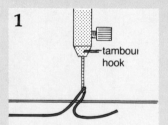

How to begin (without beads)
With the fabric mounted in the frame, wrong side up, work on the wrong side, from left to right.

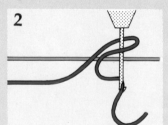

1 Insert the hook in the fabric, pick up a loop of thread and pull through.
2 Twisting the hook (one half-turn), re-insert it to the right of this loop,

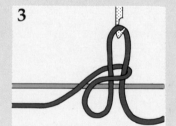

pick up a loop from the loose end and twist the hook again, maintaining tension.
3 Bring this loop up through the fabric, and

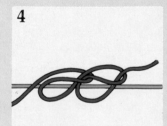

repeat step 2.
4 Pull the loose end of thread up through the fabric.

Finishing off

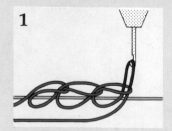

1 Pull a loop through as if making a stitch.

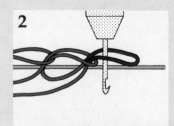

2 Re-insert the hook, almost in the same hole, but leaving the first loop loose.

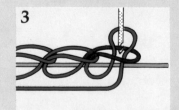

3 Pull the second loop through the first loop and remove hook. Cut thread beneath fabric.

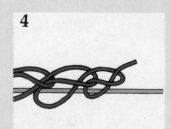

4 Pull second loop to bring cut end through. Tighten and cut off neatly.

holder so that it faces in the same direction as the screw. So you always know which way it is facing when it is in the fabric.

Materials for beadwork

You're likely to be working on a very special 'heirloom' piece, so it's worth choosing good materials.

Fabrics A transparent fabric such as organdie is a good choice to start on, as the beads are applied to the underside of the fabric and so can be seen when working. Firmly-woven fabric can, of course, also be used.

The weight of the fabric should be judged according to how solid the beadwork is going to be, as beads become quite heavy when packed close together. If the fabric was not heavy enough to support it, this could spoil the hang of a garment. In extreme cases, the weight of the beads could tear the fabric.

Thread The working thread should be a smooth, strong thread like Sylko or Gütermann pure silk which either matches the base fabric or forms a contrast. Gold and silver threads are effective, either on their own or with beads used every other stitch. Metallic threads must also be smooth and strong.

Beads There is a large range of colours and shapes available in beads, sequins and bugle beads.

Some are pre-threaded, others you will have to thread up yourself.

Designs

Linear designs are best for tambour beadwork. It is much quicker to work reasonably long lines of beading than having to keep starting and finishing in a design of mainly short lines.

Tambour beading becomes very quick with practice and that is why it is the method used for most commercial beadwork. Sequins and bugle beads can also be attached by this method, and the stitch can also be used on its own for decorative effects, particularly with gold or silver thread.

If the beads are loose, thread them on to the working thread using a beading needle.

If possible, place the reel of thread on a peg (a blunt nail is useful for this) in one of the holes on the embroidery frame. (The thread must be free-running.)

Hold the tambour hook in the right hand above the frame and the thread in the left hand below the frame, and follow the diagrams for anchoring the thread, working the stitch and securing the thread at the end of the line of stitching. It is a good idea to practise stitching

without beads until you have mastered the use of the hook.

To attach beads, push one bead up close to the fabric before the thread is wrapped around the hook to make the stitch and repeat this on every stitch for a solid line, or every other stitch for a speckled effect.

1
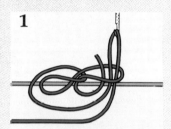

Continuous stitching
Repeat these steps following design lines.
1 Insert hook, pick up loop of thread and twist hook. Pull loop through.

2
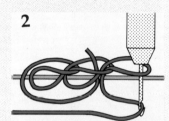

2 Twist the hook, then re-insert it to the right of where the loop came through (make stitch length as required). Pick up another loop.

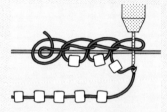

Stitching with beads
Push one bead up to the fabric with the left hand before the thread is twisted round the hook, then work the stitch.

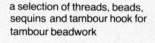
a selection of threads, beads, sequins and tambour hook for tambour beadwork

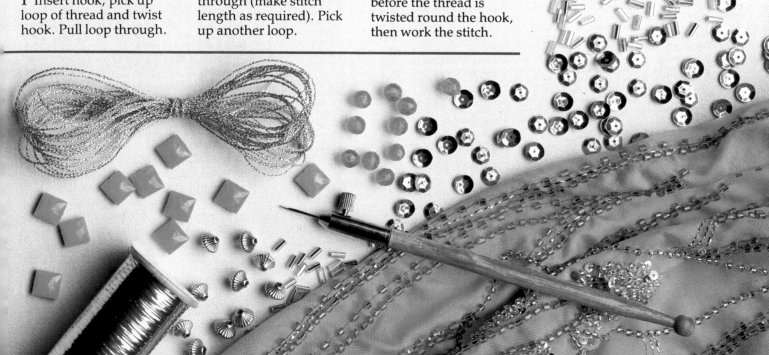

Sparkling beaded evening scarf

This beautiful beadwork design is really effective. You don't have to use the beadwork on both ends of the scarf and if you prefer, stitch them down using a beading needle.

You could use this design to give a sparkle to evening bags, a silk camisole, or even jacket pockets. The shade numbers of beads used here are given in brackets, but pick them to tone with the scarf fabric.

You will need

0.80m/⁷⁄₈yd Thai silk fabric (width 1m/40in)
2 reels Gütermann silk thread to match fabric
1 reel Rexor gold thread
2,000 CB2 beads (shade 11)
59g SB10 beads (half each in shades 2 and 30)
1,000 FS3 sequins (shade 1)
Embroidery slate frame

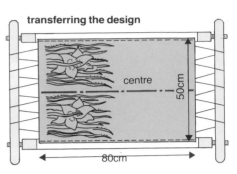

transferring the design

centre

50cm

80cm

Preparing the fabric

Cut the piece of fabric in half lengthwise and frame up one of the pieces wrong side uppermost, straight grain running horizontally. The other piece is used for backing. Run a line of tacking along the centre of the fabric, dividing it in two horizontally.

Transfer the design twice (if working both ends of scarf), centring it in each half of the framed fabric and having the lower edge of the design 5cm/2in from the raw ends.

Working the design

Following the colour key, bead the two designs as described earlier. Solid lines denote a bead on every stitch. Dotted lines should be beaded every other stitch and random dots show where you should sew the beads at random.

Making up the scarf

When the beadwork is complete, take the fabric off the frame and cut in half along tacking line. Thread the machine with the silk thread used for the beading. Stitch together the two short edges at opposite ends to the beadwork with right sides facing, taking 1cm/½in seams.

To back the scarf, cut the remaining piece of fabric in half lengthwise and machine two of the short edges together as for the scarf front. Press both seams open and place the beaded piece and the backing right sides together. Stitch all round, leaving about 10cm/4in unstitched. Turn to the right side through this opening and slipstitch closed. Press seamed edges carefully.

Left: Beadwork transforms a silk scarf.

Trace pattern for beaded scarf

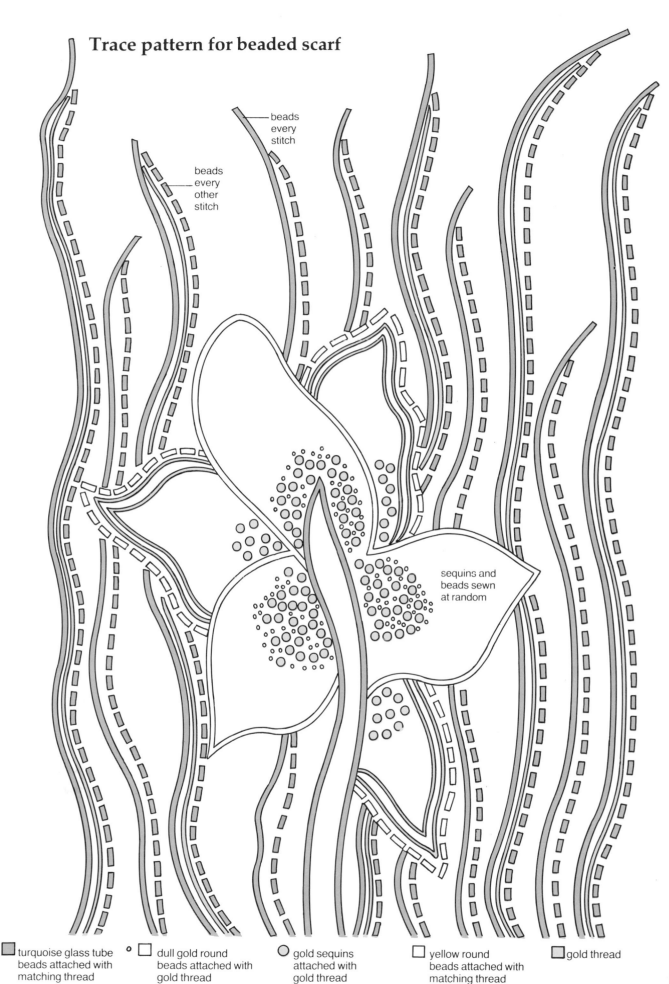

beads every stitch

beads every other stitch

sequins and beads sewn at random

turquoise glass tube beads attached with matching thread

dull gold round beads attached with gold thread

gold sequins attached with gold thread

yellow round beads attached with matching thread

gold thread

81

CHAPTER 18

Exquisite gold and silver thread work

Gold threadwork in embroidery is not reserved for coronation robes or regimental regalia. It is simple to do and the effect is glorious. Choose from a range of real or imitation gold or silver threads to stitch something really special.

Goldwork is one of the most luxurious forms of embroidery. Being one of the most expensive, it has traditionally been reserved for ecclesiastical and regimental purposes, but today, you can combine small quantities of gold thread with less expensive imitation threads to create rich effects.

The earliest examples of gold embroidery come from China and Japan – embroiderers used small strips of gold wound around a silken core. Byzantine textiles often included gold embroidery on robes and between 900 and 1500AD England became famous for *Opus Anglicanum* (English work), usually executed by men, in London, using silk and metal threads on church vestments. The backgrounds to these designs were filled with vast amounts of gold couching (gold thread caught on the fabric surface with small stitches). Between the Middle Ages and the 17th century, *or nué* became popular – a technique of couching gold with coloured silks to make a shaded pattern on the gold. Western Europe led the world in goldwork in the 17th and early 18th centuries and gold embroidery for the church was revived in England in the 19th century, but it was not until this century that any amount was done in people's homes.

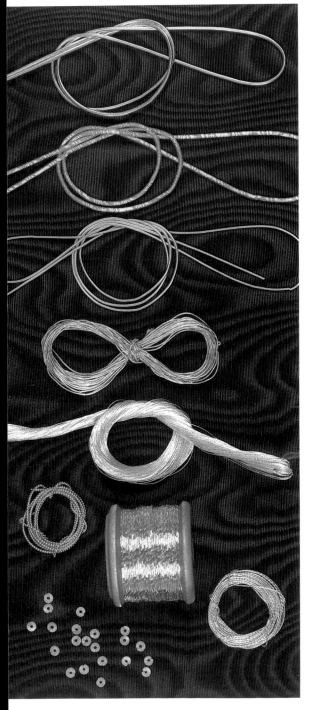

Left: A selection of materials commonly used for goldwork. Gold purl is usually sold in lengths varying from 30cm/12in to 122cm/48in. Other items come on reels or in skeins.
From top to bottom: Bright bullion No 1, bright check purl No 1, rough gold No 6, gold passing No 5, Danish silver, imitation gold Jap, gold pearl purl No 1, silver Lumi yarn No 8, gold spangles.

Types of thread for goldwork

Japanese gold (Jap) is one of the most useful and in its genuine form it is gold leaf burnished on to narrow strips of paper, lightly wound around a silk core. This is not always easy to obtain, and an imitation Jap made of lurex is suitable. Alternatives are twisted gold cord, and passing (metal threads spun round a central cotton or silk filament) which can be used doubled for extra thickness.

Gold purl, sold by weight, is a soft metal spring which is cut to the length of the stitch, threaded on the needle and sewn down like a bead. Different qualities are available, such as rough (a dull spring), smooth (a shiny spring) and bright check (a more sparkly, crinkled spring). Pieces of gold purl are known as 'chips'. There is a coarser version of purl, known as bullion.

Pearl purl is a rigid spring which looks like a string of tiny beads and comes in different sizes. It should be very slightly stretched before couching (catching down on the fabric) to allow the stitches to slip down between the coils. The thread is invisible on the finished work.

Spangles are like gold sequins, but each has a slit in it, making it more malleable over a padded or moulded surface.

Many of these items (or their equivalents) are available in silver – real or imitation – so you can create similar effects in silver.

The techniques of goldwork

Keep and cut the gold purl on a cutting board or a piece of felt. Use an old pair of scissors to cut the metal.

The fabric to be embroidered must always be mounted on a frame and also on to a backing fabric – usually holland (duck linen). This is because goldwork needs a strong foundation. The threads are heavy and need as much support as possible.

There are several different ways of working gold embroidery, but all of them consist of applying the gold or silver to the surface of the ground fabric with *couching* stitches to hold it in place. The couching is done with a double yellow polyester thread although traditionally a waxed silk Maltese thread was used.

Types of goldwork

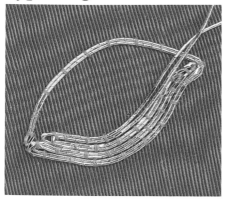

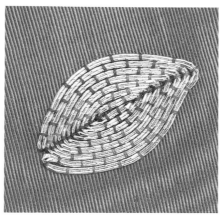

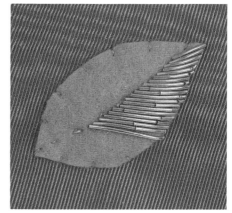

Couched gold thread can be used in a single line only, to outline work, or in flat goldwork, where shapes or background areas are filled in with solid gold couching, using a matching yellow thread.

Or nué In this type of flat goldwork, the effect is provided by the couching threads which are usually coloured and spaced out in various ways to make a shaded pattern over the gold.

Padded goldwork Padding gives a raised effect which emphasises parts of the design. To pad out a shaped, non-linear motif, cut pieces of yellow felt in the shape of the motif and stitch them in place using yellow thread.
Now work the gold embroidery over the felt, completely covering it.

Linear padding To pad linear parts of a design – making raised flower stems for instance – use fine string, which has been drawn over beeswax to strengthen it.
Couch the string down along the design line using as many thicknesses of string as you need. Work the couching, bringing the needle up and down at the same point each time.
Cover the string with purl chips. Bring the couching thread through from the back at the end. Thread a purl chip on the needle and stitch it in place so that it lies diagonally across the string and close to the fabric at either end. Work along the

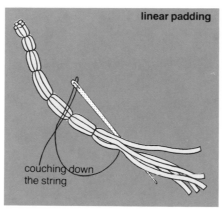

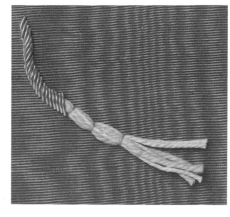

stem or line, bringing the needle up at the left and tucking it down on the right, beneath the stitch above. Use a fingertip to smooth chips.

Above: A padded line being worked over with rough gold purl chips.
Below: You could stitch any simple design on this envelope-shape bag.

Evening bag with gold embroidery

This simple, but smart evening clutch bag (14cm × 21cm/5½in × 8½in) has an exquisite gold design of a thrush perched on a rose branch. The bird and leaves gleam with a lustre that is unique to goldwork and the simple design provides you with an opportunity to explore some of the basic techniques involved in this fascinating craft.

You will need

½m/½yd furnishing fabric, moiré, velvet or silk (any width)
½m/½yd holland (duck linen)
25cm/¼yd medium interfacing
25cm/¼yd 2-3oz polyester wadding
Small piece of yellow felt
Button or press stud
1 reel Japanese gold, size 12 or smaller
About 45cm/18in each of purl in rough, smooth, check and bright check
About 25cm/10in of pearl purl
1 spangle
Yellow polyester sewing thread
Fine needle for stitching down purl
Rectangular embroidery frame
Large chenille needle

Mounting the fabric

Trim the piece of top fabric to 25cm × 50cm/10in × 20in and trim the piece of holland backing to 35cm × 50cm/14in × 20in.

To mark the bag stitching line on to the fabric, using the dimensions given in the diagram, make a paper template, pin to the fabric and run a line of tacking all round the edge. Mount the holland on a rectangular frame and then mount the fabric on the holland with the flap portion placed as centrally as possible. Oversew, beginning at the centre of each side in turn, so that no wrinkles occur. Tighten up the frame. Now trace and transfer the bird design to the centre of the bag using the trace and tack method given on page 12.

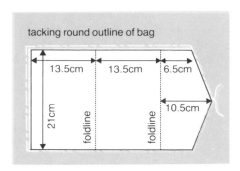

tacking round outline of bag

13.5cm 13.5cm 6.5cm

21cm

foldline

foldline

10.5cm

Stitching the goldwork design

Trace off wing and leaf shapes from the pattern, then cut them out in yellow felt, and stitch them in place on the fabric as a light padding, using yellow thread.

Use the diagram showing the position of the different materials to work the gold embroidery.

Cut a length of Jap gold about 90cm/36in long and fold it in half. Catch the loop down about halfway along the bird's back and continue catching the doubled thread down at about 4mm/⅛-¼in, outlining the head and underside of the wing. Return along the lower edge of the wing, spacing the stitches alternately with those in the row below to make a bricklike effect. Fill in the whole wing, and when you get near the top, run a row round under the upper wing outline. This makes it easier to conceal the thread ends. Two stitches away from the end, take the ends of Jap gold down through the fabric using the chenille needle, then work the last two couching stitches. This method will disturb the gold as little as possible. Fasten the ends of the Jap into the

making the bag

tacking the embroidered fabric to the interfacing

interfacing   fabric loop

back of the work.

Couch the main part of the stem and the bird's tail in the same way. Add thorns to the stem, and work the bird's downy underside using chips of rough purl. Use a spangle and a chip for the eye and a check purl chip for the beak. The legs are of pearl purl – bend two pieces over the branch for feet.

Lay purl chips over the felt for the leaves, using a different type for each side of a leaf to suggest the play of light on the leaves. Vary the length for a feathery effect, covering the felt completely.

Lastly, add a length of pearl purl down the centre of each leaf.

finishing off

fold

fold

Making the bag

Remove the work from the frame and cut out the bag shape, 1.5cm/⅝in outside the tacked seamlines, to allow for seams. Cut another piece of the same fabric to the same size for lining.

Tack the wrong side of the embroidered piece to interfacing and trim edges flush. Place lining fabric and wadding together, tack round edge and trim evenly.

To make a button fastening, position a small fabric loop on the right side of the embroidered flap, with folded end pointing towards the embroidery.

Place lining and embroidery with right sides together, pin and tack round the edges. Stitch all round with a 1.5cm/⅝in seam, leaving top straight edge open. Clip corners and trim wadding and interfacing close to seam line. Remove tacking.

Finishing off

Turn bag to right side, turn in seam allowance and topstitch opening. Fold up bag front and topstitch the sides together and continue stitching round the flap. Fold flap down and attach button or press stud to close.

Right: Black and gold is a stunning combination, but you may prefer a colour to match a special outfit.

Trace pattern for goldwork bird

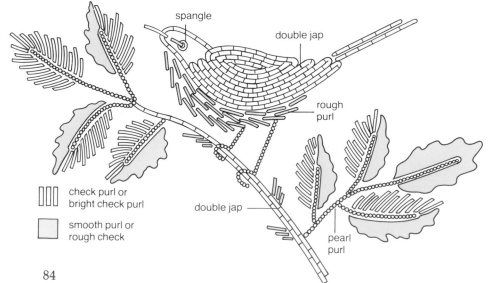

spangle

double jap

rough purl

check purl or bright check purl

smooth purl or rough check

double jap

pearl purl

Needlepoint

The craft of needlepoint is exceptionally varied. The conventional view of a skill limited to the production of tent-stitch pictures is far from the truth, although some delightful examples of this simple technique are included here. The range of canvas types and sizes and the rich choice of yarns, wools and stranded, metallic and pearl cottons now available are exciting to work with using the many techniques described in the pages that follow.

Learn how simple straight stitches can create texture as well as pattern, and give depth to your canvas work by using chunky cross stitches, surface stitches and pile stitches. Enrich your stitch repertoire still further with the many unusual sampler stitches and, as a complete contrast, achieve a delicate lacy look with pulled thread stitches. Have fun experimenting with various yarns – the effect of many of the stitches is completely changed if worked in a shiny stranded cotton and then in a chunky wool.

The choice of colour is always important and it is particularly challenging in Florentine needlepoint where it can create either bright and bold or soft and subtle effects using the traditional wave or mirror image patterns.

The projects chosen to illustrate the stitches and techniques range from designs for cushions and pictures to fashion accessories such as belts and bags, and from traditional items for the home like rugs, chair seats and picture frames to an original model house which makes a practical doorstop.

CHAPTER 19

Beginning with tent stitch

*Needlepoint is the art of creating rich and beautiful embroidery
over a firm and regular framework of canvas.
Historically it is one of the oldest forms of needlework and
many of today's designs are inspired by
glorious examples from the heritage of the past.*

Needlepoint (or canvas work as it is often called) is worked on canvas or any firm fabric with evenly spaced holes. A firm, hard-wearing fabric is produced, so needlepoint is ideal for furnishings as well as smaller items, fashion accessories and pictures.

The term 'tapestry' is frequently and wrongly used when referring to needlepoint. Real tapestry is *woven* over a framework of vertical threads on a loom. In sixteenth-century Britain, when the costly woven table rugs imported from the Near East were much admired, people found that these tapestry designs could be stitched on canvas more cheaply using needlepoint.

The English tradition

Since the sixteenth century, the fashion for making particular items has changed along with people's furniture and needs – when homes had very few chairs needlewomen worked wall hangings, table carpets and cushions for their wooden benches. In the seventeenth century people sat on comfortable, upholstered chairs, and ladies stitched Bargello work covers for them: the long stitches covered the large areas quickly.

In the eighteenth century, furniture was too delicate for needlepoint which instead was used for fire-screens, pictures and other small articles. This trend continued into the Victorian era and Victorian ladies stitched away at a vast range of items. Nowadays, keen workers of needlepoint have access to a dazzling array of threads and yarns. Designs are exciting and cover every taste. As well as stimulating new techniques, such as pulled thread and 'painting' on can-

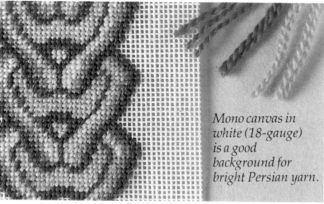

Mono canvas in white (18-gauge) is a good background for bright Persian yarn.

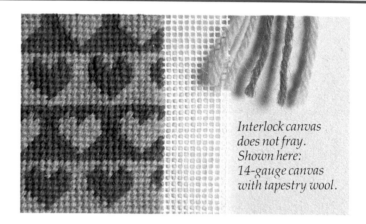

Interlock canvas does not fray. Shown here: 14-gauge canvas with tapestry wool.

Know your canvas

Most canvas is made of polished cotton or linen threads. There are two main types – mono (single thread) and Penelope (double thread). Common widths are 60cm/24in, 90cm/36in and 100cm/39in. Canvas comes in white, yellow, ecru and brown. White is best for pictorial needlepoint and for working with pale colours; ecru and brown are better for dark colours as the canvas is less likely to show between the yarn. Fine gauge canvas for petit point work often comes in yellow. When buying canvas, make sure the threads are even and shiny, not ragged or limp.

Measuring canvas mesh The measurement of canvas indicates the number of threads to 2.5cm/1in. The lower the number, the coarser the canvas: fourteen is average, and expressed as '14-gauge'. (Penelope and rug double thread canvasses are often measured in holes to 2.5cm/1in to avoid confusion over numbers of threads. Mono canvas comes in a range of 22 to 10 threads to 2.5cm/1in, and double thread canvas comes in 18 to 3 holes to 2.5cm/1in. You will soon learn to judge the most suitable canvas for your project.

Mono canvas is available in regular and interlock construction. Regular canvas has single horizontal and vertical threads woven over and under each other to form a mesh. As the threads are not bonded the canvas has a certain amount of 'give' and is the right choice for upholstery, cushions and pulled thread work.

Interlock canvas has two vertical threads woven round each horizontal one. It can be trimmed close to the finished work without fraying, so it is ideal for coasters, napkin rings, or anything with bound edges as part of the pattern. It comes in a limited number of gauges.

Penelope canvas mesh has pairs of threads – an example of a common gauge is 10/20 – ten double threads and twenty single to 2.5cm/1in. Work in a fine stitch over one thread with two strands of crewel wool, or over two threads with four.

Rug canvas has a very large mesh (usually double thread) although rugs can be worked on any canvas.

Matching canvasses and yarns When deciding which yarn to use with which canvas you can either start by choosing a canvas you enjoy working with – some people find it tiring to work with very small holes – or by choosing some particularly appealing shades of yarn. Then use the chart (far right) to guide you to a suitable combination of canvas and yarn.

vas, historical designs are being re-worked in modern colourings. People are re-discovering the pleasure of working samplers, both pictorial and geometric, to display many different stitches on one piece of work.

How to begin

When starting a piece of needlepoint make sure you are sitting comfortably in a good light.

Test the stitch and yarn on a small piece of the canvas to check that the yarn covers the canvas nicely. Thread the needle by folding the length of yarn, slipping the fold through the needle eye and pulling it through. Bring the needle through to the front of the canvas where you wish to start stitching, leaving a short length of yarn at the back. Anchor this length with your finger and work your first stitches over it to secure it. If the yarn

becomes twisted while you are working, let it dangle loosely from the work and it will untwist itself.

To finish off Run the needle under a few stitches on the back of the work and snip off.

Preparing canvas for working When cutting canvas allow at least 3cm/1¼in extra all round area to be stitched. Bind raw edges of the canvas with masking tape before you either mount it on a frame or begin stitching. Mark the top of canvas.

Transferring designs on to canvas If you are working needlepoint from a chart – usually given as squares each representing a stitch, begin working from the centre of the design. Find the centre of the chart (if not given) by counting squares horizontally and vertically. To find the centre of the canvas, measure and mark the centre of each edge and run two threads

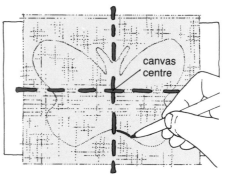

across between opposite centres using running stitch. They will cross at the centre of the canvas (see diagram above).

When using a traced design, trace off the motif in fairly thick, dark lines. Position the canvas over the tracing so that the design is central or appears wherever you want it and mark the lines on to the canvas with waterproof felt-tip pen. If necessary, hold it up to the window.

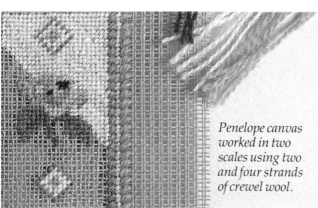

Penelope canvas worked in two scales using two and four strands of crewel wool.

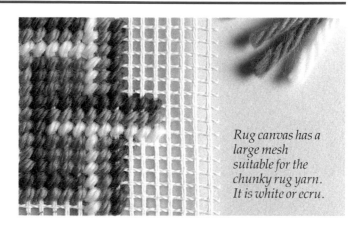

Rug canvas has a large mesh suitable for the chunky rug yarn. It is white or ecru.

Needlepoint equipment

Most pieces of needlepoint are small enough to carry around with you, and so is the necessary equipment – apart from the large floor frames.

Threads You can work needlepoint with virtually any type of thread so long as it passes easily through the canvas and covers it well.

The main types of yarn sold for needlepoint are tapestry wool, crewel wool and Persian yarn. Tapestry wool comes as an indivisible yarn similar to 4 ply knitting yarn in thickness. Crewel wool and Persian yarn are sold in thin strands that are often used in multiples for good canvas coverage. Other popular threads for needlepoint are stranded cotton, pearl cotton, metallic threads and rug yarn.

Use threads no more than 45cm/20in long to prevent them becoming weak and fluffy and so failing to cover the canvas properly.

Needles You should use a tapestry needle with a blunt point to avoid splitting the canvas threads. These come in sizes 13-24, the higher the number the finer the needle. The correct size depends on the canvas mesh and the yarn thickness – the needle

must pass through the holes comfortably without dislodging the threads and the yarn must pass through the needle eye easily without friction.

Scissors You will need a large pair for cutting canvas and small sharp embroidery scissors for the work.

Common canvasses and yarns for tent stitch

Canvas (threads to 2.5cm)	Yarn (number of strands recommended)	Size of tapestry needle
mono (22 or 24)	C (1)	24
mono (18)	C (2) P (1) T (1)	22 or 24
mono (16)	C (3) T (1)	22
mono (14 or 12)	C (3-4) P (2) T (1)	20
Penelope (10/20) over 2 threads	C (4) P(2-3)	18
over 1 thread	C (2) P (1)	24
rug (7 or 6 or 5)	P (8-9) rug (1)	16

KEY C=crewel wool, P=persian yarn, T=tapestry wool

Choosing the right tent stitch

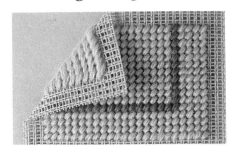

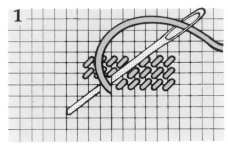

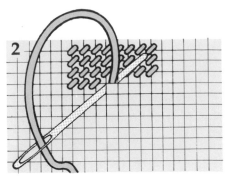

Tent stitch is the most often used needlepoint stitch. It is very versatile and is worked over only one canvas intersection making small, neat stitches on the front, longer ones on the back. It is ideal for pictorial designs, intricate patterns and smooth plain areas of background. Tent stitch forms a hard-wearing, well padded surface. There are two common forms of tent stitch – continental and diagonal.

Continental tent stitch
This is worked in horizontal rows across the canvas – from right to left and back again – and is used for outlining and small details. The back of the work is filled with long, sloping stitches (see above left).
1 Bring the needle out at the right-hand end of the row; re-insert it one hole to the right and one above, making a diagonal stitch, and bring the needle up again one hole to the

left of where it first came up. Continue along the row like this.
2 On the next row (return journey), if you are holding the work, turn it upside down and work as for Step 1. Otherwise, bring the needle out in the second hole of the top line and re-insert it one hole to the left and one below to form the tent stitch. The needle comes out on the top row one hole to the right of where it first came up.

Quick and easy fragrant sachets

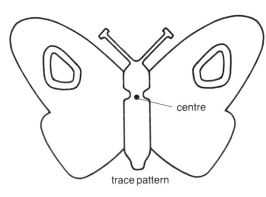

trace pattern

centre

These pretty butterfly motifs can be stitched in an evening if you leave the white canvas all round the butterfly unworked. Add a canvas backing and some fragrant pot pourri or lavender – and it makes a pretty present personally stitched by you.
A fairly fine canvas is used, to prevent the pot pourri coming through. If it seems powdery, make a little muslin bag for it before inserting it into the sachet.

Two-coloured sachet
This is a simple traced butterfly in two colours framed by a double border.

You will need
One small skein each Appleton's Crewel Wool in Royal Blue 1 (821), and Sky Blue 1 (561), *or* one each of

Coral 1 (861) and Coral 3 (863).
Tapestry needle size 22
20cm piece of white 18-gauge mono canvas (narrow width)
5g dried lavender or pot pourri

Preparing the canvas
Cut two 15cm squares from the canvas, (10cm x 15cm oblongs for the smaller sachet). Bind the edges of one of the pieces with masking tape Mark the centre of the canvas and trace the butterfly outline directly on to it from the trace pattern (left), matching the centres as already described. (The centre of the trace butterfly is marked with a dot.)

Stitching the butterfly
Using the paler yarn for the body and wing markings, and the darker one for the main wing area, work in tent stitch over one thread of canvas using two strands of crewel wool. Use continental tent for the body, wing markings, and wing outline and diagonal tent to fill in. The left hand antenna is worked in stitches sloping to the left.
Remember not to leave any trailing ends of yarn which might show through. Finish them all off neatly. Next mark a square or oblong border with a pencil, 2.8 cm from the canvas edge all round and work a row of

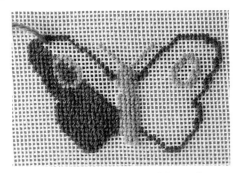

Above: Diagonal tent stitch fills in the main area of the butterfly wings.

Right: These sachets are quick to work and use both forms of tent stitch – continental and diagonal.

continental tent stitch in the paler shade. On the square sachet work a row of zigzag tent stitch border top and bottom in the dark shade as shown on page 90.

Backing and finishing
Take the other square or rectangle of canvas. Put the worked piece on top and grasp the two together so that the canvas holes align. With two strands of the darker yarn in your needle, start with a knot between the two pieces. Come through to the front and work a second row of continental tent, one thread away from the first, round three sides of the canvas. You will need to work each stitch in two movements to

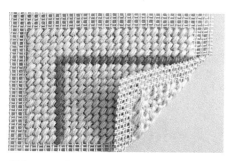

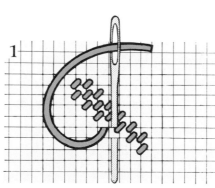

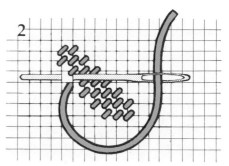

Diagonal tent stitch

This form of tent stitch is even more popular than the continental because it does not pull the canvas out of shape so much – the stitches at the back of the work being made both vertically and horizontally. It is mainly used for filling in motifs and working large areas of background.

1 Make a diagonal stitch from bottom left to top right as for continental. Then bring the needle out directly below where it goes in so that it passes under two horizontal threads, ready to make the next stitch. Your stitches will form a diagonal, downward line on the right side.

2 On the next row (return journey), the stitches are worked into the 'gaps' in the first row and the stitches on the back pass behind two vertical threads. On the front, a diagonal upward line is formed. There is no need to turn the work. The basketweave effect on the back of the canvas (see above left) means it is also sometimes known as 'basketweave tent stitch'.

make sure the border is very neat and the holes constantly aligned. At the corners, work a stitch on the end of each row to form a crossed stitch. This strengthens the corners. Fill the sachet with the pot pourri or lavender, then work the fourth row of continental tent to close. Trim the canvas surround to within six threads of the border and pull away the loose threads to leave a pretty fringe all round.

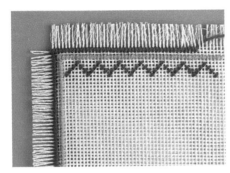

Above: After stitching the border row, fray the canvas threads to make a fringe.

Multi-coloured sachet

This highly decorative charted butterfly in misty blues, subtle corals, yellow and white can easily be worked without a frame.

You will need

1 small skein each Appleton's crewel wool in Royal Blue 1 (821) Sky Blue 1 (561), Coral 1 (861), Coral 3 (863), Bright Yellow 1 (551), and White (991)
Tapestry needle size 22
20cm/8in piece of white 18-gauge mono canvas (narrow width)
5g/¼oz dried lavender or pot pourri

Working multi-coloured sachet

The working method is very similar to the first sachet, except that the butterfly design is worked from a chart (right).
Cut two 17cm/7in squares of canvas, as this sachet is slightly larger than the two-coloured sachet.
Mark the canvas centre, and begin stitching from the centre, using two strands of yarn in the needle.
Work the stitches marked in black on the chart first – the body, antennae and main wing framework. Then work those marked in red. The repeat line on the chart shows you where to begin working the same portion of the chart on the right hand side, so that the wings are

Working chart for multi-coloured butterfly

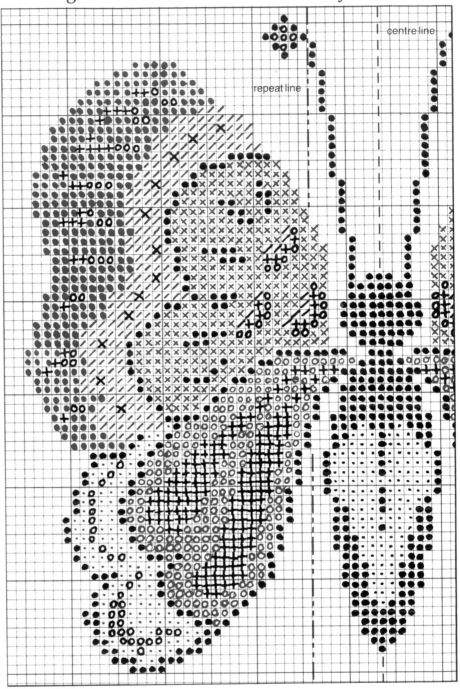

Above: Note that the chart gives the whole of the body and the left wing. To complete the right wing, work from the repeat line and reverse the pattern.

symmetrical.
Work a single border row in Royal Blue 1, positioning it about six threads away from the butterfly on each side. This row must be worked through both layers of canvas to secure the backing.
Finish off as for the two-colour sachet.

Key to chart		
yarn shade	work first	work second
821	●	●
561	·	·
861	+	+
863	o	O
551	×	×
991	/	/

90

CHAPTER 20

A single stitch creates a picture

In appearance this stitch is similar to tent stitch but it is worked differently. Less yarn is carried across the back of the canvas making it economical but not so hardwearing. Use it to make a cushion or picture with this delicate orchid design.

As its name suggests, half cross stitch is worked like cross stitch, but without adding the second row of crossing stitches. Do not mix this stitch with either form of tent stitch or the work will look uneven.

Half cross stitch is sometimes worked on Penelope (double thread) canvas as well as on mono canvas. Use a frame if possible because half cross stitch can pull the canvas out of shape.

Although not as hardwearing as tent stitch, half cross stitch is popular for pictures, fire screens and other items which do not get a lot of wear.

Mounting the picture

To make a needlepoint picture, mount the finished canvas on a piece of hardboard or heavyweight card. If the picture is to be framed, allow a margin all round for the frame overlap. Otherwise, take a piece the same size as the work and stretch the canvas over it. Secure the canvas along the cut edges of the board with pins or tacks, fixing one pair of opposite edges and then the other. Lace opposite edges tightly across the back with fine string or strong thread. Cover with backing fabric, the edges turned in and slip-stitched to the work. Screw two ring-hooks into the board (through the fabric) and tie string between for hanging. It is not always a good idea to use glass. Beware especially of non-reflective glass: it can rot canvas. Never cover textured stitches.

A beautifully designed cushion like this fits easily into a sitting room or bedroom scheme. The design would look equally good as a picture and you could then omit the border and use a frame instead.

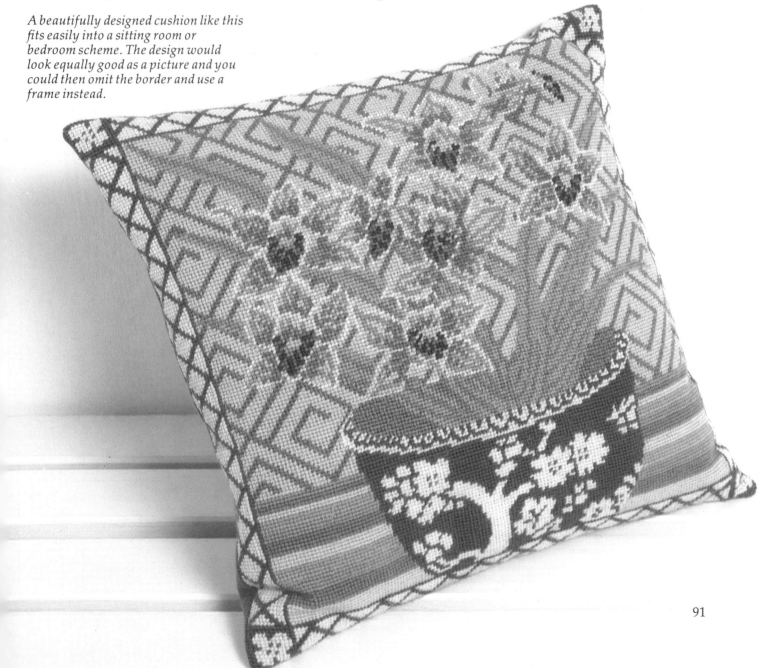

Working chart for orchid design

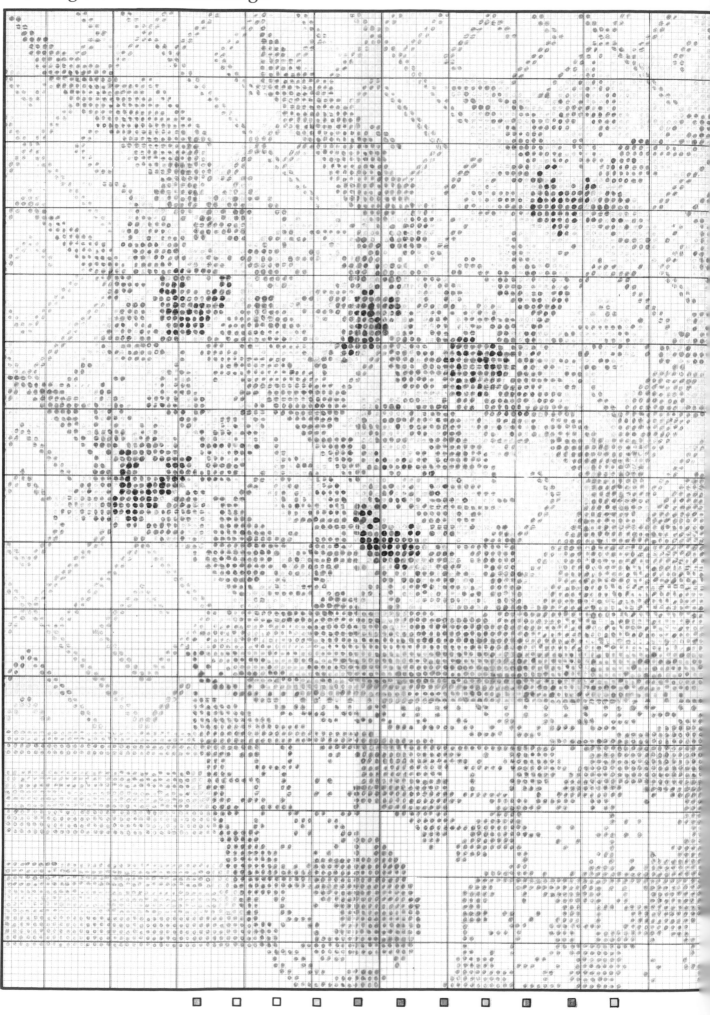

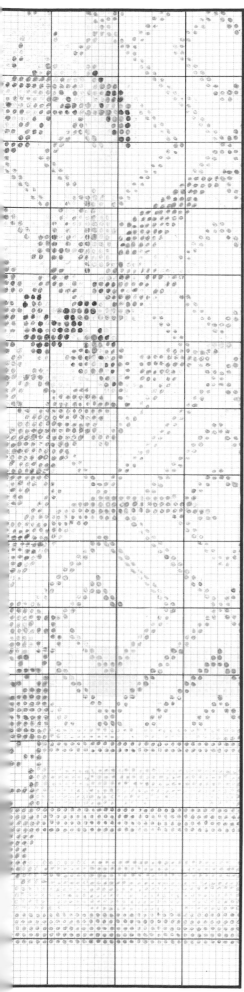

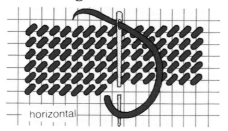

Working half cross stitch

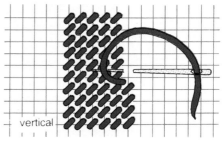

To work horizontally
Stitch from left to right as shown and turn the work at the end of each row. Straight upright stitches are formed on the back of the work.

To work vertically
To work vertical parts of a design pass the needle behind a vertical thread instead of a horizontal one.

Orchids in a Chinese bowl

This design of exotic pink orchids with a pretty blue and white lattice border is worked entirely in half cross stitch. The finished design measures 36cm/14½in square.

You will need
45cm/18in square piece of 12-gauge mono or Penelope canvas
25g/1oz hank each Appletons tapisserie wool in Bright China Blue 5 (745), Custard (851) and Off-white (992)
3 small skeins each Bright Rose Pink 1, 3 and 4 (941, 943, 944), Flame Red 4 (204), Early English Green 1 (541)
2 small skeins Grey Green 4 (354)
1 small skein each Rose Pink 7 (757) and Autumn Yellow 1 (471)
Tapestry needle size 18

Stitching the design
Bind the canvas edges with masking tape and mark the centre of the canvas. If possible, mount in a frame (see page 105).
The chart is divided into blocks of ten stitches square, so divide the

canvas in the same way using a waterproof marker to make accurate working easier. Stitch the flowers and bowl which form the main part of the design first; the background last. Use a single thickness of tapisserie wool.
Lattice border pattern Start with one of the corner squares and repeat the lattice pattern along the border beginning with a whole diamond and ending with a half diamond before the next corner square. Take care not to trail any blue yarn behind an area that will be stitched in white. When the design is complete, block and set the canvas as shown on page 99.

Making up the needlepoint
There are several ways of making up a finished needlepoint design.
Knife-edged cushion cover Take a piece of backing fabric 2.5cm/1in larger all round than the worked part of the canvas. Suitable backing fabrics are twill, rep, brocade, heavy linen, velvet and other furnishing fabrics.
With right sides together machine the canvas and backing along three and a half sides, leaving an opening along the lower edge of the cushion. Turn to right side, insert a cushion pad slightly larger than the cover and hand stitch the opening.
Cushion with border To make a larger cushion, buy a ready-made cushion cover of the required size and mount the needlepoint on it. Trim the edges to 1cm/½in and turn under. Pin the canvas centrally in place and slipstitch firmly all round the edge.

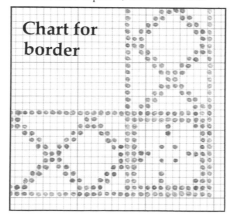

Chart for border

Note: On both charts each dot represents one half cross stitch

CHAPTER 21

Rug yarns and canvas for large-scale projects

Much historical needlepoint consisted of working rugs in imitation of Oriental woven designs. You can still do this today – in fact all kinds of designs make beautiful rugs. This colourful cow design is fun to work and looks good in a child's room.

Needlepoint rugs can be both lovely to look at and practical providing you choose yarn and stitches carefully. Rugs tend to be too ambitious a project for needlepoint beginners, so perfect your stitches and techniques before attempting one.

Planning a needlepoint rug

Take plenty of time to decide on the size, shape and colour of your rug – once begun, it may take you some time to complete and you must be sure it suits your requirements exactly.

Now decide whether to make it all in one piece, or in smaller squares which you can join together when complete. A rug worked in one piece, or as a central panel with borders added will wear far better than a rug consisting of several joined panels. However, a large, single piece of canvas is less convenient to work on than several smaller pieces.

Choosing materials and stitches

In theory, you can stitch a rug on any gauge of canvas from very fine to the coarse rug canvas – finer canvasses will take longer! Check the different widths in which your chosen canvas is available – you could save yourself some unnecessary joining of pieces. If you plan a separate border or a design of different squares, all the canvas for the rug must be cut from the same roll. Adjoining squares with a discrepancy of even one canvas thread will not match up satisfactorily.

Suit the yarn to the canvas in the usual way, making sure canvas coverage is as good as it can be for maximum wear, whether you are working in crewel, persian, tapestry, thrums (carpet manufacturers' off-

cuts), or rug wool. Of course, the finer the yarn and canvas, the longer it will take you to cover a given area. Chunky four or six-ply rug wool makes lovely stitched rugs – use a heavy, blunt rug needle. It is sold in skeins and can be used for cross or half cross stitches, straight gobelin stitch and gobelin filling stitch.

Other suitable stitches for the finer yarns which are available are basketweave tent stitch and all types of cross stitch including the decorative crossed corners.

Florentine patterns make dramatic rugs which are quick to make. Always choose designs with stitches that are not too long as these can snag when the rug is in use.

For a rug with a fluffy, raised pile, use one of the looped or cut pile stitches.

If the design requires a number of skeins of yarn in one colour, these must come from the same dye lot to ensure colour matching.

Working a needlepoint rug

It is easier, but not essential, to work heavier rugs in a frame. If possible, work on a frame with a floor stand and mount the canvas with the selvedges at the sides. Allow at least 4cm/1½in of canvas outside the stitching on each piece. Transfer the design to the canvas in the normal way, unless you are working from a chart. Start stitching at one end with the unworked canvas away from you. As far as possible, work in horizontal rows but, obviously, work separate motifs as they appear in the design. Block and set the finished work as described on page 99.

Joining the rug sections

If your rug is in several square, or

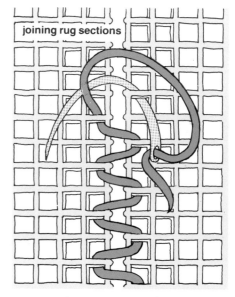

joining rug sections

rectangular sections, or has an added border, join the worked squares together by hand, using blind stitch and invisible thread, or, for very heavy pieces, carpet or button thread. Lay the canvas right side up on a table so that the pieces are supported. Press unworked canvas to the back on both edges to be joined and lay them together so that they just meet. Using a curved needle pick up one thread of large gauge canvas or two threads of 10-gauge canvas or finer canvas on the folded edge of one of the pieces. Now pick up a corresponding number of threads on the folded edge of the other piece, exactly opposite the point where the needle emerged from the last stitch. Continue in this way until all pieces and borders are joined.

If you are joining larger pieces of canvas for all-over designs, overlap the edges 4cm/1½in and tack with strong thread. Work through double canvas when stitching the design.

Finishing off the rug

It is important to turn over the edges and mitre the corners of the rug neatly.

If you're adding a fringe to the ends of the rug, leave one or two rows of canvas showing on the right side and mitre canvas and stitch edges as described below.

1 Trim unworked canvas equally all round to about 3cm/1¼in and fold the four corners diagonally towards the centre on the back.

Press the fold firmly to keep it flat.

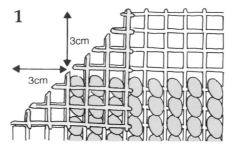

2 Fold one straight edge over to the centre and press well. Fold and press the other edge and stitch along each diagonal seam.

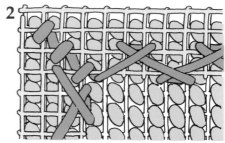

Secure all the edges on the back with herringbone stitch. This is all the finishing that some rugs will need unless a fringe is required.

Cows in a field rug

A softly twisted rug yarn makes this chunky rug a welcome addition to a playroom. It measures 69cm ×102cm/27in×40in. Work the rug on double thread (Smyrna) rug canvas. Use cross stitch for a hard wearing rug or half cross stitch as shown here to cut down on time and cost.

You will need

1.15m/1¼yd DMC rug canvas (width 69cm/27in, 5 double threads to 2.5cm/1in)

Rug needle

DMC Soudan wool, to work in half cross stitch:

5 skeins in 7344, 3 skeins in 7469, 2 skeins each in 7314, 7428, WHITE, 7184 and 7341, 1 skein each in 7435, 7164, 7351, 7133, 7310 and 7445

For fringe: 1 skein each in 7314 and 7344 (optional)

To work in full cross stitch, buy 5 extra skeins in 7344, 3 in 7469, 2 each in 7314, 7428, WHITE, 7184 and 7341, and 1 in 7351

Working the rug

Stitch the design from the chart – one square equals one half cross stitch. Use a single thickness of Soudan wool, in 45cm/18in lengths. To complete, fold back the two short ends of the rug leaving two double rows of canvas showing and secure with herringbone stitch. Add a sky colour fringe at the top and a grass colour at the bottom.

Finally, overcast the two long edges.

Right: An appealing rug in a lovely combination of colours – try adapting other simple children's pictures, too.

Chart for rug

1 square = 1 half cross stitch

■ 7184　■ 7469　■ 7445　■ 7133　■ 7344　□ 7164　□ 7351　■ 7314　■ 7428　□ 7341　□ 7435　■ 7310　□ white

Rug and carpet fringes for trimming

You may wish to add a decorative fringe to the ends of your rug.

In general, it is best to use the same yarn as that used for stitching the rug, but for Persian-type designs, a traditional cotton fringe is often knotted on to either end to look like the warp threads of a real woven rug. You'll need a crochet hook and a pair of sharp scissors for trimming the finished fringe. If possible, the strands should share holes with the outside row of needlepoint stitches to avoid having a row of bare threads showing.

Cutting the fringe

Depending on the yarn, 15cm/6in strands will give you a fringe of about 5cm/2in. As a rough guide, double the depth of fringe required and add 5cm/2in for the knot. Cut even strands by winding yarn round a piece of cardboard the depth of the fringe plus 2.5cm/1in and cutting through the yarn along one side.

Simple knotted fringe

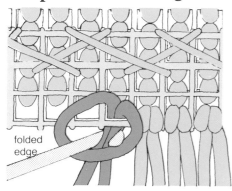

folded edge

With the back of the rug upwards, insert crochet hook through edge hole close to stitching. Catch the cut length (or lengths) of yarn in the centre, and pull a loop through to the back.
Pass the loose ends through this loop and pull tight.
A smoother effect is obtained by working with rug front uppermost.

Plaited heading with knots

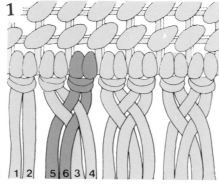

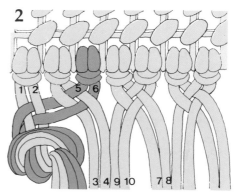

This adds decoration to a plain fringe and looks attractive worked in rug yarn.
1 Plait the ends in groups of four. Leave first pair of strands (1/2) loose.
Pass strand 5 over strand 4, strand 3 over strand 5 and strand 6 under strand 4 and over strand 3. Repeat with the next four strands.

2 Now hold strands 1 and 2 with strands 5 and 6 and knot them. Continue plaiting and knotting along the fringe making sure the knots are tied at exactly the same level as the first one.

Overhand knot fringe

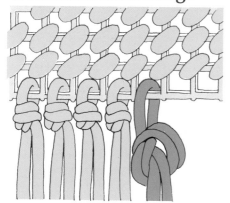

To make more of a feature of the knots, thread the length (or lengths) of yarn through the hole. Hold the back and front ends together and tie tightly in an ordinary overhand knot, close up to the edge of the canvas.

Alternating knots fringe

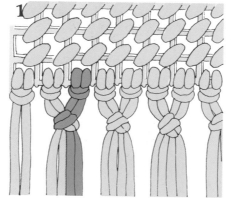

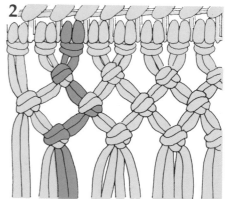

A pretty fringe with a diamond pattern at the top which requires a little extra yarn. It can be worked in groups of four on a simple knotted fringe or under a plaited heading.
1 Knot pairs of strands together all the way across the fringe to form groups of four, having all the knots level about 1cm/½in away from the top of the fringe.

2 Now work a second row of knots, about 1cm/½in below the first, taking two strands from one group and two strands from the next. Work as many rows of knots as you like before trimming the fringe evenly, but the loose fringe should be left longer than the knotted band.

CHAPTER 22

Variations in straight stitch create texture and pattern

Straight stitches in needlepoint are easy to work and cover the canvas quickly. Exciting patterns and textures are made simple and show the colours of the yarn to best advantage, so enjoy the freedom of straight stitches and embroider a colourful picture in several stitch variations.

There are several different types of straight stitches for use on canvas. Many different textures and effects can be created by varying the length and direction of the stitches.

Straight stitch techniques

Straight stitches are ideal for pictorial needlepoint and form clean-edged areas of colour. Subtle, shaded effects are also possible and often found in Florentine stitchery – one of the most well-known forms of straight stitch work.

Straight stitches are often worked over several canvas threads at a time. This is why you can finish a piece of straight stitch work comparatively fast. It is important to get canvas coverage right, and you will probably find you need a thicker thread than for tent stitch on the same gauge of canvas. (Use the guide given for tent stitch on page 87, and add an extra strand to the recommended thread thickness.)

Some types of straight stitch are not very hard-wearing. If stitches are very long, they can become loose and fluffy with too much wear, so they are best confined to pictures, wall-hangings and the like.

Working methods

You can work straight stitches horizontally, vertically, in neat rows, geometric patterns or at random – in fact, almost any way you like. Experiment on small pieces of spare canvas when you are testing for good canvas coverage. By changing the direction of stitches on a piece of work, you can emphasize different parts of a design. The light will catch them in a different way.

Where possible, bring the needle up in an empty hole, and push it down through a filled one. The yarn will pass more easily through the canvas and will not bring up fluffy strands of other colour yarns to spoil the look of the finished work.

In general, straight stitches do not distort the canvas nearly as much as tent and other diagonal stitches. You will often find that you can work effectively without a frame, particularly on smaller pieces of canvas. Mono canvas is the most suitable for this type of work.

Texture and pattern

The house picture (left) is an ideal example of how you can use straight needlepoint stitches to create different textural effects. All the stitches in the picture lie vertically yet, by varying their length and the way they are worked together, you can portray sky, roofs, trees, bricks and paving.

Try out different stitches on spare canvas. Find out which stitch is most effective for each part of the picture you are working. Here, the walls of the house are worked in blocks of straight stitches positioned to look like bricks. The sky, in gently undulating graduated straight stitch, is a good foil for the foreground detail. Notice the clever tile effect on the red roof, and how the same stitches, reversed, are used for the paving stones on the path. A diagonal line pattern makes a perfect front door. The ends of the stitches are used to 'draw' the lines in the picture.

Left: This colourful house picture incorporates several different textures. Right: Take a closer look at the patterns. From top left to bottom right: sky, roof, bricks, tree, garden path, front door.

Four well-known straight stitches

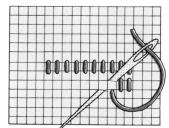

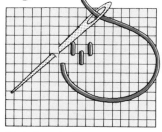

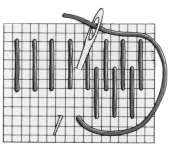

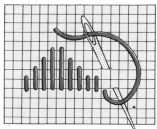

Straight gobelin stitch

This simple stitch resembles those on the famous Gobelin tapestries. The stitches are worked to a uniform length in horizontal rows, and are good for borders and for large areas.

Work over two to five canvas threads, from left to right and back again. Bring the needle out on the left and reinsert it two threads above. Bring it out again in the next hole to the right of where it first came up.

Brick stitch

This stitch is normally worked over two or four canvas threads. The interlocking rows form an all-over texture that is a useful filling. When changing colours the slight overlap between the rows creates a pleasing shaded effect. Work alternate up-and-down stitches as shown to make a zigzag row. The next row is worked directly underneath, so that the stitches lie end to end, and each one shares a canvas hole with the one in the row above.

Gobelin filling stitch

A close relation of brick stitch, gobelin filling stitch gives a slightly different effect, being worked over six threads or more (but it must be an even number). Work each row in vertical straight stitches, leaving an empty row between each stitch. On the next row, work stitches in the empty rows, three threads lower than those in the first row. For a straight edge, work stitches over three threads to fill the gaps left by the last full row.

Graduated straight stitch

By working straight stitches of varying length, you can fill almost any shape satisfactorily. Geometric patterns can be interpreted very well in this stitch, and many interesting textures can be created. Try aligning one end of all the stitches to create a 'wave' effect (as shown above), or working an area of horizontal stitches. The working method is the same as for straight gobelin stitch, except for the length of the stitches.

Blocking and setting needlepoint

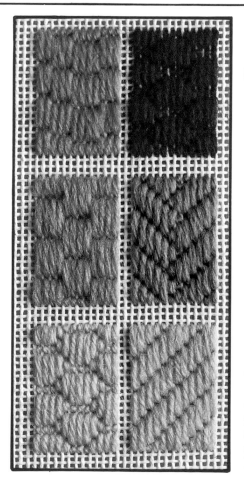

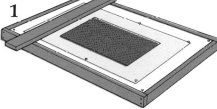

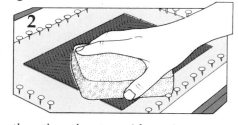

All needlepoint benefits from being blocked when completed. The process ensures that all the canvas threads end up straight, with any patterns or pictures the right shape and not distorted in any way. It also gives a smooth texture to the stitchery.

Dampening the canvas and allowing it to dry will reset the canvas threads correctly. Check that you have not missed any stitches – hold it up to the light and fill in gaps.

1 Take a piece of wooden board larger than the piece of work, which will take tacks. Fix a piece of white sheet over this and nail the canvas on to it, right side upwards so as not to flatten any raised-texture stitches. Use a steel ruler to get the edges absolutely straight.

Nail down two opposite sides and then the other two sides using rust-proof tacks at about 2cm/¾in intervals. Stretch the work into shape as you go. If necessary, use a tracing of the design placed over the worked canvas to get it exactly straight.

2 Dampen the canvas by dabbing with a wet sponge until it is really wet. Do not scrub, but use a blotting motion. You should not dampen any work incorporating silk threads, and some of the very dark shades of crewel wool and tapestry wool are not guaranteed colour-fast, so be very careful with these where they adjoin pale colours. Be sure that any markers or paints used on canvas are colour-fast before you dampen it. Leave it flat to dry naturally and completely. This will take at least 48 hours.

CHAPTER 23

Chunky cross stitches

The cross stitch family is one of the largest in needlepoint.
All the stitches are sturdy and suitable
for working handsome geometric designs on useful items
that need to be strong and hardwearing, such
as the glasses case and clutch bag in this chapter.

Cross stitches can be worked on mono or Penelope canvas. Some form square patterns, some diamonds and some rectangles. This geometric character makes them simple to master – from the basic cross stitch over two canvas threads, to the larger eye-catching triple cross stitch.

Tent stitch is a good accompaniment to some cross stitch variations – filling in spaces between them.

Basic know-how

The general rule that applies to the whole cross stitch family is that the last part of the stitch worked should always lie in the same direction. When a stitch incorporates an upright cross stitch, it is always the horizontal thread that is placed last. It is well worth trying out all the variations on spare canvas before tackling any projects.

Regular cross stitch

Cross stitch can be worked either horizontally or vertically, in single complete stitches, or in two-stage rows of half cross stitches. To be sure of always having the crossing stitches sloping in the same direction, work along a row in half cross stitches, and then back again to complete the crosses. For small motifs such as initials, you will find it easier to work in complete stitches.

Horizontal cross stitch

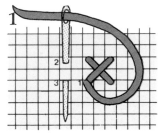
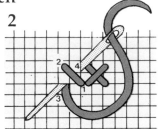

Working from right to left, over two threads:
1 Bring the needle out at (1) and re-insert at top left (2) to come out at bottom left (3).

2 Re-insert it at top right (4) to complete the stitch, and bring it out again at bottom left, ready to work another stitch.

Oblong cross stitch

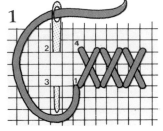
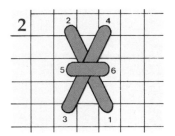

1 To work it over two threads, make an elongated cross stitch over four horizontal threads and two vertical threads.

2 Create a more decorative effect by adding a small catching stitch across the centre, over two threads as shown.

Vertical cross stitch

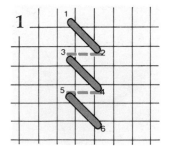
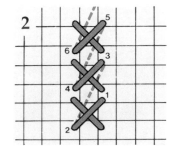

Working in two-stage rows of half stitches:
1 Make a diagonal stitch from top left (1) to bottom right (2) over the required number of threads (in this case, two). Bring the needle out at bottom left (3) and continue making downward diagonal stitches to bottom of row.

2 Beginning at top right of bottom stitch (1), make a diagonal stitch to bottom left (2), crossing the first one, and bring the needle out at top right of the stitch above (3). Continue to the end of the row. This makes long crossing stitches on the back of the work.

Crossed corners

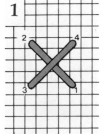
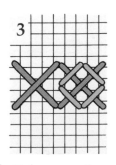
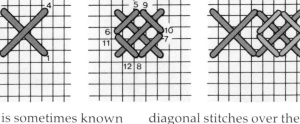

This is sometimes known as rice stitch, and is a useful hardwearing filling or border stitch. It looks striking when the corner stitches are worked in a contrasting, sometimes finer, yarn.
1 Work a large cross stitch over four threads.
2 Work four small

diagonal stitches over the corners as shown.
Always bring the needle up in the hole opposite to where it last went in.
3 When the corner stitches are in a contrasting yarn, work a row of large cross stitches first, and then 'cross the corners' using the new yarn.

Double cross stitch

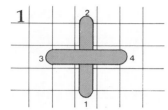 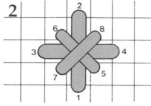

This pretty stitch is often worked in two shades.
1 Work an upright cross stitch over four canvas threads.

2 Next work a small diagonal cross stitch over two threads on top of it, forming a diamond pattern. Remember to keep the last stitches sloping the same way.

Below: Two needlepoint gifts to make. The bag and glasses case are worked in a combination of blue and deep rose pink. They would look just as good in black with gold thread.

Triple cross stitch

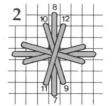 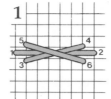 

This exciting stitch gives the effect of raised star shapes. Fill the gaps with cross or tent stitches.
1 Make a horizontal stitch over eight threads and work an oblong cross stitch on top (over six vertical threads and two horizontals).

2 Make a vertical stitch over eight threads. Now work another oblong cross stitch on top of this, (over six horizontal threads and two verticals).
3 Finish with a central regular cross stitch (two threads) over all these stitches.

Delightful small gifts in cross stitch variations

The geometric shapes of the cross stitch family make them suitable for working all kinds of simple items based on square and rectangular shapes. To start you off, here are patterns for two quick-to-make gifts – a glasses case and a clutch bag with a needlepoint flap.

The raised texture of the cross stitches gives a strong as well as pretty finish. Notice how the stitches complement the designs. Oblong cross stitch in the glasses case is combined with crossed corners, which sets up an unusual rhythm. The bag flap features two diamond shaped stitches to echo its V-shape.

Clutch bag

This beautiful clutch bag has a richly embroidered needlepoint flap, divided into vertical panels bordered by cross stitch. It includes the decorative triple cross stitch in two shades of pink. The stitched flap extends just over the top of the bag, but if you wish, you can continue the stitchery right down the back of the bag and up the front, too.

You will need
25cm/¼yd piece of 14-gauge mono canvas (narrow width)
3 small skeins each Appleton's crewel wool in Bright China Blue 7 (747), Bright Rose Pink 8 (948) and Bright Rose Pink 5 (945)
Tapestry needle size 20
Waterproof marker, masking tape

Below: The chart shows half of the symmetrical design for the clutch bag flap. Just work the other half of the design in reverse to complete the flap.

For making up
50cm/½yd toning fabric (any width)
25cm×50cm/9¾in×19¾in piece buckram (optional)
Large press stud fastening

Working the flap
Bind the canvas and mark the flap outline on to it by counting threads. The stitched area is 136 threads wide and 84 threads deep at the point.
Work very carefully from the chart by counting threads. Each of the five vertical panels covers 24 vertical threads, and the lines of cross stitches between them are worked over two threads. Begin at the centre and work outwards.
After completing the charted design, work one row of tent stitch in blue round the edge of the whole

Glasses case

The glasses case, stitched in an all-over pattern, is a smaller project. Each diagonal row of crossed corners is worked in a different shade of pink or burgundy in a random order so it is marvellous for using up oddments of leftover yarn. Only one side of the case is embroidered.

You will need
20cm/¼yd piece of 18-gauge mono canvas (narrow width)
3 small skeins Appleton's crewel wool in Bright China Blue 7 (747)
Skeins of yarn in 5 other shades of pink and burgundy such as Appleton's Bright Rose Pink 1, 3, 4, 6 and 8 (941, 943, 944, 946, 948) or Paterna Persian yarn 850 and 855
Tapestry needle size 20
Waterproof marker, and masking tape.

For making up
25cm/¼yd toning fabric (any width)
40cm/16in square buckram
Fabric adhesive

Working the glasses case
Cut the canvas to 20cm×27cm/7¾in ×10¾in and bind edges with masking tape. Mark canvas centre, and mark the outline of the case with a waterproof marker by counting the threads. (The length covers 100

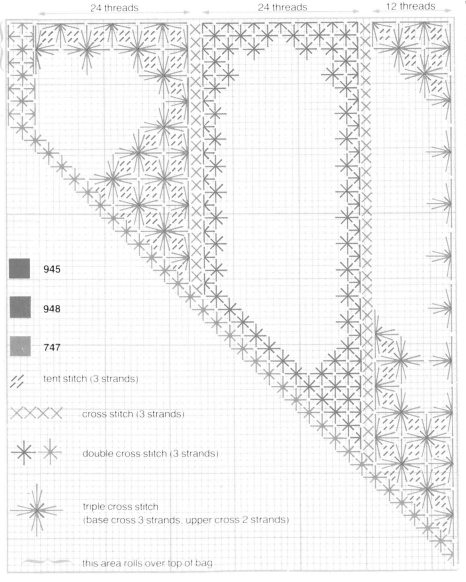

▨	945
▨	948
▨	747
╱╱	tent stitch (3 strands)
✕✕✕✕	cross stitch (3 strands)
✳ ✳	double cross stitch (3 strands)
✳	triple cross stitch (base cross 3 strands, upper cross 2 strands)
～	this area rolls over top of bag

24 threads   24 threads   12 threads

worked area to make the turnings neat. Work an extra row across the back edge.

Making up the bag

You can either have the bag made up professionally, or assemble the simple envelope shape yourself. Cut a paper pattern with measurements as shown. Draw sides AB, CD, and AC. Next draw EF down the centre. Join FB and FD to make the V-shaped flap. Fold fabric in half lengthwise and cut out the bag piece (double). Block needlepoint, or press carefully, pulling it to the correct shape. Trim canvas border to 1cm/½in and turn under canvas on long back edge of flap, tacking it in place. Place wrong side of needlepoint on right side of one bag piece with edges flush. Tack in place, and stitch all round close to needlepoint

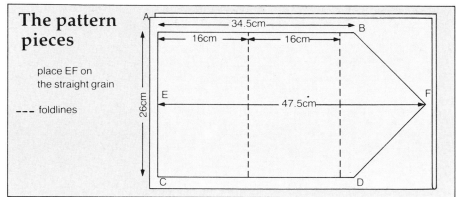

The pattern pieces

place EF on the straight grain

--- foldlines

on sloping edges, and between two tent stitch rows on back edge. Place bag pieces right sides together. Stitch all round with 1cm/½in seam, stitching close to needlepoint on flap and leaving short edge open for turning. Turn to right side and press carefully. To give the bag extra stiffening, cut buckram to fit exactly inside

and slip into place. Tack round bag edges, turning in 1cm/½in allowance on open edge. Topstitch round needlepoint flap inside tent stitch row and along short edge. Fold bag into shape, bringing short edge up to base of needlepoint, and stitch side seams close to the edge by hand or machine. Attach press stud fastening. Remove all tacking.

---

canvas threads, and the width, 54.) Following the chart, beginning in lower right corner, work the design of diagonal bands, using two strands of crewel wool in the needle or one strand of Persian yarn. Work in oblong cross stitch (with a centre catching stitch) and crossed corners. Fill in each oblong gap along the edges with two regular cross stitches over two threads. The oblong stitches are all in blue, and the crossed corners in alternating shades of pink and burgundy.

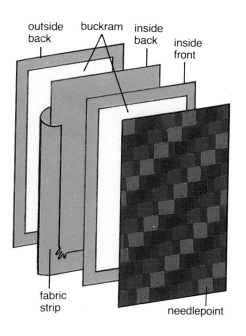

outside back · buckram · inside back · inside front

fabric strip · needlepoint

Making up the case

Block needlepoint, or press, face downwards, on a well-padded ironing board. Cut four pieces of buckram (for stiffening) measuring same as stitched area (16.5cm×9cm/6½in×3½in). Cut three pieces of fabric measuring 18.5cm×11cm/7¼in×4¼in, and one strip measuring 2.5cm×40cm/1in×16in.

Inside and outside back, inside front Cover one side of three of the buckram pieces with the fabric, turning 1cm/½in to the other side all round, clipping corners slightly. Pull fabric tight and stick down round the 1cm/½in turning, handling fabric carefully so that no adhesive spoils the right side. Trim canvas border round needlepoint to 1cm/½in. Lay canvas on one side of the other piece of buckram and stick the border down on the other side. Neaten both short ends of fabric strip with a 1cm/½in turning.

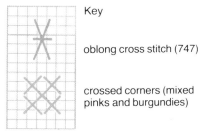

Key

oblong cross stitch (747)

crossed corners (mixed pinks and burgundies)

Assembling the back Lay outside back wrong side up. Lay right side of strip on buckram, 2cm/¾in down from top edge on each side, and overlapping so that 1.5cm/⅝in of the strip protrudes all round. Stick. Lay inside back on top, wrong sides together, so that strip protrudes between layers, except on top edge, and stick in place.

Assembling back and front Lay inside front on assembled back, right side of inside front to inside back. Wrap the protruding strip tightly over edge of inside front and stick in place. Lay the needlepoint piece in place on inside front and stick.

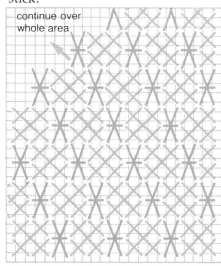

continue over whole area

pattern repeat for glasses case

CHAPTER 24

Working on a frame using a range of sampler stitches

This chapter give you guidance on choosing and using frames for needlepoint – a good idea for neat stitchery. Frame up your canvas and start stitching the sampler cushion cover – each area of the beautiful design is worked in a different stitch.

Although it is not essential, a frame keeps needlepoint evenly stretched – and you will find it is much easier to count threads and keep work neat when canvas is taut. The finished piece will also need less blocking.

It is always advisable to use a frame for pieces incorporating different stitches, diagonal stitches, couched threads, beads, laid threads in silk or stranded cotton, and for pulled-thread work.

Choose the type of frame most suitable for you and the space available – if possible, one that allows you to use both hands.

Artists' stretcher bars

These are the least expensive and most widely available type of frame. Bars come in pairs, and lengths from 25cm/9¾in upwards. Buy two pairs, one about 10cm/4in longer than the width and one about 10cm/4in longer than the depth of the design (not the canvas), you are working. For example, a design 25cm×30cm/9¾in ×11¾in on a canvas 35cm×40cm/ 13¾in×15¾in would need one pair of 35cm/13¾in and one pair 40cm/ 15¾in bars – they slot together at the corners. The canvas is mounted as tightly as possible, with drawing pins so it can be re-tightened as work progresses. To work with two hands, rest the frame on the edge of a table or the arm of a chair.

Below: Frames for needlepoint come in various different shapes and sizes.

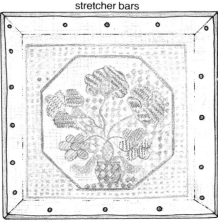

stretcher bars

Ring frame

This type comes in several sizes and consists of two hoops that fit one inside the other. A frame with a stand is best because it leaves both of your hands free. Choose from a knee or table stand, or table clamp, according to how you prefer to work. The knee/table stand frame is the most convenient to work with because the canvas can be mounted in seconds, so you are not tempted to work some areas without the frame (it really does show).

To mount the canvas, place it over the inner ring, place the outer ring on top and tighten the side screw to hold the work taut.

Sometimes, when working a large canvas, you will need to cover stitches with the ring. Wool yarn is unaffected, but when working with fine, fragile threads, it is best to cover the work with tissue paper before mounting on the frame, and tear away the paper just over the area being worked.

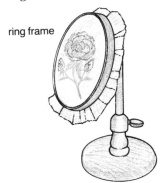

ring frame

Slate frame

This square or rectangular stretcher frame comes in several types and sizes, from 45cm/17¾in square upwards. It consists of taped rollers top and bottom and adjustable side stretchers with either screws, ratchets, pegs or split pins to hold the taped bars apart – giving the correct size and tension for the work.

The canvas is stitched to the tape on the top and bottom rollers and laced to the side bars (so it must not be wider than they are).

If you choose a slate frame drilled to fit a floor stand, you can buy a stand (now or later) which will make it easier to work with both hands.

Travelling frame

Sometimes called a rotating frame, this works on a similar principle to the slate frame. After stitching the work to the taped rollers, these can be rolled and fixed so that only the area being worked is exposed. This frame comes in two sizes, 30cm/11¾in square and 30cm×45cm/11¾in×17¾in.

Stitching on a frame

Have your right hand under the canvas to guide your weaker (left) hand which stays on top. If you are left-handed, simply reverse these positions. Pass the needle between your hands as if it were a weaving shuttle, making the stitches with a stabbing motion.

Renaissance Garden sampler cushion

The design of this beautiful cushion – worked in a stunning combination of coffee and cream crewel wool and stranded cotton – is based on the geometric layout of a French chateau's formal garden – each flowerbed is worked in a different stitch and bordered by cross stitch hedges and square mosaic stitch paths.

You will need

1½×25g hanks Appleton's crewel wool in off-white (992)
1×25g hank in fawn (952)
7 skeins Twilley's Lystra stranded cotton in camel (836) and 8 in cream (843)
2 tapestry needles size 20, 1 size 22
Large blunt rug needle *or* curved needle
40cm/½yd piece of white 14-gauge mono canvas (narrow width)
Pencil *or* grey Nepo waterproof marker
2 pairs of 40cm/16in stretcher bars *or* a slate frame (if possible)
40cm/½yd fawn or cream heavy

backing fabric (any width)
35cm/14in square cushion pad
Working hints Always keep the canvas selvedge at the side when working. You may turn the canvas completely upside down to reach an area more easily, but never turn it on its side. This rule helps you to work all the stitches in the right direction.

Remember that it is always better to come up in an empty hole, if possible. Use the key to the chart to find out which thread, shade and how many strands to use.

Needles Two size 20 needles are recommended, because in areas of the design where you are using two different colours or threads together, it is easier to have a needle for each.

The large rug needle or curved needle is used for smoothing out stranded cotton stitches before pulling them down on to the canvas. Hold it in the hand which is not holding the main needle, and make the stitches over it, gently

easing it out as you pull the stitch tight.

Crewel wool When working with the uncut 25g hanks of crewel wool, cut each hank through once at each end to obtain threads of the correct length.

Stranded cotton This thread needs 'stripping' before you begin stitching, to make it lie smoothly and give the best canvas coverage. Cut a piece 50cm/20in long and pull the six individual strands apart. Lay them flat, side by side, before gathering together and threading the needle with the number of strands recommended for the particular stitch.

Beginning threads When working a needlepoint sampler with different stitches, you will find yourself constantly beginning new threads in different parts of the canvas. There may be no stitching nearby (for anchoring the thread) so make a knot and insert the needle at the front of the canvas, fairly near the point where you are working.

Above: Pale and subtle colouring in this elegant cushion gives maximum effect to the texture of the stitches. The soft sheen comes from the stranded cotton which has been combined with the wool.

When the knot is eventually reached by stitching, cut if off close to the canvas. The stitches will have caught the 'tail' firmly on the back. Finish off threads in the usual way, running through the back of several stitches.

Marking the canvas
Cut canvas to a 40cm/16in square. Bind the edges with masking tape and mark the centre.
Mark the design on to the canvas by counting threads – each square on the chart equals two threads. Use the pencil or waterproof marker and work outwards from the centre. Each line on the chart corresponds to a line of *holes* on the canvas. To mark straight lines, simply place the

point of the pencil or marker in the channel between two threads and run it along for the required number of threads, counting each one as the pencil or marker bumps over it. If you use a pencil, give the canvas a good rub with white kitchen paper before you start to work or some of the graphite may come off.

Beginning to stitch the cushion
First, work all the paths between the blocks in square mosaic stitch. Now work the hedges round each flowerbed in padded cross stitch. Lay the padding stitch with three strands of crewel wool and work the top cross stitch over two threads in stranded cotton using the 22 needle, so that the wool shows through. Once you have worked the paths and hedges, the working order is not crucial. If you work outwards from the centre, your hands will not rest on areas you have already stitched.

Key to chart
The paths are shown in yellow, the hedges fawn and the flowerbeds salmon on the chart opposite. Use the photograph above as a guide to the colour scheme.
Paths: Square mosaic stitch
2 strands crewel wool.
Hedges: Padded cross stitch
Padding stitch: 3 strands crewel wool, cross stitch: 3 strands stranded cotton (22 needle).
A1 Diagonal tent 6 strands stranded cotton with single Leviathan stitch in centre of square: 3 strands crewel wool (large cross), 6 strands stranded cotton (upright cross).
A2 Diagonal tent 6 strands stranded cotton, four Leviathan stitches in square (threads as A1).
B Crossed corners Large cross: 3 strands crewel wool, small crossing stitches: 6 strands stranded cotton.

C1 and C2 Milanese stitch 6 strands stranded cotton, 2nd row: 6 strands stranded cotton, reverse diagram for C2.

D1 and D2 Oriental stitch 6 strands stranded cotton, 2nd row: 6 strands stranded cotton, reverse diagram for D2.

E Double brick stitch Work over 4 threads, 6 strands stranded cotton. (Work horizontally.)

F Chequer stitch Diagonal tent: 3 strands crewel wool, boxes: 6 strands stranded cotton.

G Ray stitch Diagonal tent: 3 strands crewel wool, rays: 6 strands stranded cotton.

H Cushion stitch Alternately 6 strands stranded cotton, 3 strands crewel wool.

I Small waffle stitch Alternately 6 strands stranded cotton, 3 strands crewel wool.

J Eyelets and crossed corners Eyelets: 6 strands stranded cotton, crossed corners: 6 strands stranded cotton.

All the new stitches are described in detail below and on the following four pages.

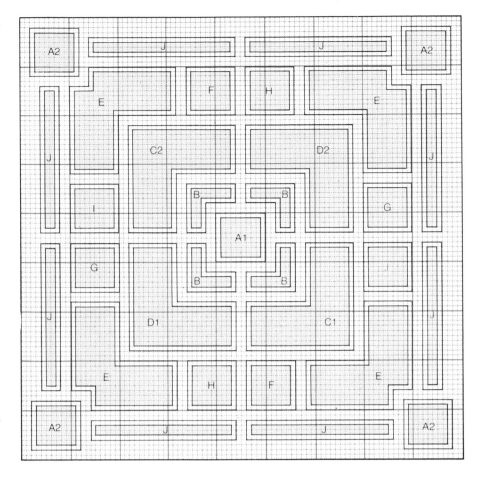

New stitches for the sampler cushion

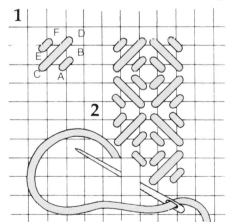

Square mosaic stitch
This stitch is composed of small blocks of three stitches each.
1 Begin with a short tent stitch over one canvas intersection (A–B), a longer stitch above it over two canvas intersections (C–D). Finish off the block with another short tent stitch (E–F). All three stitches slope in the same direction.
2 Adjacent blocks should slope in alternate directions, forming a chequerboard effect. The blocks will share the same canvas holes along the edges.

Square mosaic stitch is a useful filler.

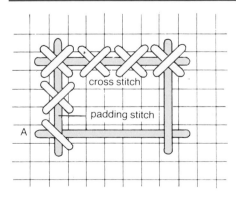

Padded cross stitch
To give a raised and decorative effect to cross stitch, work it over a straight 'padding' thread laid along the canvas in advance.
The diagram shows you how to turn corners with padding stitches, outlining an oblong shape, beginning at point A.
Work regular cross stitch over two threads, using a contrasting thread for the best effect.

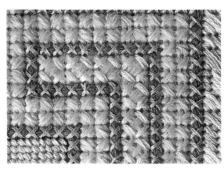

Padded cross stitch makes a good border.

Chequer stitch

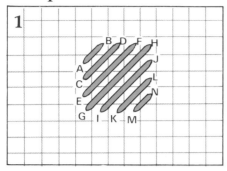

This stitch is formed of square boxes, as its name suggests. It looks very effective worked in two different threads.
1 Work diagonal straight stitches over one, two, three, four, three, two and one canvas intersections as shown. Leave alternate squares free.

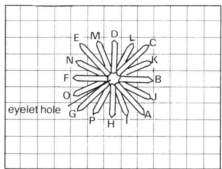

2 Now work the alternate squares in diagonal tent stitch, with the stitches all sloping in the same direction. The outer stitches on this box share a hole with stitches in the four adjacent straight stitch boxes. The boxes are alternated throughout.

Ray stitch

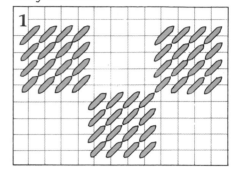

This very attractive stitch is also based on square units.
1 Work a series of square blocks of diagonal tent stitch, four stitches wide and four stitches deep. Leave alternating squares free.

Cushion stitch

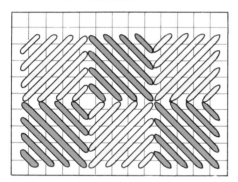

This stitch is very effective when light catches the alternating blocks of diagonal stitches.
For each 'square', work seven diagonal stitches, with a central one over four canvas intersections, and three more on each side, graduating in size over three, two and one intersections.
Each hole along the edge of a square will be shared by two stitches.

Eyelets

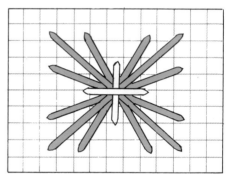

Often used in pulled thread work, this stitch incorporates 16 straight stitches, all converging in the same hole at the centre. If you wish to create a lacy look enlarge the central hole first with a large rug needle. Follow the stitch order carefully from the diagram, so that no threads run across the hole on the back of the work.

Leviathan stitch

This is similar to triple cross stitch but the long stitches are worked over eight canvas intersections (instead of eight threads) causing the whole stitch to lie at a different angle. And the small central cross stitch becomes an upright. Working this in a contrasting thread looks most effective.

An alternate colourway

Stitch the Renaissance Garden cushion in any colour. The one in the picture opposite has been worked in blue and cream using the same stitches given with the chart on pages 106 and 107. By working paths and hedges in two shades of blue crewel wool the whole emphasis of the design is changed giving a more vibrant look to the pattern when compared with the cream and fawn colour scheme.

You will need
1½×25g Appleton's crewel wool in pale blue (743)
1×25g Appleton's crewel wool in dark blue (746)
7 skeins Twilley's Lystra stranded cotton in blue (641) and 8 in cream (843)

Starting to stitch
Try out each new stitch on a spare piece of canvas and make sure you can work it confidently before filling the appropriate area on the canvas. Square and diagonal pattern stitches like these are wonderfully versatile, neatly filling geometric shapes and creating fascinating textural effects. Experiment by using two different colours in one stitch or work in cotton and wool of the same shade.
Use the picture opposite and the detail on page 111 as a colour guide.

Small waffle stitch

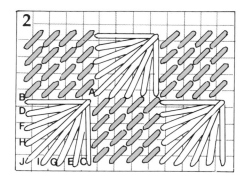

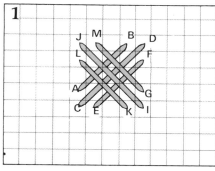

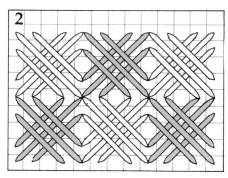

2 Now, in the alternating squares, work the blocks of ray-like stitches in the suggested order (A-B, A-C and so on). Each one uses the same hole (A) in the upper right corner, and the other end of each stitch shares a hole with one of the tent stitches in the next block.

Another stitch which forms a square pattern.
1 Work three stitches over 3, 4 and 3 canvas intersections in one direction and then work three stitches over 3, 4 and 3 threads in the opposite direction, on top.

2 Continue working in square blocks with all the top stitches sloping in the same direction. Two different shades or types of thread can be used very successfully.

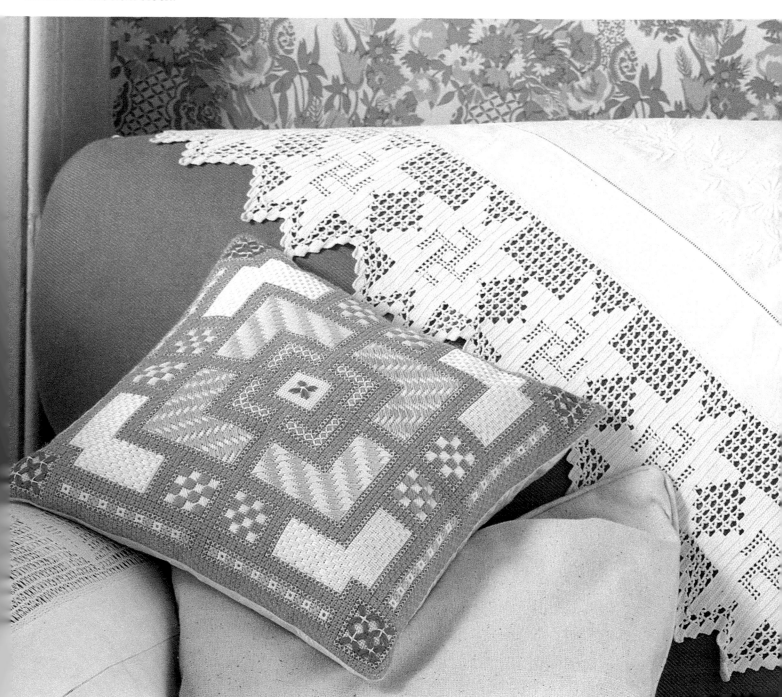

Milanese stitch

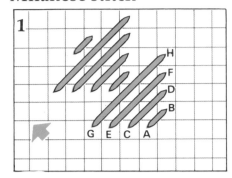

This striking stitch forms a diagonal pattern of triangular arrowheads running in alternate directions, making a good all-over zigzag design.
1 Begin with a tent stitch over one canvas intersection (A-B), then work over two, three and four intersections in turn (C-D, E-F, G-H) to make the triangle. Begin the

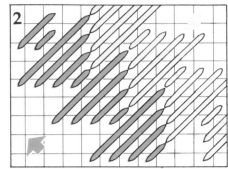

next arrowhead with another short tent stitch centred over the longest stitch of the first arrowhead, and continue working diagonally upwards.
2 Reverse the direction of the arrowheads for the downward row. Working alternate rows in different colours creates an even more attractive pattern.

Oriental stitch

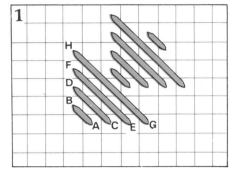

This pretty variation of Milanese stitch looks like steps.
1 Begin with a row of Milanese stitch arrowheads running diagonally in whichever direction you wish to work.
2 For the second row, change threads if you wish, and make groups of three even stitches over two canvas intersections, sloping in

---

Finishing the sampler cushion

Continue to refer to the key to the working chart on pages 106-107.

Milanese stitch
Areas C1 and C2, which are diagonally opposite to each other, are worked in Milanese stitch. Work the stitches over a rug needle to keep the stranded cottons smooth. To work area C1, begin in the outer corner with a short stitch and work first row of triangles in one colour. Work downward row of triangles above in second colour stranded cotton. Near the outside edge, work compensation stitches of irregular length to obtain a straight edge. When you begin the second colour

thread, work some pattern stitches in the correct position first (begin at the dot in the diagram), then go back and fill in the compensation stitches. The diagram shows you how to deal with the inner corners as well as the outer ones.

Oriental stitch
Now work areas D1 and D2 in Oriental stitch, reversing the stitch diagram for D2. Begin at the outer corners as for the Milanese stitch and use two needles – one for each shade of cotton.
To work the row containing compensation stitches, begin at the dot in the diagram.

Double brick stitch
Fill the areas marked E with double brick stitch (which is worked in the same way as brick stitch, but with the stitches in identical pairs), worked horizontally. If the work is not on a frame, you may turn it sideways in order to work the brick stitch vertically.
To obtain a straight edge, work the compensation stitches over two threads, as shown. Add these after working the complete row nearest the edge.

Working the small squares
Now work the squares of chequer stitch, ray stitch, and small waffle stitch, taking care to slope all the

Milanese stitch

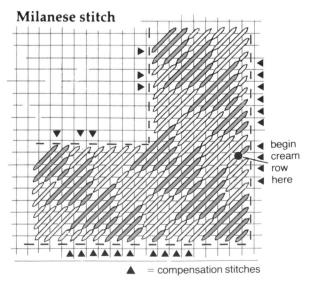

begin cream row here

▲ = compensation stitches

Oriental stitch

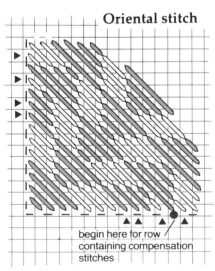

begin here for row containing compensation stitches

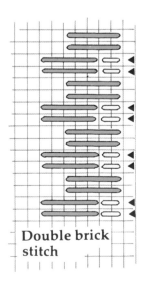

Double brick stitch

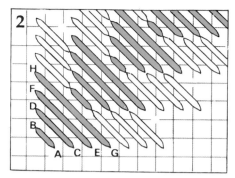

the same direction as the first row stitches. Work them into the same holes as the ends of the three smallest stitches in each triangle. When you have done this along the upper and lower edges of the Milanese stitch, you will see shapes developing into which you work the next row of arrowheads pointing in the opposite direction.

stitches in the correct direction in relation to the top edge.

When stitching the areas marked H (cushion stitch), run a diagonal thread across the two squares to be worked in stranded cotton before adding the stitches, to give extra body. The diagram shows you how to run the thread from the lower left corner of one square to the upper right corner of the one diagonally nearest.

Crossed corners and eyelets
All the long bars marked J are worked as rows of alternating crossed corners and eyelets. Work all the crossed corners first (beginning each one at top right –

see dots), leaving a gap four threads wide between each. The crossed corners should be at the inside ends of each bar.
To make a pretty lacy effect, enlarge the eyelet holes as described.

The finishing touches
Finally, add the striking Leviathan stitches – one in the centre of area A1 and four in each square marked A2.
Work them on top of the tent stitch background already worked. Each stitch spans eight canvas threads in either direction. The diagrams show you exactly where to place stitches. Check the work for any missed stitches and remove from the frame

Above: Geometric designs are ideal for samplers: each area contains a new stitch.

– if you are using one. Block and set the canvas, making sure that the edges are straight.

Making up
Trim the canvas border to 1cm/½in. Cut the backing fabric to a square 34cm×34cm/13½in×13½in (the same size as canvas).
With right sides together, machine stitch three sides of cover, taking a 1cm/½in seam. Stitch fourth side, leaving a central gap of 20cm/7¼in. Trim corners, turn and insert cushion pad through opening. Slipstitch opening neatly.

Cushion stitch

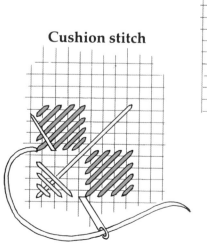

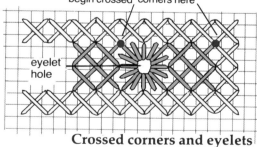

Crossed corners and eyelets

begin crossed corners here
eyelet hole

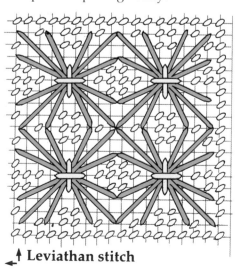

↑ **Leviathan stitch**

111

Design ideas for sampler cushions

These three cushions use patterns based on diamond and lattice shapes to evoke the delicate tracery you might find in a Moorish mosque. A subtle mixture of wools with matt and shiny cotton threads, together with a few ribbons for highlights, have been used. Some of the stitches allow the white mono canvas to show through which keeps the overall effect light and lacy. Others use the pulled thread technique described in detail on pages 126-7. The square cushion in the foreground has a Gothic Florentine border.

The chart for this and information on how to work a variety of border designs are given on page 141.

Plan your own geometric design on a sheet of graph paper first and then transfer it accurately to the canvas using a pencil or waterproof marker. You will find the stitches described in chapters 23, 24, 28, 29 and 31 particularly useful for this type of needlepoint.

Always work any design outline first to set the pattern; it is then easy to fill in the diamonds, triangles, etc, with the appropriate stitches.

Making up a cushion With the right side of the work and backing fabric together, stitch round three sides as close to the edge of the work as possible (about 2.5cm/1in seam allowance). Trim seams to 1cm/½in, cutting across each corner diagonally to reduce bulk.

Turn to the right side and insert the cushion pad. Oversew the fourth side by hand. (Simply unpick this seam by hand to remove the pad.)

CHAPTER 25

Pile stitches add a third dimension

Needlepoint stitches which give a soft pile effect are fun to do and cover the canvas quickly. Once you have mastered the three shown here, plus three new background stitches, you can make an appealing panda picture for a favourite child.

Some needlepoint stitches produce a raised pile, creating a rug-like effect. In fact these stitches are sometimes used to make needlepoint rugs – the loops formed can be left uncut, or trimmed evenly to make tufts. They can also be used for any project where you want a raised texture, for abstract designs with textural variations, or for novelty effects in designs such as animal pictures.

The three pile stitches introduced here should all be worked in horizontal rows from left to right and upwards over the canvas. This is because the pile tends to lie downwards once it has been stitched, covering the few rows of canvas threads underneath. If you find it tricky keeping the loops uniform, work over a knitting needle chosen to give the required size.

This chapter also shows you three new textured stitches, useful for building up backgrounds in pictorial needlepoint.

Below: Stitch this brightly-coloured needlepoint picture or design your own using simple shapes.

Three pile stitches

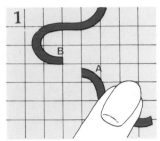

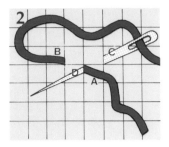

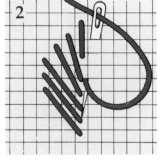

Single knotted stitch
This stitch gives a dense pile effect. The loops can be left uncut, cut through or trimmed short.
1 Insert the needle at A, leaving a short length of yarn anchored by the left thumb. Bring the needle up at B (1 canvas thread up and 2 to the left).

2 Reinsert the needle at C (3 threads to the right of B) and bring it out again at D, pulling firmly to make a tight knot. Make the next stitch, leaving a loop between the two stitches.

3 Continue along the row in this way, so that each tight horizontal stitch shares a hole with the next one. Try to keep the loops regular. Leave a free row of horizontal canvas thread between each row of stitches (leave two for a less dense pile).

Velvet stitch
This stitch gives a pile similar to that of an Oriental carpet.
1 Bring the needle out at A; re-insert it at B (2 threads to the right and 2 up), bring it out again at A. Now re-insert the needle at B leaving a loop of thread and bring it out under the loop at C (2 threads down). Re-

Three useful textured stitches

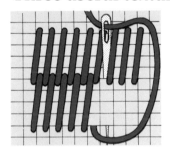

Encroaching gobelin stitch
This stitch is closely worked and gives an

attractively textured background useful for colour shading effects – each row of stitches overlaps slightly with the rows above and below it. Start at the top of the area and work each stitch over five horizontal canvas threads, and diagonally over one vertical one as shown. Work backwards and forwards in rows.

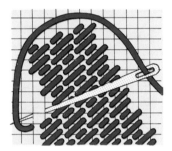

Cashmere stitch
Another useful texture stitch – this one looks almost like woven fabric

with a diagonal grain. Work in units of three stitches over 1, 2, and 2 canvas threads, progressing diagonally down the canvas by moving one thread to the right after each three-stitch unit. On the return journey, work diagonally upwards, this time moving one thread to the left each time.

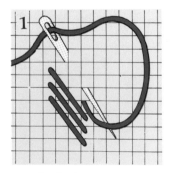

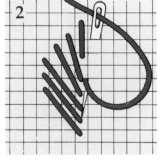

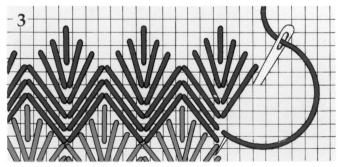

Leaf stitch
This pretty stitch forms a series of 'leaves' on the surface of the canvas. Use it as an all-over texture or in leaf and tree pictorial designs.
Each leaf consists of 11 straight stitches – three at

each side and five fanned out at the top.
1 Beginning at the base of the leaf, follow the working order given in the diagram. The three stitches on each side of the leaf lie directly in line with one another.

2 Continue round the top of the leaf. Note that all the central ends of the stitches lie along the same vertical row of canvas holes.
3 When the leaf is complete, begin the next one six holes to the right

(or left) of it, so that the side stitches of the leaves share the same holes. For an all-over texture, begin the leaves for the row above in the hole where two top side stitches converge.

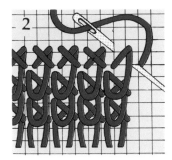
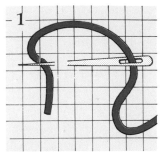
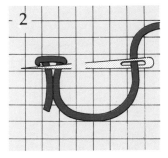

insert it at D (2 threads up and 2 to the left, bringing it out again at C ready for the next stitch.
2 Continue working upwards over the canvas, and when the whole area to be worked is covered, cut through the centre of each loop to form the pile, trimming them evenly to the desired length.

Rya stitch
Dense, overlapping loops make this a good 'special effects' stitch.
1 Holding the end of the yarn on the right side of the canvas, pass the needle from right to left under a vertical canvas thread and pull through. Make the next stitch in the next thread to the right, pulling tightly.

2 Pass the needle under the next vertical thread to the right, pull through forming a loop and hold this loop in place with your thumb while you make the next stitch under the next vertical canvas thread. Pull through tightly to secure the loop. With the next stitch, form the next loop.

3 Continue along the row, alternately forming loops and tight stitches and keeping all the loops even. Work the next row in the horizontal line of holes just above this one.

Playful pandas nursery picture

The colourful needlepoint nursery picture of pandas shown on page 113 will delight any young child and remain a favourite for many years to come. It's fun to work and includes several different stitches which bring the picture alive with their interesting textures – fluffy clouds and pandas, leafy trees and daisy-scattered grass.

You will need
50cm/½yd white 14-gauge mono canvas
Appletons crewel wool:
5 small skeins white (991), 3 skeins each black (993), grass green 1, 3 and 5 (251, 253, 255)
2 skeins each grass green 6 (256), sky blue 1 and 3 (561, 563)
1 skein each red fawn 5 (305), iron grey 7 (967), scarlet 3 (503), bright yellow 2 (552), royal blue 4 (824) and turquoise 4 (524)
Tapestry needle size 22
Nepo waterproof marker

Preparing the canvas
Bind the edges of the canvas with masking tape and mark the centre. Boldly trace the design outlines from the life-size photograph (overleaf) on to tracing paper. Centre the canvas over the tracing and re-trace the outlines with a waterproof marker.
If possible, mount the canvas on stretcher bars or a slate frame.

Working the design
As far as possible, stitch from the centre of the picture outwards, but leaving the two pandas till last. Use three strands of crewel wool throughout except for the lake area where you should use four strands.
Lake Gobelin filling stitch over six threads.
Bees Tent stitch.

Below: For a smaller project, pick out a panda motif from the picture, and add a plain, primary colour background.

Trace pattern for panda picture

Centre field Cashmere stitch.
Left hand trees Trunks in tent stitch, foliage in leaf stitch.
Sky Encroaching gobelin stitch, becoming darker towards the top.
Clouds Single knotted stitch, cut to a short pile when complete.
Left hand field background Work this area in Milanese stitch in a single colour.
Right hand field background Using the same green, change to brick stitch.
Ball Continental tent stitch.
Right hand tree This tree has a cross stitch trunk and rya stitch foliage – leave rya stitch loopy.

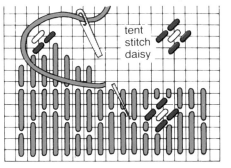

Working the foreground field First scatter the foreground with tent stitch daisies, each one worked as five stitches – a central yellow one and four surrounding white ones. Fill in the remaining area with graduated straight stitch in a zigzag pattern as shown.
Pandas The eyes, noses and bamboo shoots are all worked in tent stitch. Use tent stitch for the inside of the paws too. The fluffy bodies of both pandas are worked in velvet stitch, cut to a short pile.

Finishing off

Check your work for missed stitches and take it off the frame. It's not a good idea to dampen this design as black wool can run when used on white canvas, but these stitches should hardly distort the canvas.
Stretch the canvas tightly over a piece of strong card or hardboard and lace firmly at the back (see page 91, Mounting the picture). Use a purchased frame to display the picture or have it framed professionally.

Left: Use this lifesize photograph as your trace pattern. Remember that pile stitches tend to overlap the outlines.

CHAPTER 26

Four textured stitches

*Complete your collection of textural needlepoint stitches
with the four shown here. Make a cheerful
picture of a plump black and white cat sitting on a busily-
patterned carpet. A well-designed picture
succeeds even with this many colours and stitches.*

Needlepoint pictures can be fun to
work and provide the perfect chance
to try out unfamiliar stitches to build
up interesting textures.

The four new stitches, shown right,
have been incorporated into the colourful domestic scene that makes up
the enchanting picture above.

Full working instructions are given
in this chapter plus a close-up of the
actual-size picture to use as a trace
pattern, instead of having to draw it
from a graph.

Four new textured stitches

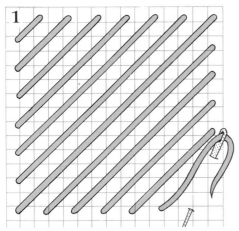

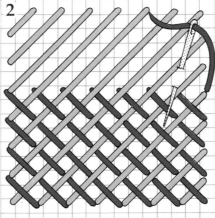

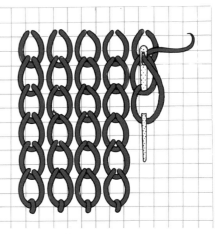

Web stitch

This firm, all-over texture stitch gives a woven effect when worked in two colours.

1 With the first colour in the needle, lay a series of diagonal threads across the canvas, so that they run across each alternate line of holes. The thread does not pass through the canvas except at the edge of the stitching area.

Left: Pictures like this jolly cat in an interior are fun to stitch in several different textured stitches.

2 With the second colour, work stitches diagonally in the opposite direction.
Work stitches in horizontal rows like half cross stitches but only working into every alternate hole, to 'tie' the long threads in place. Where these stitches meet in one hole, make sure the long, laid thread runs between them.
No stitch should 'tie' the same thread as the stitch before or following it.

Chain stitch

Needlepoint chain stitch is worked in exactly the same way as on fabric, except that stitches are regulated by the canvas threads.
Working vertically, bring the needle up in the first hole, loop the thread and hold with a finger. Re-insert the needle in the same hole and bring it up two holes further down, catching the loop of thread as you pull it through. Make the loop for the next stitch, and so on.
At the end of a row, hold the final loop in place with a catching stitch.

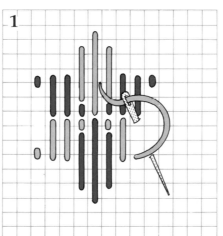

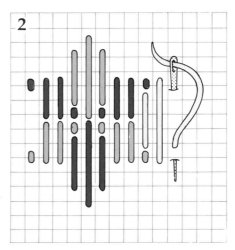

Dutch stitch

This stitch, useful for all-over patterns, is formed of interlocking stars. Begin each stitch by working an oblong cross stitch horizontally – that is, spanning four vertical canvas threads and two horizontal. To finish off, work a single vertical straight stitch over four horizontal threads, in the centre to complete the star. The ends of these straight stitches should share holes with the ends of adjoining stars, as shown.

Interlocking diamond stitch

Another 'pattern' stitch formed of closely-interlocking geometric shapes. Six diamonds make a six-pointed star. You can either work each 'star' in one colour, or use different colours for individual diamonds.

1 Work the upright diamonds as straight stitches over 4, 6 and 4 threads. The sideways diamonds which interlock with them are worked over 1, 3, 3, and 1 threads.

2 Having completed a star shape, work an upright diamond in the space created by two of the sideways diamonds. You need another upright diamond and three more sideways diamonds to complete the second star.

Contented cat picture

Stitch yourself a purring pussycat sitting in a colourful roomscape, and getting into mischief with a ball of wool! As well as the cat, the window scene, wallpaper and carpet are all fascinating to work. There are lots of different stitches to hold your interest as well as a colourful mixture of different threads – soft, matt cotton, stranded cotton, pearl cotton and tapestry wool. A web stitch 'frame' finishes the design; choose neutrals for this, to enhance the picture.
(Note that you need three sizes of tapestry needle to suit the various threads.)

You will need
28cm×36cm/11in×14in piece of 16-gauge mono canvas
Tapestry needles size 20, 22, 24
Tracing paper
Thick black felt-tip pen
Waterproof marker
for the cat
1 skein each DMC tapestry wool in 7192 noir, 7285 blanc, 7911 and 7604
1 skein bright green stranded embroidery wool
Oddments of silver metallic thread for whiskers (Twilleys Goldfingering is a suitable choice)

for the window frame and border
2 skeins each DMC cotton Retors à broder in 2938 and 2939
for the wallpaper
1 skein each DMC pearl cotton No 5 in 437, 223, 920, 301, 841 and ecru
for the carpet
1 skein each DMC stranded cotton in 900, 352, 741, 321, 3041 and 725
for the sky
1 skein each DMC cotton Retors à broder in 2825, 2826, 2798, 2799, 2828, 2800 and 2933
For the hedge
1 skein each DMC cotton Retors à broder in 1956, 2907 and 2957

Working the needlepoint design

Mark the centre of the piece of canvas and bind the edges with masking tape.
Trace off the main design outlines using a thick, black felt-tip. Lay the canvas centrally over the design and transfer the outlines to the canvas with a waterproof marker. Mount the canvas on stretcher bars or a frame if possible.
Stitching the cat Use tapestry wool and a size 20 needle. Work in vertical straight stitches, using the ends of stitches to define the contours of the cat. Using this heavier yarn makes the cat stand out well against the patterned carpet and wallpaper.

Stitching the carpet Using a size 22 needle and stranded cotton, stitch the busy, multi-coloured pattern on the carpet in interlocking diamond stitch.
Strip down the stranded cotton into separate strands before using it and work each stitch with six strands in the needle, then with another six so that each stitch has the weight of 12 threads. This gives good canvas coverage.
Stitching the wallpaper Use Dutch stitch and a size 24 needle to fill the wallpaper area. Random shades of pearl cotton form the all-over interlocking design. They complement the carpet colours, but are more subdued and the difference in thread texture enhances this effect.
Stitching the sky Stitch the sky in blended blues from light to dark, using encroaching gobelin stitch worked over four horizontal threads. Change the thread colour

after each row, shading from dark at the top to light at the bottom.
Stitching the hedge The green hedge outside the window is stitched in three different greens using Hungarian stitch. Work small random patches in each of the colours.
Stitching the basket of flowers First work the basket in straight stitch, then fill in with multi-coloured flowers formed by mixing together freely embroidered French knots, eyelets and double cross stitches. Add touches of green for the leaves.
Stitching the ball of wool Rows of chain stitch make a realistic ball of wool. Work several vertical rows to form the main ball shape, then add a few rows worked diagonally across the ball and a wandering thread festooned around the cat. Use one strand of stranded wool and a size 24 needle.
Stitching the frame Web stitch in two colours makes an effective border. Use the beige soft cotton for the laid threads and the brown for the tying stitches.
Lastly, using silver, add the highlights in the cat's eyes (French knots) and the whiskers (straight stitches). Take the work off the frame or stretcher bars, mount and frame if you wish.

Left: There's a wealth of different colours and threads in the cat picture. Right: Use this actual-size photo as your working chart.

CHAPTER 27

Freestyle needlepoint for subtle tones and textures

Try your hand at freestyle stitchery, even if you're not a dab hand with a paintbrush. This technique relies on simplicity of design, enriched by mixing textures and materials. Stitch a beautiful square picture with subtly mixed tones and a random border.

To build up a freestyle design, use a mixture of stitches, threads and colours carefully chosen to reflect the quality of the subject. Decide where you want solid blocks of colour and where subtle tonal mixtures are required, where you need texture or smoothness, and where you need matt wools, or the slight sheen of silk or cotton.

Choosing stitches

Different textures and the way they interact play an important part. French knots, a stitch usually associated with embroidery on fabric, can be suitable for natural foliage and flowers on canvas. In contrast, satin stitch or encroaching Gobelin stitch work well as flat surfaces – wood or bricks, for instance. Tent stitch is always a useful standby.

Consider whether your stitches are intended for the foreground or background of the needlepoint. Flatter stitches make shapes recede into the background while textured stitches appear to move to the front of a picture. Used with discretion, this technique helps to create three-dimensional effects, as in the centre

Interesting stitches for freestyle needlepoint

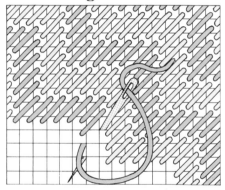

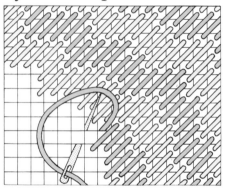

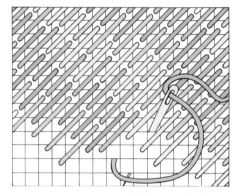

Byzantine stitch
This stitch consists of diagonal satin stitches worked over two, three or four canvas intersections, forming a zigzag pattern of steps. The finished effect looks like woven fabric. This stitch is quick to work and a useful background filling.

Random Byzantine stitch
For freestyle designs, stitch in a less regular way. Try working over two canvas intersections for a more detailed effect. Work out an irregular step pattern across the motif, keeping all stitches the same length, then repeat to fill the area.

Random Gobelin filling stitch
Work as Gobelin filling stitch but this time diagonally over odd numbers of intersections.
Work a row of level stitches (with a row of empty holes between each stitch for the next row).
Occasionally, move the stitch one hole to the left or right and make the other rows follow suit.

Freestyle garden picture with border

This beautiful picture with its subtly-toned central landscape and riotously coloured border uses a combination of stitches and materials. The square panel in the centre of the picture gives the impression of looking through a camera viewfinder. The colours are mixed and the stitches more highly textured, whereas in the rest of the picture they are flatter. Stretch the finished needlepoint over hardboard before framing but do not place it under glass.

You will need
33cm/13in square of white 18-gauge mono canvas
Coats Anchor stranded cotton, 1 skein each in 1212, 0212, 0851, 0899, 0210, 0216, 0218, 0245, 0261, 0258, 0888, 0264, 0266, 0281, 0400, 0398, 0397, 1087, 1214, 063, 096, 0107, 0108, 095, 0349
Coats Anchor tapisserie wool, 1 skein each in 096, 0105
Small pale green and pink glass beads, about 80 in each colour

Tapestry needle size 18
Crewel needle size 10
Square or rectangular frame, or stretcher bars
Masking tape
Waterproof marker
Tracing paper

Preparing the canvas
Bind the edges of the canvas with masking tape and mark the centre. Trace the main design outlines on to the tracing paper using a thick,

section of the square picture. This represents a more detailed view of the scene, so massed French knots add heavy texture to this area. Smoother stitches in the rest of the picture area look more distant.

Canvas has a regular, grid-like structure, normally reflected by the stitches worked on it. Experiment by ignoring the grid, working mixtures of random stitches in all directions, combining colours and threads. The border of the square picture shown below is a perfect example of disguising the canvas grid.

Using borders

Borders work well on freestyle stitchery. They help to balance and frame pictorial designs that have no geo-metric structure of their own and are pleasing to the eye. Careful colour and stitch choice can co-ordinate the different elements of the main design. Border patterns can be in random or geometric designs, or a combination of the two.

Colours, threads and canvas

Choosing colours and materials is one of the most exciting parts of this type of needlepoint. Select several tones of the same colour rather than unrelated colours.

Colour mixing To capture the subtle colours of Nature successfully, try mixing and blending threads as you would if using paint. Instead of using just one colour in the needle, mix different tones. Stranded cottons are available in ready-shaded colours, but provide only random tonal changes. To control the effect your-self, mix the colours as you work – versatile stranded cotton has six separate strands. Change the colour balance after each needleful – sooner if your design requires.

Mono canvas is the best choice, and the threads you use depend on the gauge of the canvas – any weight and combination as long as coverage is good. Cottons, silks, metallic threads and wools even with beads added, can work happily side by side, so go ahead and start mixing.

Below: On a detailed picture like this one, keep the main shapes simple. Use up thread oddments on a random border.

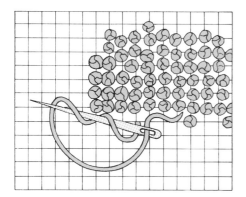

French knots

Bring the thread out where you want to make the knot, anchor it with a finger and wind the loose thread twice round the needle. Still holding the thread, re-insert the needle close to where the thread first emerged. Pull the thread through to the back.

black felt-tip pen. This makes the design easier to see through the canvas. Transfer the outlines to the canvas using the waterproof marker. Mark the position of the inner and outer borders shown in the positioning diagram by counting threads.

Mount the canvas on a frame large enough to accommodate the whole design. Once the canvas is fixed in place, do not remove it until the design is completed.

Stitching the freestyle picture

Work from the centre outwards. The design uses mainly stranded cotton. Use three strands of each colour, separating the strands as you need them to avoid tangles and help the stitches lie smoothly.

The centre square Begin with this area – sections A, B, C and D are all stitched in close French knots using mixed greens. Follow the same method for each section. In area A, there are five shades of green. Start with three strands of the first green in the needle. Scatter the French knots in the first area until the first needleful is finished. Then change to the second, third and fourth greens and drop the first one. Continue like this until the whole area is filled. Repeat for areas B, C and D using the colours shown in the picture.

Area M Work the sky area in the centre square using the shaded blue stranded cotton. This automatically produces an effect of 'clouds'. Work the random Gobelin filling stitch in patches, moving to a new patch when the thread colour changes. All the stitches should end in the same horizontal top row.

The main picture area Work the beautifully trimmed trees in random Byzantine stitch as described on the previous page. Fill in the main part of the sky (area K) using tent stitch. Try as far as possible to make the different colours link up with those in the centre square.

Add the two L areas in random Gobelin filling stitch, with the three strands of shaded thread, this time taken from different cut lengths so that they are mixed in the needle and form mottled areas.

The crazy paving First establish the dark grey tent stitch lines which run between each paving stone. Use the three lighter greys for the stones (random Gobelin filling stitch). Thread the needle with three strands of the first grey. Change the colour for each paving stone as for the central trees.

The border Stitch one row of jade green tent stitch all round the design, working into the same holes as the outer picture stitches. Next, work two rows of sloping satin stitch in wools, over three horizontal and three vertical threads. Stitch outer border in a completely free way, using a random mixture of stitches and colours. Those used here include French knots, slanted Gobelin stitch, straight stitches at any angle, cross stitch and oblong cross stitch. Sew on the pink and green beads at random using the crewel needle and one strand of stranded cotton.

Finishing off Check the whole picture for any missed stitches and take it off the frame. Stretch carefully and frame.

Stitch guide

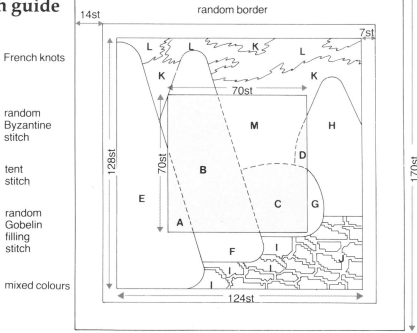

A
B
C
D } = French knots

E
F
G
H } = random Byzantine stitch

J
K } = tent stitch

I
L
M } = random Gobelin filling stitch

☐ = mixed colours

random border

14st · 7st · 70st · 128st · 70st · 170st · 124st · 166st

CHAPTER 28

Lacy pulled thread stitches

With its open mesh and even weave, canvas makes an excellent ground fabric for pulled thread work. The finished surface looks delicate, but is surprisingly tough. Much of the canvas is left showing, so it's quick to work and gives a lovely pale effect.

Eighteenth century white openwork embroidery of Germany and Denmark contains early examples of pulled thread work. It was called Dresden work or Dresden Point and originated as a time-saving alternative to real lace, often used for ladies' caps, fichus and aprons.

Pulled thread work should not be confused with drawn thread work, where threads are cut and completely removed from the ground fabric. In pulled thread, fabric threads are moved out of alignment by making different embroidery stitches and pulling these up tightly. This creates holes which form the pattern and give the work a delicate, lacy look.

Colour schemes
Traditionally, white thread on a white background was the rule. While you can use bold colour, it is usually more successful to make a soft combination of white, cream and beige with possibly a gentle accent of pale pink, green or blue. The reason for this is that the pattern is formed mainly by the *holes*; the thread only serves to bind the canvas threads together, so it should blend with the ground fabric as unobtrusively as possible.

For a project like a pulled thread cushion cover, mounting the worked canvas on a deep-coloured backing accentuates the pattern.

Materials
Canvas White mono canvas is the

Pulled thread stitch patterns for needlepoint

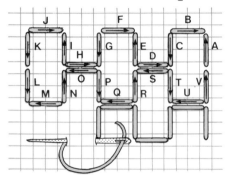

Honeycomb filling stitch
This pretty stitch leaves much of the canvas showing. Single vertical stitches and double horizontal ones create a honeycomb effect when pulled. Work all the stitches over three canvas threads.

Work from right to left on the first row. The letters indicate the order

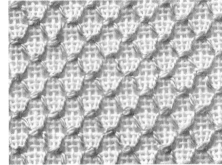

of holes in which to bring the needle up for each stitch.

On the second row, work back from left to right after taking a stitch into the surrounding canvas between the last stitch of the first row and first stitch of the second. Pulling the horizontal stitches tightly makes the pulled thread pattern.

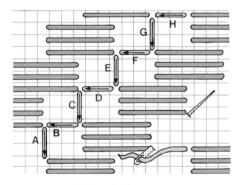

Blocks and single faggot pattern
Satin stitch blocks which are not pulled run between the diagonal lines of pulled stitches in a step pattern. The blocks are worked first, over six threads, the step pattern stitches next, over three. Use two different shades for the best effect.

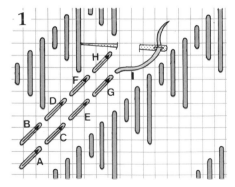

Diagonal chain and straight stitch
Pulled thread chain pattern is not related to regular chain stitch, on fabric or canvas.

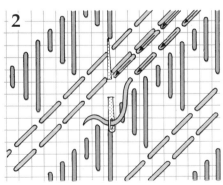

Here, little straight stitch triangles (not pulled) are used in diagonal rows between rows of the chain pattern.

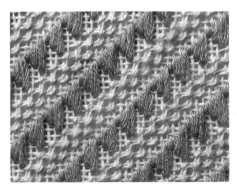

Follow diagram letters for the working order of the chain pattern as before, stitching two parallel rows at once.

only choice. Take care not to buy interlock canvas – the threads will not pull nicely.

Thread This must be strong enough to withstand constant pulling. Pearl cotton, crochet cotton, stranded cotton and fine string are all suitable. In general, the working thread should be the same thickness or finer than the canvas.

Stranded cotton should be stripped down as usual before use. Take care to align the thread plies when stitching, for a smooth finish.

Frames It is essential to use a frame for successful pulled thread work.

Needles It's a good idea to use a tapestry needle one size larger than that usually recommended for the canvas gauge. This helps to enlarge the decorative holes. Use the normal size of needle for non-pulled thread stitches; a fine, sharp needle is useful for finishing off threads in the back of the work.

Pulled thread techniques

Try to work any areas surrounding pulled thread stitchery first. This gives you a firm area to anchor the thread used for pulling the stitches. Make sure no loose threads trail across the back of an area to be pulled. If there are no surrounding stitches to anchor a new thread, leave an end about 6cm/2¼in long, running away from the work, and darn it into the back of the completed work later, using a sharp needle.

Following charts To obtain the correct 'pull' over a whole design, follow any working order instructions carefully. If, when starting a new line, you need to bring the needle up in the same hole as the last stitch finished, take a small stitch into the surrounding canvas, then return to the occupied hole.

Tension and pulling Everyone's tension varies and there's no right or wrong, but keep it constant and watch working charts for stitches that don't need to be pulled at all. Pull upwards evenly on each stitch and ease the canvas threads together by pulling directly above where the needle will next go down through the canvas. Below the canvas, pull down evenly beneath the hole that is the up-point of the next stitch.

Below are some attractive patterns. Try creating your own effects combining pulled and regular stitches.

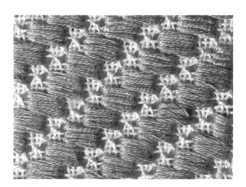

Working from right to left and upwards, begin at the lower right-hand corner of the stitching area with the first block of three stitches. The next block is positioned three horizontal threads higher than the first. Turn and work the pulled stitches in the order indicated.

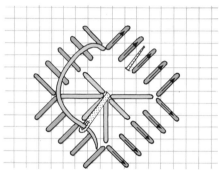

Diamond eyelet stitch
This example shows the diamond eyelets in a framework of diagonal overcast stitches worked in a different shade of thread.
Work the diagonal overcast stitches first, in zigzag rows from left to right, then from right to left, to create the diamond-shaped spaces.

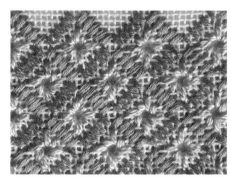

Then add the diamond-shaped eyelets using eight stitches for each one, worked into the same central hole.

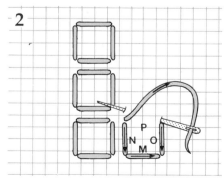

Four-sided stitch
1 Work each stitch over three threads, forming a design of squares which makes an attractive pattern when stitches are pulled.
2 Work in vertical rows in the order shown in the diagram. The letters indicate where to bring the needle

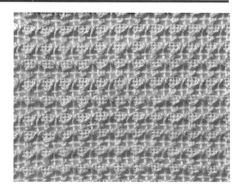

up for each stitch and the arrows show the direction of the stitch.
A series of large cross stitches forms on the back of the work.

127

A pretty mirror frame

Gluing a square of worked canvas over an ordinary mirror-tile makes an attractive piece of needlepoint to hang on the wall. The cut-out centre of the canvas shows the mirror which also glints behind the holes in the pulled thread work, accentuating the lacy look. Toning ribbons secured with oblong cross stitch make a pretty frame for the squares.

You will need
30cm/12in square mirror-tile
40cm/16in square 18-gauge mono white canvas
4m/4⅜yd satin ribbon, width 10mm/⅜in, in coffee colour
4 skeins DMC stranded cotton in fawn (543)
2 skeins DMC pearl cotton No 5 in salmon (948), 1 skein in ecru
2 small skeins Appleton's crewel wool in Flame Red 3 (203)
1 ball DMC Cotonia (a soft knitting cotton) in shade 2429 (cream)
Stretcher bars or frame.

Tapestry needles size 20 and 22
Fine, sharp needle

Marking the canvas
Using the chart (below) mark the square of canvas with the positions for the ribbon and cross stitch borders framework. (When working the design these should be stitched first and the other stitches – shown in detail earlier – filled in afterwards). Mark in the lines with a pencil on lines of *holes*, not threads. **Note:** one square on the chart represents *two* canvas threads. The ribbon and cross stitch bands span eight threads so that they are four squares wide on the chart. The padded cross stitch borders on either side of the bands cover two threads and the pattern squares each span 36 threads in either direction.

Right: If you prefer to make a cushion, work the centre square area as well.

Chart for mirror frame

1 square = 2 threads

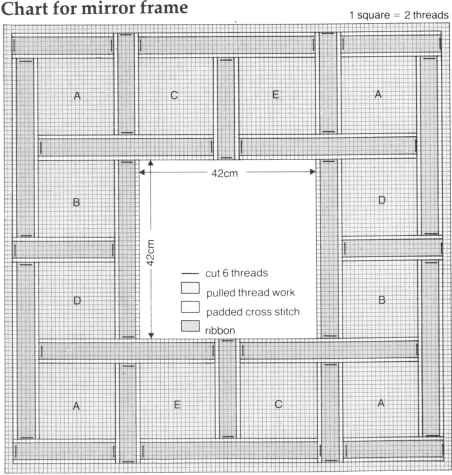

42cm

42cm

— cut 6 threads

pulled thread work

padded cross stitch

ribbon

A   C   E   A

B   D

D   B

A   E   C   A

Working the needlepoint

weaving ribbon through 6 cut threads

red dots show position of padded cross stitch

The ribbon framework
Having pencilled in placement lines, make slits in the canvas where indicated, in order to pass lengths of ribbon through to the back of the canvas. With a pair of small, sharp scissors, carefully snip through six threads in the centre of the eight-thread band at the points marked on the chart.

From the ribbon, cut eight 35cm/
14in lengths and four 10cm/4in
lengths. Keeping the canvas and
ribbon flat, weave the ribbon into
place, following the over and under
pattern, see chart, pushing one
ribbon through to the back every
time two ribbons cross, to avoid a
double thickness.

Padded cross stitch
When the ribbons are all in place,
work round all edges of each piece
(except where ribbons finish at
outer edge of design) using padded
cross stitch. Use three strands of
crewel wool for the straight
padding and three strands of the
stranded cotton for the cross
stitch on top. Pierce the ribbon
where necessary to hold it in place.
On back of canvas, trim ribbons and
stick ends to canvas.

Completing the framework
Now work oblong cross stitch
across each section of ribbon
using the soft knitting cotton and
making the stitches over four
vertical and eight horizontal canvas
threads.

Work a border of crossed corners
round the outside of the whole
design using one strand of the ivory
pearl cotton.

Working the panels
All the stitch patterns you need are
described in this chapter.
Begin with the four corner squares
(A) which are worked in diamond
eyelet stitch in a diagonal overcast
stitch framework. Use six strands of
stranded cotton for the overcast
stitches and one strand salmon
pearl cotton for the eyelets, going
round each eyelet twice.
Stitch the panels marked B using
four-sided stitch over three threads.
Use one strand of salmon pearl
cotton.
Next work the panels marked C in
the diagonal chain and straight
stitch pattern. Use six strands of the
stranded cotton for the triangles
and do not pull the stitches. Then,
using one strand of salmon pearl
cotton, work the pulled diagonal
chain stitch.
Use blocks and single faggot pattern
for the two panels marked D. Use
six strands of the stranded cotton

for the upright satin stitches and
one strand of salmon pearl cotton
for the pulled single faggot stitch.
Finally, fill the two panels marked E
with honeycomb filling stitch using
one strand of salmon pearl cotton.

Making up
Take the worked canvas off the
frame and cut out the central
unworked area to within five
threads of the inner cross stitch.
Now turn back the canvas all
round, close to the cross stitch and
snipping diagonal cuts at the
corners, being careful not to snip
the threads holding the cross stitch.
Glue the canvas back behind the
ribbon border.
On outside edge, trim canvas back
to within eight threads of edge. On
all sides, remove the canvas thread
immediately adjacent to the outer
worked edge (this helps the canvas
to fold more easily) and trim
corners. Fold excess canvas to the
back and glue lightly. Finger-press.
Now glue canvas over mirror-tile –
outer edges should be flush.
Fix on the wall using the adhesive
pads supplied.

CHAPTER 29

Simple straight stitches form Florentine wave patterns

Florentine stitchery forms striking zigzag patterns. The tradition goes back a long way, particularly for soft furnishings, and it's satisfyingly quick to do. Patterns are built up from a basic pattern row – start by following these charts and you'll soon be designing your own.

The dramatic and attractive effect of Florentine stitches, and the simplicity and speed of working them has probably done more than anything else to make needlepoint so popular. Florentine embroidery has several other names – among them, Bargello, Hungarian point, Flame stitch and Irish stitch. Its origins are rather obscure, but it was certainly popular on both sides of the Atlantic in the 18th century where it was worked in wools for upholstered wing chairs, and in silks for small items such as purses and belts.

What is Florentine stitchery?

Traditionally, Florentine stitch is a series of upright stitches, worked in repeating patterns. In its most basic form it covers four canvas threads with a jump up (or down) of two horizontal threads between each stitch, making a zigzag effect of alternate peaks and valleys. Countless variations are made by altering the stitch length, the size of the jump up or down, or by working two or more parallel stitches. The two most important characteristics of any design are its pattern repeat and its colours.

Florentine patterns

There are several easily recognisable types of Florentine design. Charts for some simple wave patterns are shown right. Once the basic row is established on the canvas, it is often just a matter of progressing down the canvas, copying the pattern underneath it in the chosen colours.

Florentine stitch The most basic wave pattern is the traditional Florentine stitch itself. The peaks and valleys are all the same depth, so the stitch forms an even zigzag. The yarn colour is usually changed with every row.

Deep wave stitch By making some of the stitches longer, or increasing the step height (jump between stitches) deeper pattern rows can be planned. These patterns look best worked over larger canvas areas – cushions, carpets and chair or stool covers. If the area is not deep enough, the design cannot be developed fully, so choose patterns carefully. With simple, shallow patterns, you can stitch smaller and narrower items such as belts.

Rounded patterns Curves can be introduced into classic Florentine

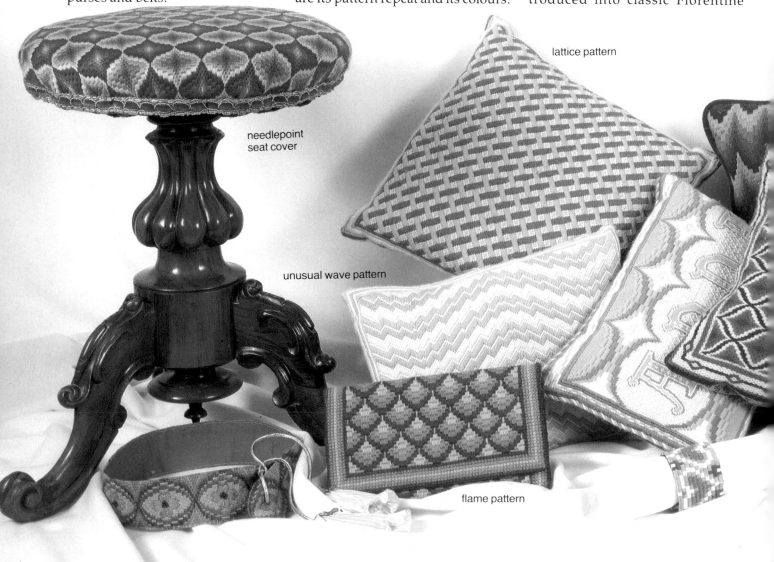

needlepoint seat cover

lattice pattern

unusual wave pattern

flame pattern

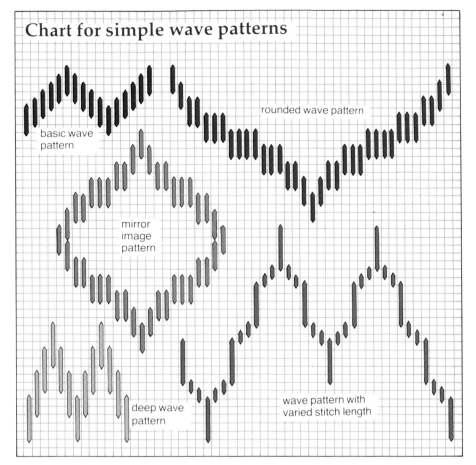

Chart for simple wave patterns

basic wave pattern

rounded wave pattern

mirror image pattern

deep wave pattern

wave pattern with varied stitch length

flame patterns by working blocks of stitches of the same height next to each other. The step height between blocks or between a block and a stitch determines whether the curves are gentle or sharp.

Mirror image patterns By repeating a pattern upside down underneath itself, a mirror image pattern is formed. These patterns form rows of symmetrical motifs such as diamonds, or curved onion shapes. The new spaces which may appear between these motifs need to be filled.

Working techniques

Mono (single thread) canvas is the most suitable for Florentine work. Work into each vertical row of holes, and make each stitch in two movements. The stitches should share holes with the ones above and below. Canvas coverage is most important. Remember that straight stitches do not cover the canvas as well as diagonal ones, so you may need extra strands of yarn, or a finer canvas than you normally use for tent stitch with a particular yarn. Always test the stitch and yarn first to check coverage.

mirror image medallion pattern

classic rounded wave pattern

garland pattern

four-way design of repeated hearts

four-way heart design in contrasting shades

four-way design in toning shades

Florentine pattern charts are usually given as grids where each square represents one canvas hole. Begin by working a complete pattern row or repeat from the chart. Take great care to stitch accurately, taking note of the length of each stitch and the step height between stitches.

Colour planning

Florentine designs provide an opportunity to create stunning colour effects. Traditionally the patterns are worked in subtle tonal gradation, the colours shading from light into dark and back. Two, or perhaps three basic colours are combined – each represented by several different tones. Nowadays, bolder colour combinations are also seen – several unrelated colours in the same design can look effective.

The interaction of neighbouring colours is important – closely related colours like green and blue blend quietly together, whereas more distant colours like red and blue look

Above: The jazzier contrasting effect.
Top: The calm and harmonious effect.

much jazzier. The wide colour range of embroidery yarns means that you can stitch magnificently-shaded designs and even the simplest wave repeat can look sophisticated in subtle shades.

By changing the order of colours, the same design can be given a completely different look, using exactly the same shades. To experiment, take two shades of brown, two of coral, and white. For a calm and harmonious effect work a simple wave pattern in the order: light brown, dark brown, light brown, white, light coral, dark coral, light coral, light brown, dark brown, etc.

Now work the same pattern in white, dark coral, dark brown, white, light coral, light brown, white, dark coral, dark brown, etc. This jazzy effect is much more contemporary and the colours 'jostle' with each other more. This is because a higher proportion of white is used and because the stronger colours are not next to their own lighter tones.

Florentine belt

Here's a pretty Florentine belt. The very simple zigzag pattern is worked as a mirror image to give a row of diamonds in the centre.

You will need

For a belt up to 76cm/30in waist:
Piece of 18-gauge mono canvas (white), canvas width×15cm/6in
Small skeins of Appleton's crewel wool: 1×Bright rose 6; 3×Royal blue 1; 3×Scarlet 1; 2×Leaf 6; 2×Bright China 7; 2×Fuschia 4
Tapestry needle size 22
Metal belt clasp
10cm/4in moiré or acetate backing fabric
Masking tape

Stitching the belt

Measure the depth of the shank of your chosen belt clasp – the width of the finished belt depends on this. The belt in the picture has a shank size of 5cm/2in. To make a wider belt, work extra pattern rows or, if the increase is slight, work on a slightly coarser canvas – check that the thread still covers the different gauge of canvas and if not use a thicker thread.

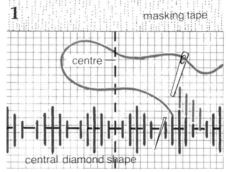

1 Bind the piece of canvas. Stitch the simple zigzag design from chart, using three strands of crewel wool and beginning at the centre of the canvas. Start with the central diamond shapes – each one is worked over two, four, six, four and two threads. Then stitch the rows of zigzags over three threads and fill in with the triangles to make a straight edge.

2 When the exact waist measurement is reached, bend the unworked canvas over along both long edges, leaving two threads on the right side, next to the stitched area. Pinch this turning well with your fingers. Work a row of straight gobelin stitch over the two threads along both sides of the belt. Stitch through both thicknesses of canvas, aligning the holes as you work.

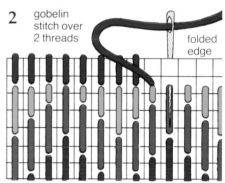

Making up the belt

Trim the short ends of the canvas to 2cm/¾in. Turn under and catch stitch.

3 Turn in the long edges of the backing fabric. Using a small, sharp needle, stitch backing to the needlepoint along all edges, having the fabric extending 5cm/2in at each end. Thread the extended backing fabric through the clasp at both ends, trim and stitch in place. This avoids damaging the needlepoint by having it constantly pulling against the metal.

Chart for belt

Appletons crewel wool shade nos.

▬ = 946		▬ = 426	
▬ = 821		▬ = 747	
▬ = 501		▬ = 804	

Using Florentine stitch patterns

Use the chart for simple wave patterns to experiment with different colour combinations and, at the same time, make a variety of useful and colourful needlepoint items for your wardrobe and home.

A single mirror repeat along a length of canvas can make a strong and practical shoulder strap for a favourite bag. Double the mirror repeat for extra depth to make a belt to fit a wider fastening.

Parallel bands of deep wave pattern can build up graded tones of colour for a cushion cover. Use a medium gauge canvas and crewel or tapestry wools for this greater area.

Pick out one or two colours from a pair of curtains to make some simple tie backs using the rounded patterns for extra depth.

The method for backing and finishing off given for the Florentine belt can be adapted for all these projects.

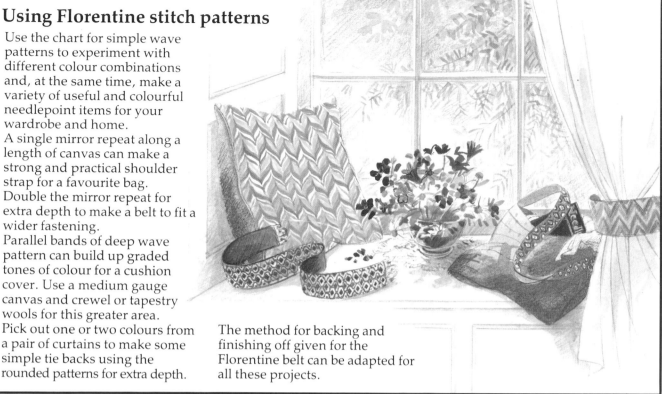

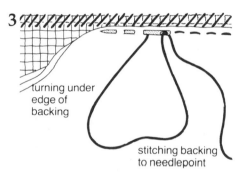

turning under
edge of
backing

stitching backing
to needlepoint

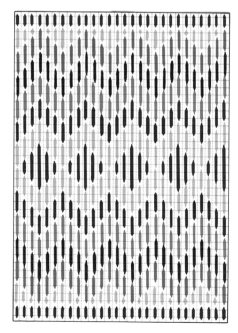

Above: These bright colours create an ethnic effect. The more muted colourway (right) shows a more traditional alternative.

133

CHAPTER 30

Planning a Florentine design

*Try working out pattern repeats and pretty four-way designs
using simple wave, mirror image and
medallion patterns and use variations in scale to fit these
patterns to a pre-determined shape. Stitch
a stunning shaped cummerbund using this technique.*

Planning a whole design depends on the shape and size of the project as well as on your chosen pattern. The Florentine sampler picture below shows you how several different kinds of design – all-over, linear or single motif patterns – can be planned to fit in a definite area, and at the same time, how well they can work together.

Different patterns, same shape

Adapting a favourite pattern to an item you are making is much easier than you might think. To understand how patterns fit into areas, take a basic shape such as a rectangle. This could be made into a long stool cover, a glasses case, a matchbox cover, a cheque book cover or an evening bag – objects of differing scales.

All-over patterns with small repeats are useful and will fill any shape easily – the exact final size of many items is not critical, so begin at the centre and work outwards, balancing pattern repeats until the whole area is filled. A good example

of this is trellis pattern. With all straight-edged items, work compensation stitches when you reach the top and lower edges to make them straight, maintaining pattern on inner ends of stitches.

Basic wave or mirror image designs can be planned for this shape in various ways. Obviously, the larger the project, the more stitches there will be in each pattern repeat (for added width) and the more horizontal rows there will be (for added height).

Uneven numbers of repeats seem to make for the most interesting designs – three, five or seven

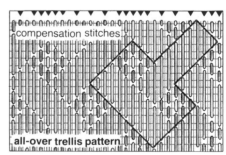

'peaks'. If your calculations suggest an even number will fit best, try to split the last motif in half to give an odd number of whole peaks with a half at either end. Whether working a mirror image or simple wave baseline, always establish the centre pattern lines on the canvas first.

Same pattern, different shapes

The diagram (right) shows how the same design – in this case a single or repeated medallion motif can be used to fit different basic shapes like squares and rectangles. A motif like this appears in the Florentine sampler. Although its height measures slightly more than its width, this is a design that will easily adapt to a square.

Taking the idea a step further, some designs can decide the shape of the project for you – for example the shaped cummerbund overleaf. The outline of the belt front follows the mirror-image pattern – curves are kept gentle by using blocks of same-length stitches (see below).

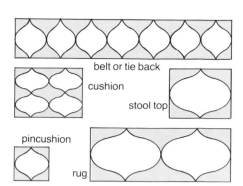

belt or tie back

cushion

stool top

pincushion

rug

Charting a pattern repeat

If you've already decided how many peaks you want across the design, divide the number of vertical canvas threads by this number to find the width of each peak and enable you to work out a pattern repeat. Do this in chart form, on a piece of graph paper. Remember that high and low pivot stitches on a pattern repeat must only be counted once.

If the height of the pattern needs to fit the item exactly (for instance the mirror-image band placed vertically in the sampler) take this into account, otherwise make as deep or shallow pattern as you wish, and work as many pattern rows in your chosen colour sequence as necessary to fill the area.

Left: All-over flame pattern (top left), single medallion motif with tent stitch surround (top centre), mirror-image wave border used vertically (right), single motif ribbon border with straight stitch background (centre), four-way rose motif (bottom left), all-over trellis pattern (bottom centre), initials in a pair of mirror-image medallions (bottom right).

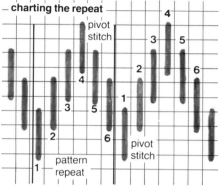

charting the repeat — pivot stitch — pattern repeat — pivot stitch

Working the pattern baseline

Make an accurate paper template of the area to be worked. Lay this on the canvas and mark the area with a pencil. Cut out, leaving a good border. Count horizontal and vertical threads and mark the canvas centre. Always begin stitching at the centre.

Curves The more same-length stitches worked together in a pattern repeat, the flatter will be the curve and the wider the repeat. To increase width without affecting height, include some larger groups of same-length stitches and increase their height in small increments. For a smooth curve, increase stitch

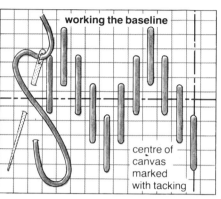

working the baseline

centre of canvas marked with tacking

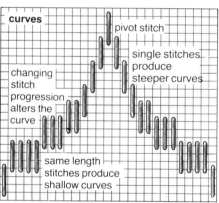

curves — pivot stitch — single stitches produce steeper curves — changing stitch progression alters the curve — same length stitches produce shallow curves

lengths in mathematical progressions such as 1, 2, 3 threads, 1, 3, 5, 7 threads, never in unrelated jumps such as 7, 2, 10, 4 threads.

Four-way Florentine patterns

An example of this appears at the bottom left of the sampler. These beautiful designs are based on a square divided diagonally into repeated quarters, the straight stitches lying in four different directions, radiating outwards from the centre hole.

Begin working at the centre. If necessary, you can stop wherever you like to fit an area exactly, although you should be able to determine this by counting threads. Mark the canvas centre and divide it diagonally in four with lines of tacking. Adjoining design repeats must share holes along these lines.

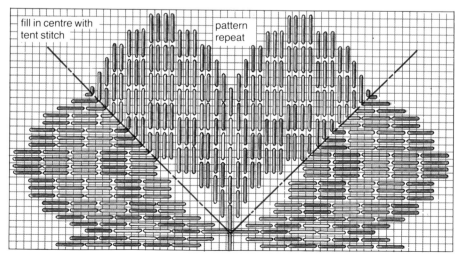

fill in centre with tent stitch

pattern repeat

Dazzling evening cummerbund

Above: Quick to stitch, this cummerbund makes a very versatile evening accessory.

This wide cummerbund with its eye-catching combination of glowing colours framed in black and given a sparkle with gold embroidery thread, will be a stunning addition to evening outfits. The mirror-image Florentine design is based on rounded pattern lines.

You will need
Piece of 14-gauge mono canvas
 (canvas width ×20cm/8in)
1 skein each Paterna Persian yarn in
 pale emerald (501), dark emerald
 (500), magenta (645), blue (763)
8 skeins black (050)
5 reels Balger gold embroidery
 thread
Tapestry needle size 20

For making up
2m/2yd black bias binding
20cm/¼yd backing (plastic
 furnishing fabric such as Lionella)
4 large black hooks and eyes

Stitching the belt
First measure your waist accurately for a comfortable fit. The belt shown here fits a 71cm/28in waist. It has three of the lozenge motifs (marked D on the diagram) at each end. To enlarge or reduce the size, add or omit as many D motifs as necessary to obtain the nearest measurement *below* the waist measurement. (The width of each D motif is 6.5cm/2½in.) Continue the pattern symmetrically at each end of the belt until the waist measurement is reached.

Most of the stitches in the design are worked over four threads. Some of the gold stitches are worked over two.

Begin at the centre front of the belt – see chart – with three strands of the black yarn in the needle. Work the framework of black stitches first. Now fill in the green, blue and magenta stitches. Finally, add the gold stitches, using two thicknesses of the gold thread.

Fill in the area between the Florentine stitches and the edge of the belt as shown on the chart with diagonal tent stitch in black, using two strands of yarn.

136

Making up the belt

With brightly coloured tacking thread, tack round the edge of the belt. Place the tacking line between the second and third rows of tent stitch from the edge of the straight part of the belt and along the top of the long black stitches on the curved parts.

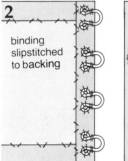

tacking bias binding along guide line

1 Using this line as a guide, tack one edge of the bias binding (along fold) to the belt, right sides together.

Wrong sides together, pin canvas centrally into position on piece of backing. Machine stitch along the tacked line through binding, canvas and backing fabric.

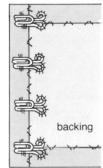

binding slipstitched to backing

backing

2 Remove tacking and trim canvas so there is one free thread lying between the needlepoint and the edge, with backing flush. Fold bias binding to inside of belt and slipstitch in place.

Bind the ends in the same way and attach the four hooks and eyes to close.

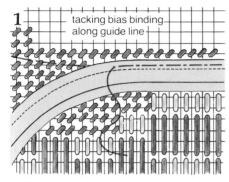

positioning guide for Florentine belt motifs

centre

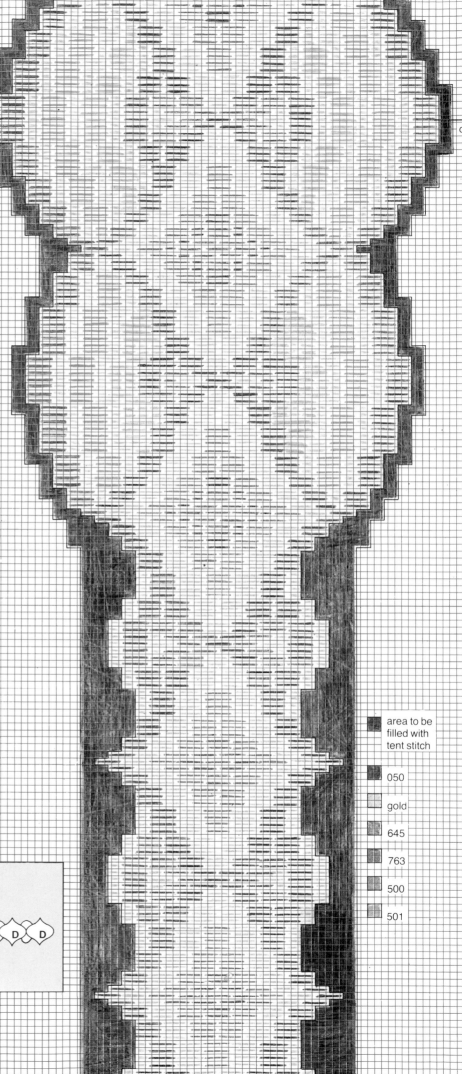

centre

area to be filled with tent stitch

050

gold

645

763

500

501

CHAPTER 31

Borders, corners and frames for Florentine needlepoint

*Many needlepoint pieces benefit from having a stitched border.
A border helps to link different colours
in the main area and gives it a firm edge. Here's a choice
of attractive borders to suit all kinds of
design. Use one to stitch a photograph frame.*

Needlepoint borders can be richly-coloured and intricately designed like the ones used on old Persian carpets. They may include several stitches. Often, however, all that's needed is the narrowest band of straight gobelin stitch or a few rows of tent stitch. Between these two extremes there are countless possibilities – learn how to choose the right one for your piece of work.

Types of border

Geometric borders are equally effective on geometric or pictorial needlepoint. A lattice border on a half cross stitch floral design is a good example see cushion, page 91). An effective trick with designs like this is to stitch part of the main picture so that it breaks out of the frame, actually overlapping it. This gives a three-dimensional feel.

A randomly-stitched border also works well on a picture (see page 124). You can make a pretty border from a repeated motif like hearts (see page 86). Florentine designs, too, make lovely borders (see page 134) and they're highly adaptable.

Borders can be used on their own as a straight band for items like belts and curtain tie-backs. Generally, any design will do provided it can be adapted to the required depth.

Frames Projects like mirror, picture and photograph frames, consist of the worked border on its own. This is a chance to use some of the more ornate borders. It is important to choose a design which turns corners happily.

Planning a border

Some borders will fit any size of design, others need careful counting of threads to make them fit. You may need to add stitches to the outer edge of the main design to match up the thread count with the border. With a geometric design in the centre, it's likely to be easier to adapt the border. Always mark the centre of the canvas before beginning to stitch, extending both tacking rows to the edge of the canvas. This means you have the centre of each side marked – important for border patterns which reverse in the centre or for repeated motif designs.

Borders with an exact thread count need more careful planning. Even with rows of a comparatively simple stitch such as crossed corners, the length of each side of the border must be a multiple of four threads – the number of threads spanned by each stitch – so an exact number of stitches can be fitted. Adjust the central design accordingly.

For a picture, it's a good idea to stitch the border after the main part of the design but *before* the background is worked. This means you can make alterations to your border plan when you see the effect of the pictorial design. Then you can work the all-over background in the spaces between the design and the border.

Borders to fit any size of design

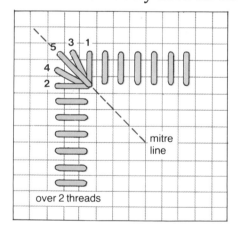

over 2 threads

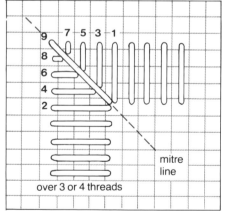

over 3 or 4 threads

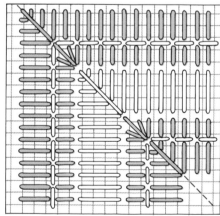

Straight gobelin stitch borders
This is a very useful stitch and adaptable to any size of border. When turning a corner with this stitch, you need to work in a slightly different way, depending on the number of threads you are working over.
Over two threads In this case, note

that you should stitch into the inner corner hole five times.
Follow working order on chart.
Over three or four threads Work each stitch into the diagonal mitre line of holes, the outermost ones being over one thread, then work a long stitch from inner to outer corner, to cover the ends.

Simple straight stitch border
Pick out one of the deeper colours in the central design for the outer and inner rows of straight gobelin stitch. Fill in the border area with more rows, varying the width of the bands.
Backstitch in pearl cotton between some of the rows looks very pretty.

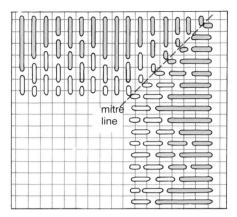

Planning a corner

The best way to deal with most border corners is to pencil a diagonal mitre line from the inner border corner to the outer. The border design should 'change direction' along this line, with stitches being worked into the holes along the line, keeping to the pattern as far as possible, shortening stitches where necessary. Patterns such as square motifs, do not need a mitre line – they fit naturally into the angle of the corner. This is clearly shown in the cushion stitch example (below right). Other ideas for corner squares are blocks of chequer stitch or a Florentine medallion.

Right: Use one of the borders in this chapter to stitch a pretty frame with a hanging ring or a standing support.

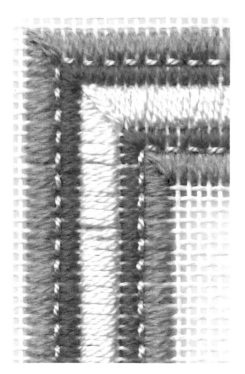

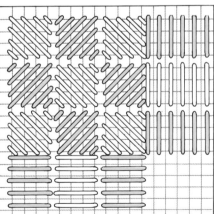

Cushion stitch striped border

Cushion stitch makes an ideal corner decoration on a straight gobelin stitch border. Use two different colours to make the diagonal stitch pattern show up. You could also work a block of cushion stitch at the centre of each side of a rectangular border.

139

Borders that can reverse in the centre

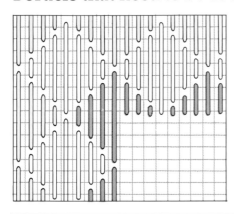

Plait border
This pretty border pattern must be worked in three colours to emphasize the plait effect.
It is worked entirely in straight horizontal or vertical stitches with an edging of straight gobelin stitch. Make it wider if you wish.
Reverse the pattern along the centre marked line of each side and follow the photograph to see how to treat the corner.

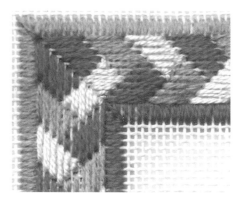

Borders that need to be counted

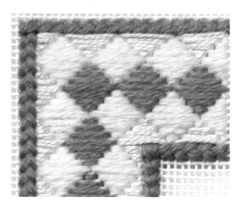

2, 4, 6, 8 stitch border
This diamond pattern fits well as long as each border side is a multiple of eight threads. Try working some of the 2, 4, 6, 8 stitches horizontally.
To adjust the measurement of the central design, add a row of cross stitch or straight gobelin stitch round the edge. If you add a row of straight gobelin over two threads, you have added four threads overall.

Ribbon border photograph frames

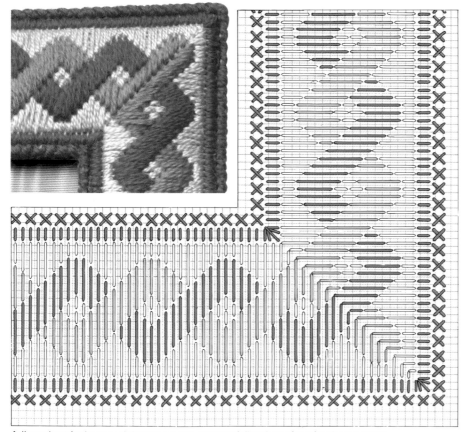

These professional-looking photograph frames are quick to stitch using a pretty Florentine ribbon border.

You will need
For a frame 18cm×21cm/7in×8¼in (picture area 8cm×11.5cm/3¼in×4½in)
Piece of 14-gauge mono canvas 28cm×31cm/11in×12in
3×4g skeins Appleton's crewel wool in Flamingo 3 (623) and 3 skeins in Grey Green 1 (351)
2 skeins DMC pearl cotton No 5 in ivory (948)
2 tapestry needles size 20
For making up
Stiff card
Fabric adhesive
Oddment of lining fabric or moiré
For a frame 21cm×25.5cm/8¼in×10in (picture area 12cm×15.5cm/4¾in×6¼in)
Piece of 14-gauge mono canvas 31cm×36cm/12in×14in
1×25g/1oz hank Appleton's crewel wool in Flamingo 3 (623)
All other requirements as given for the smaller size frame.

follow chart for bottom right and top left corners; follow inset for other two corners

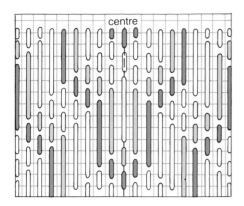

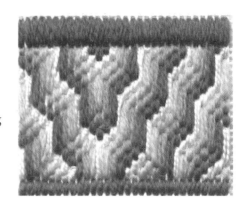

Gothic Florentine border

This spectacular border adapts well to any size. Begin on the centre line of one of the sides with a straight stitch over six threads, having one end at the border edge.

Work the design outwards on both sides of this central stitch, following the chosen colour sequence and reversing pattern on either side.

At corners, work stitches into the mitre line, shortening them where necessary.

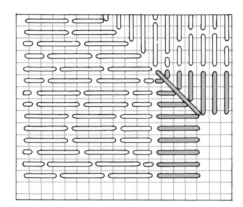

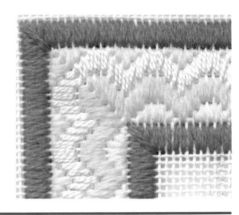

Double wave border

This Florentine-type border also has an eight-thread pattern repeat, the pivot stitch being counted once only (see page 135).

To stitch this border to a particular width, add extra row of the Florentine design, or build up with straight gobelin stitch, here used on either side of the pattern, over four threads.

Stitching the frame

Mark the centre of the piece of canvas. Roughly mark out the central picture area of the frame (size as given in You will need, left) placing it centrally.

Work the ribbon pattern and the mitred corners from the chart. Use four strands each of the coral and green wools in the needle. It is easier to have one needle for each colour and work a little in each at a time.

Leave two free canvas threads outside the ribbon band and work straight gobelin stitch over two threads either side of them, using four strands of the coral wool. Add a row of cross stitch outside of these lines, using three strands.

Work the background to the ribbon pattern in satin stitch using two strands of the ivory pearl cotton.

Making up the frame

Cut two pieces of stiff card to the finished size of the frame you are making. Using a ruler, mark and cut out the central picture area

appropriate to the size, from one of the card rectangles.

Cut two pieces of the backing fabric to the size of the whole rectangle, plus 1.5cm/⅝in for seams. With right sides together, machine round two long sides and one short. Trim seams and corners and turn to right side. Press seams under on remaining short raw edges, insert uncut card rectangle and slipstitch edges closed. This is the back of the frame.

Make a fabric loop, insert through hanging ring, and stitch both ends to upper edge of frame back.

Take the worked canvas and machine all round inner and outer edges of border, close to the needlepoint using the closest shade of thread possible. Make slits in the canvas as shown, trim inner and outer canvas rebates to 1cm/½in. Make diagonal cuts at outer corners. Stick needlepoint to card frame, pull rebates to the back, and lace opposite edges tightly with strong thread.

Apply fabric glue carefully to front

side and lower edges of frame back. Stick needlepoint border portion carefully in place. Photographs can be inserted between the two layers at the top.

For a frame with a standing support, omit the hanging ring and cover a blunt-ended wedge shape of card with fabric, securing with fabric adhesive. Leave a small tongue of free fabric (at the narrower end of the wedge) and stick this to the back of the frame so that it is supported at the correct angle.

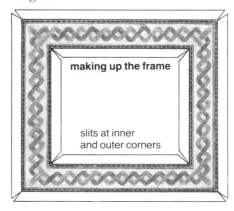

making up the frame

slits at inner and outer corners

CHAPTER 32

Using Florentine needlepoint for upholstered furniture

Hardwearing needlepoint is an ideal covering for upholstered furniture and Florentine patterns have been traditionally used for seats and stools. Learn how to stitch and cover a drop-in seat and experiment with medallion patterns to make up your own designs.

Upholstered pieces of furniture undergo considerable wear and tear and the materials used must be chosen accordingly. Wool yarns wear better than any others.

Do not choose too large a gauge of canvas or a pattern with very long stitches. A stitch worked over six threads of 10-gauge canvas will be almost twice as long as the same stitch on 18-gauge canvas, and twice as likely to fluff up and catch. As a guide, try not to use stitches worked over more than six threads and work on canvas no coarser than 14-gauge.

Choosing patterns

The scale of the pattern must complement the size of the piece – don't choose a very large pattern repeat for a small item. Rules are made to be broken, however, and a single bold Florentine motif can look stunning on a round stool.

Asymmetrical designs never seem to work well on upholstered pieces – they make a chair or footstool look as though it might fall over!

Long stools can be made more interesting by working a pattern reversed along a central line.

A richly-hued drop-in seat in Florentine stitchery is the perfect partner for an antique chair. Gently curving patterns echo the lines of the chair.

Chairs with an upholstered back panel can have the seat pattern adapted to the long narrow shape. Pairs or sets of chairs can either be stitched in the same pattern, changing the order of the colours, or in different patterns, using the same colour scheme. Make sure that the scale and colour balance of the different patterns is the same.

Choosing colours

Try to choose harmonious colour schemes for your upholstered pieces. Avoid loud, jazzy colour combinations which are best kept for cushions. A chair, or a set of dining room chairs, will be more adaptable and easier to live with if the colours are fairly muted and they will probably become family heirlooms.

Check that your chosen colours harmonize with the wood of the furniture and if the needlepoint is intended for a room which is often used in the evenings, look at the colours in the room itself by artificial light.

Do not include too much white or pale colours – they are not as practical as the medium or dark shades.

Chair seat variations

Here are some different patterns obtained by arranging medallions in various ways. Try to balance pale medallions with darker ones and remember that a filling pattern can look quite different in new colours or when inverted.

1 Mix your medallions for a random, patchwork-like effect.
2 Include a central vertical band of identical medallions.
3 Another symmetrical pattern with the centres in dark brown.

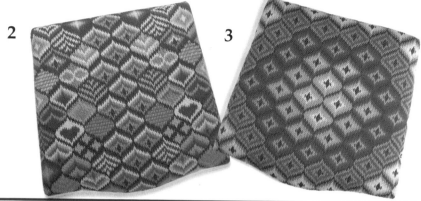

Techniques for drop-in seat covers

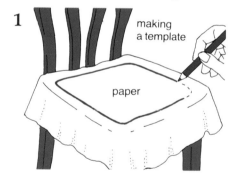

1 making a template

paper

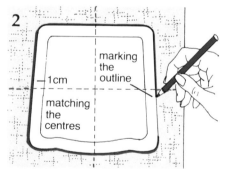

2 marking the outline
1cm
matching the centres

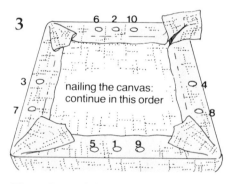

3 6 2 10
3 nailing the canvas: continue in this order 4
7 8
5 1 9

First check that the finished seat when covered will still fit in the chair framework, removing any previous covering if necessary.

If you are making covers for a set of chairs, buy all the canvas and yarn you expect to need at the same time. Keep a record of the amount of yarn used on the first cover so that should any errors or changes of plan occur, more supplies can be purchased in good time.

1 Make a template of the cover from paper or, better still, from a piece of old sheeting. Lay the paper or sheeting over the seat and mark all round where the wooden part of the seat begins. Add 1cm/½in extra

all round and cut out the pattern.
2 Lay the pattern on a piece of canvas which has at least 5cm/2in extra all round the template. Mark the outline with a pencil or waterproof marker. Do *not* cut it out.

Mount the canvas on a frame if you have one – but with these straight stitches this is not essential. Begin in the centre of the canvas and work the first pattern rows horizontally to establish the design. Begin each subsequent row at alternate ends – first work from left to right, then from right to left. This gives an even amount of yarn on the back, helping it to wear well.

The edges of the stitches do not need to be particularly straight – they'll be turned under on the finished seat.

Block and set your finished needlepoint (see page 99).

Upholstering the seat Unless you are confident, it is probably best to have the finished needlepoint mounted professionally. If you wish to do it yourself, make sure that the design is centred on the seat and the canvas is stretched evenly round to the underside.

3 Nail down all round on the underside working from the centre of each edge and alternately from front to back and side to side.

143

Medallion patterns for a dining chair

The dining chair and seats shown in the picture are part of a set – each one unique. They harmonize well because the medallion outlines are identical on each one and worked in the same rich shade of brown. The same colours – five shades of coral, off-white and two browns – are used throughout in different combinations.

The instructions given here are for the V-shaped seat design which is formed by working different filling patterns in diagonal lines which come to a point at the centre front of the seat. Medallion patterns one to six (opposite) are used for this design – number one in three different colourways.

Use the other medallion patterns to develop your own seat designs. Once you have stitched the basic medallion outlines, have fun mixing and matching the filling patterns in random designs or regular geometric patterns. For examples of both see the Design Extra on the previous page.

You will need

For one chair seat:
1 × 25g/1oz hank each Appleton's crewel wool in off-white (992), flesh 5 (705), coral 1 (861), coral 2 (862), coral 3 (863), coral 4 (864), chocolate 2 (182)
2 × 25g/1oz hanks in chocolate 5 (185)
Mono canvas (ecru) 14-gauge
Tapestry needle size 20

Linking the medallions

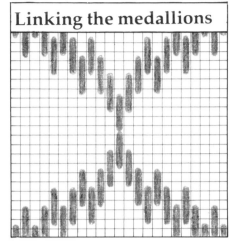

Making the seat

Make a template for the chair seat and mark the area to be worked on the canvas. Mark centre of area. Make a sketch as a reminder to yourself which patterns you intend to place in what order. A scheme is given for the actual design of the V-shaped seat design.

The design motif is formed from a simple curve and peak pattern in mirror image. Stitch the framework of interlocking medallions first, then work one complete chevron of filling patterns to establish the design.

Work the subsequent chevrons starting at the centre out towards each edge. Block and set your finished needlepoint.

Chart for V-shaped seat design

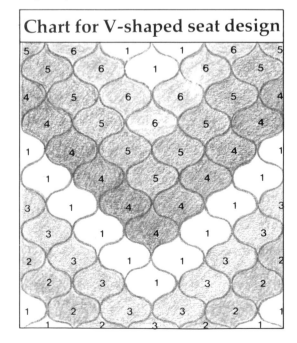

(705) flesh 5
(861) coral 1
(862) coral 2
(863) coral 3
(864) coral 4
(992) off-white
(182) chocolate 2
(185) chocolate 5

Appleton's crewel wool colours

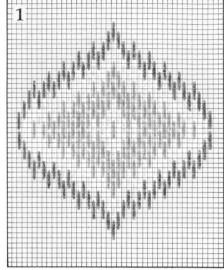

flesh 5, off-white, chocolate 2, chocolate 5

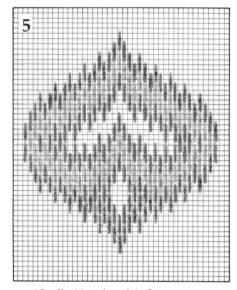

coral 3, off-white, chocolate 2, chocolate 5

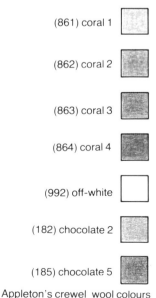

coral 1, coral 2, coral 3, chocolate 5

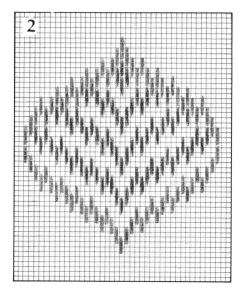

coral 4, off-white, chocolate 5

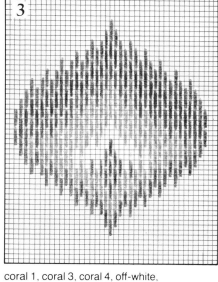

coral 1, coral 3, coral 4, off-white,
chocolate 2, chocolate 5

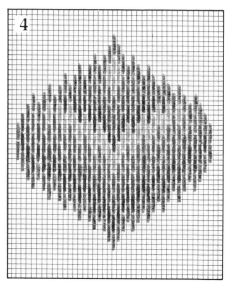

coral 1, coral 2, coral 3, coral 4,
chocolate 5

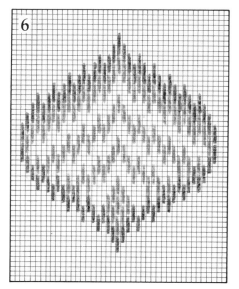

flesh 5, off-white, chocolate 5

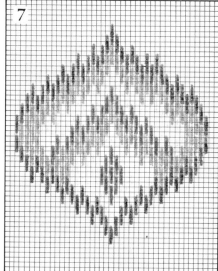

coral 2, off-white, chocolate 2,
chocolate 5

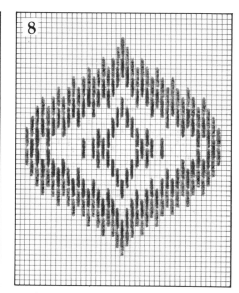

coral 4, off-white, chocolate 5

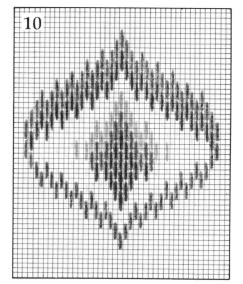

coral 1, coral 3, coral 4, off-white,
chocolate 5

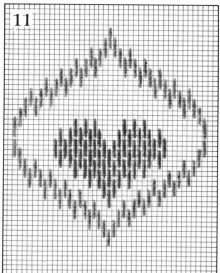

coral 4, off-white, chocolate 5

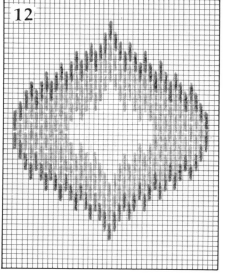

coral 1, off-white, chocolate 2,
chocolate 5

CHAPTER 33

Three-dimensional projects

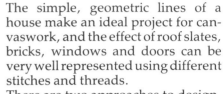

With careful planning, it's quite simple to stitch an accurate representation of any house you like on canvas. Work it as a picture which can be framed or make it three dimensional for the ultimate doorstop! All the basic know-how for stitching is given here.

The simple, geometric lines of a house make an ideal project for canvaswork, and the effect of roof slates, bricks, windows and doors can be very well represented using different stitches and threads.

There are two approaches to designing a stitched house – you can either work a flat picture *or* work all four elevations of the house, together with the roof as a three-dimensional piece that could become a doorstop, a large paper weight, or just a unique ornament.

If you choose to make a picture, a front or back view of the house, straight on, works best, because perspective is difficult to represent on canvas.

Left: A house can be fun to stitch and makes an unusual doorstop.

Checklist

1 What canvas do you wish to use? This depends largely on the finished size required and the amount of detail. For a fairly small piece showing a large house with good surface interest such as brickwork and mullioned windows for instance, use a fine-gauge canvas. A plainer (stucco or plastered) exterior with picture windows would be better stitched on a coarser canvas.

2 What colour canvas? This is a personal choice to a certain degree but if the main house walls are white or a pale shade, white canvas is easier to cover, likewise a deep colour house will work up better on ecru or brown canvas.

3 What are the house's dimensions? Check the relative height and width of the house from your photograph or drawing. Do they give you a tall

Three-dimensional, free-standing projects work well if the house is fairly compact. When stitched and made up, these pieces can be filled with wood or foam blocks, cut to fit. Bear in mind, though, that features like low-built back extensions could be tricky to fill.

End (side) walls of houses are often rather ugly – they may have frosted bathroom windows or untidy plumbing, and terraced houses don't have side walls at all.

To solve these problems, work both end walls in an attractive brick pattern to link the front and back. Or use one of the ends to personalize the piece with a stitched 'family tree' showing its occupants.

Preparation

All you need to work from is a straight-on photograph of the view you wish to stitch. An ordinary snap is adequate but a slightly enlarged print is better. If available, a good alternative is an architect's elevation, which is drawn to scale.

If you don't have a colour photograph to go by, make notes on the actual colours. The house will be more fun to stitch if you can include any bushes, plants or trees that grow close to it, so try to take the photo-graph in summer when the garden is looking at its best.

It is very important to look really hard at the house to assess the scale and relationship of doors to windows, depth of roof to overall height, etc, before drawing the design on the canvas. To do this, take a ruler and notepad and ask yourself ten simple questions (see below).

Choosing materials

Canvas See checklist questions 1 and 2 – the guiding factors being what you are most happy to work on and the quality of detail you wish to represent on the house.

Yarn It is unlikely that this kind of piece will need to be hard-wearing but you will probably be looking for maximum texture and surface interest. Crewel and Persian yarn, stranded and pearl cotton or crochet cotton are all excellent, but anything which appeals to you in knitting or weaving yarns, with regard to colour and texture, is worth experimenting with.

Any kind of thread or yarn can be couched (caught in place with small stitches) on to the canvas surface to add interest and depth to the design. Try this with rug thrums, linen weaving thread, chenille, fluffy mohair or nubbly knitting yarns.

For regular stitching through the canvas, choose a smooth thread and one which is not too thick for the canvas, or it may wear thin before a needleful is finished.

Bushes, plants and flowers

It is only satisfactory to work these in a solid stitch directly on the bare canvas if they are very bushy. Usually it is better to stitch the fabric of the house then use surface embroidery stitches like chain stitch, split stitch, and French knots to add climbing plants to the walls of the house. This is particularly effective on free-standing houses.

To stitch a larger area of garden when working a picture, choose several different shades for foliage and use the darker ones at the back for depth, paler shades towards the front. Pick a small, repeating stitch for small areas and use larger, individual stitches such as triple cross stitch or eyelet to represent single blooms.

Leaf stitch is ideal for leaves and trees, and various other stitches may appeal to you as suitable for plants and gardens. If you don't manage to include them all in the picture, how about using the extra ones in a sampler border round the outside?

---

or flat finished shape? Is this what you want or do you wish to adjust the shape by adding trees and bushes to the side of the house or grass, paths and hedges to the front, lengthening the foreground? (This applies mainly to flat pictures.)

4 What size do you want the final piece of needlepoint to be? Having decided roughly, work out the relationship between the dimensions in the photograph/plan and the projected finished piece. This will help you both to draw up the design and choose materials.

5 What is the proportion of the roof to the frontage? Many houses, Alpine chalets and thatched cottages for example, depend on their deep roofs for much of their character, so remember this when planning the design.

6 Where is the front door, what is its scale, is there any detail? Again, the 'identity' of a house can depend on its front door. Does it line up with other features such as windows beside or above it?

If the front door has a porch, keep this face-on and flat when stitching a picture. For a free-standing house, it's possible to add the porch as it actually is.

7 Where are the windows? For an accurate representation, look carefully at the arrangement of windows on the house and see if they all align. Are there the same number of panes in each window? Are the panes square or rectangular? If the house has a later extension, or French windows, narrow metal window frames may have been used which are not so wide as those on the rest of the house.

8 Is there any surface decoration that will affect the thread count? As the design must be worked out accurately on the canvas before you begin stitching, take account of any features such as bricks or shutters which require a particular number of canvas threads to be fitted in. If you're using a stitch such as cushion stitch, remember to allow for its thread count, too.

9 Any bushes or climbing plants? Any flowers or foliage you wish to include is best worked as surface embroidery on the stitched house. In this case, choose tent stitch for the walls.

10 Any other detail you wish to add? Besides using artistic licence with the size of bushes (see above), you may wish to add other details such as window boxes, a garden gate, or a different door.

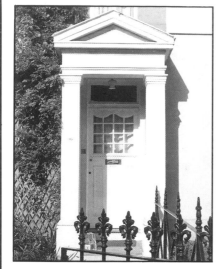

Roofs, walls and windows

Have fun experimenting with colours and stitches to obtain the best effect for the house you are stitching. Spend a little time trying them out on a piece of spare canvas before actually working the house. Here are some commonly-found roof, wall and window effects to start you off. Save up yarn oddments – they could be useful for a house feature.

Roofs

1 and 2 show two different scales of red-tiled roof. Both use double brick stitch, worked horizontally in mixed brick red and brown yarn.
3 and 4 show two variations of grey slate roofs, using straight and sloping gobelin stitch.
Backstitch in a darker thread gives added definition where separate tiles stand out.
5 and 6 show two thatched roof effects – 5 has one end of the couched flecked weaving yarn taken through to the back of the canvas, the other trimmed. 6 shows you the effect of couching a bouclé yarn, both ends are trimmed.

Adding perspective

The photograph of a house is bound to contain areas of shadow which give definition and perspective to it. To portray these realistically on flat or three-dimensional pieces, mix in one or two strands of grey or a slightly darker shade thread than the main colour you are using.
Not all houses are flat-fronted.

Some have projecting areas and extensions, so use scale as well as the shadow techniques to help define them. Consider using a stitch with a smaller thread count for the walls and roof of the recessed part and a larger stitch effect for the forward part (see the two sizes of brick pattern shown opposite).

Special effects stitches for house stitchery

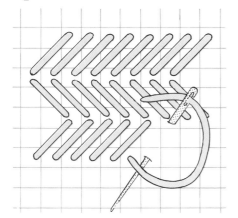

1

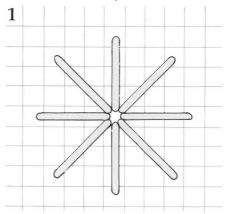

2

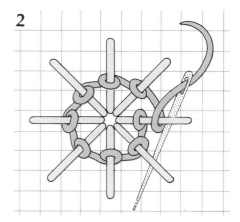

Horizontal knitting stitch

This is a good stitch for surface interest and gives a zigzag effect, used on the chalet shutters.
Knitting stitch can also be worked vertically.
Work diagonal stitches spanning two threads in each direction, then work the next row in the opposite direction, but so that the stitches share holes with the first row.

Whipped spider's web stitch

This is fun to do and useful for details like flowers. It is used in the chalet design for the logs.
1 First set up the framework of straight stitches, converging in the same hole to form a star-shape as shown. Work the stitches in the basic cross over three or four threads, depending on the size you want.

2 Bring the needle up close to the centre of the star-shape and whip it, making sure the needle does not pierce the canvas.
To do this, pass the needle forward under two 'spokes', and back over one, working outwards until all the spokes are covered.

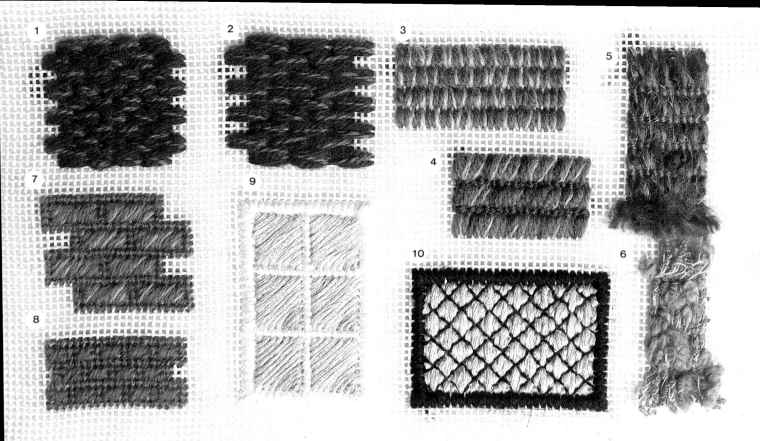

Walls

7 and 8 show the pretty effect of traditional red brick in two scales. The sloping gobelin stitch 'bricks' are surrounded by tent stitch 'mortar'.

Windows

9 and 10 Sloping gobelin stitch used again – here in two different shades of grey to enliven window panes on a white-framed window.
For a diamond-paned leaded window, Hungarian stitch is ideal. Diagonal rows of backstitch in black add the lines of leading.
Other stitches that might well be useful are square mosaic and double brick stitches.

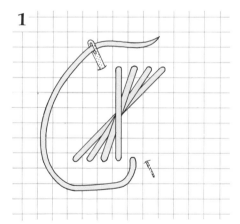

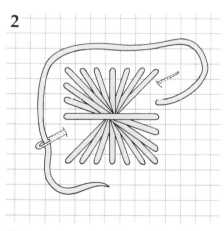

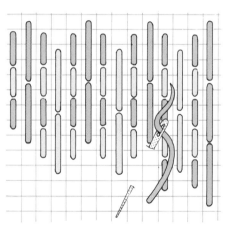

Rhodes stitch

This spectacular stitch forms a large padded square. Work it in single squares or as an all-over filling. The square can cover any number of threads as long as the same basic method is used.
1 Begin at one of the corners of the square and make a diagonal stitch to the opposite corner.
Bring the needle up in the next

hole, going round the edge of the square anti-clockwise, and re-insert it opposite in the hole next to the one where it last went in. A square over six threads is shown here.
2 Continue round the edge until the whole square is filled. If desired, you can add a small upright stitch in the centre to 'tie' all the threads in place.

Hungarian stitch

This is ideal for diamond-paned windows and could come in handy for roofs or gardens.
Working horizontally to form diamonds, make upright stitches over two, four and two threads, leaving two vertical threads free between each diamond.
On the next row, make the long stitches between the previous diamonds. The short stitches should share holes with the previous row.

149

Needlepoint houses

The instructions which follow apply equally to a two dimensonal house picture or three dimensional model.

Planning the design

Whether your photograph is an angle shot, or not, make a straight-on sketch/diagram of the front of the house, as accurately as possible. Mark on it the dimensions you have already taken from the photograph. For three-dimensional houses, make a straight-on sketch of one of the sides as well.

Points to watch

The main exterior features to be fitted in on the chalet shown opposite are the windows, shutters and balconies. Walls and roof can be stitched as all-over effects, adaptable to the rest of the design. Notice that the windows and shutters line up on both storeys, both balconies are the same depth, and the roof overhang is equal all round.

14-gauge canvas was chosen for the chalet piece but study your answers to the checklist given on pages 146-147 to establish what is best for your intended design. The relative dimensions for the finished piece are based on the desired height. For instance, if the height of the building is to be five times its photograph height, multiply all the dimensions by five to keep the house to scale.

Modifying the design

It is sometimes a good idea to use 'artist's licence' and modify the design to make it simpler to stitch. For instance, the actual chalet on which this chapter's project is based is a very deep building with jutting balconies which extend out at the back. It was decided instead to include only one set of windows on each side, foreshortening the side walls, and to work the chalet as a regular rectangle, with the front and back identical and the two sides identical.

The front and one side wall are worked as one piece, likewise the back and one side wall. The roof is worked in one piece.

To provide interest and attractive detail, window boxes, flowers,

stacked logs and a bank of snow are added to the design. Sketch these in your first drawing to see the effect. Although the roof is snow-covered, work it in a more interesting mixture of grey and brown, rather than stark white. Scallop satin stitch with Rhodes stitch timber ends makes the roof more attractive.

Transferring design to canvas

Working horizontally The desired width for the chalet was about 25cm/10in, so on 14-gauge canvas, this gave a count of 140 threads. Increasing this slightly to 150 gave 7 threads for each window pane and inside shutter and 2 for each window frame and shutter border, plus an equal amount of plain wall at each end (14 threads).

Working vertically Notice that the roof space is one of the main features and takes up almost one quarter of the total height.

The window panes are shorter than their width and so should span 5

threads or less (width is 7). The horizontal glazing bars are narrower than the main frames, so must be one thread.

Make balconies slightly deeper than windows and plan for a bigger stitch to help the illusion of relief. The desired height gives a thread count of about 175. Allowing 40 for the roof space, you arrive at 24 for balconies, including handrail, 21 for windows, timber cladding under balcony at 16, basement at 30, giving the required window pane count of 5. Calculate for the side and back walls in the same way.

Marking the design Mark all these calculations on a second diagram. Cut and bind the piece of canvas and mark the centre. Mark all the design lines for the front and side walls on the canvas with a pencil, counting threads carefully. Mark the corner of the house. Remember your marks should run along lines of *holes* as this is where stitch ends will fall.

Stitching and decorating the chalet

It is difficult to talk specifically about amounts of canvas and thread you need as these are so variable. For a three-dimensional project like this, (28cm/11in tall, 24cm/9½in wide and 13cm/5in deep), you'll need about two large hanks (25g) of crewel wool in each of nine colours (including, in this case, four different browns and three different greys) plus three or four shades of stranded or pearl cotton for flowers, curtains and highlights.

It is always a good idea to strip down stranded cotton before use as this helps the threads to lie smoothly over the canvas.

Working the walls

Work the house front plus one side first, then the back plus one side. As when you are planning the design, try to establish features like windows and shutters on the canvas first. Work window frames and shutter outlines, using the neat cornering of straight gobelin stitch on both.

Now fill in these areas with the chosen stitch. Horizontal knitting stitch makes the red shutters here look very attractive.

Balconies are another feature to fit in early on. Padded satin stitch makes handrails stand out – lay a double thickness of yarn along the stitching line first of all.

The eight window boxes filled with flowers are fun to include – work the boxes in cushion stitch.

Most of the balcony bars are in straight gobelin stitch in mottled brown yarns; the bars directly above window boxes are worked in tent stitch as the flowers are embroidered later on top.

Timber cladding Before filling in the main body of timber cladding, ensure that you have stitched all irregularities such as shadows and beams.

Encroaching gobelin is a good choice for effects like painted clapboard and natural timber cladding. Try to make the surface as interesting as possible with colour shading, beginning with the two darkest tones in the darkest area, (probably beneath the roof overhang) gradually changing to the lighter shades.

Lower storey area The basement floor of the chalet has stone walls with stone piers supporting the

Below: A three-dimensional Alpine chalet makes an attractive ornament and may bring back holiday memories.

weight of the balcony above. One of them falls at the corner of the house and appears on both front and side walls, so is double the width of the other two on the canvas.

Double brick stitch in mottled grey and white makes effective stone piers; a darker combination is used for the stonework of the walls.

The only other feature to be fitted in is a door (horizontal straight gobelin stitch for contrast).

Work the background areas, where you intend having surface embroidery, in tent stitch, (in this case, the pile of logs on the front wall of the chalet).

Leave the area for the bank of snow unworked – the French knots used for the snow can be worked so densely that there is no need to stitch the canvas underneath as it will not show through.

Surface embroidery
Now add the pile of logs using mixed browns and whipped spider's web stitches placed at random.

Finally, fill the window boxes with pretty flowers using detached chain stitches for green leaves and French knots for the flowers themselves. Work an identical piece for the back and other side wall of the chalet.

Working the roof
For the chalet roof, work a simple rectangle of needlepoint. The width should be the measurement of the side wall, plus back and front overhang allowance (about 1cm/½in) and the length should be the length of both upper sloping chalet front walls plus overhang allowance for both sides. Mark the edges of the roof on the canvas, as well as

the centre fold.

To make an interesting feature, work timber ends in a row in chunky Rhodes stitch on either side of the centre top of the roof.

Apart from any foldlines which are worked in straight gobelin stitch, work the main roof area in an attractive scallop pattern satin stitch using a mixture of grey and brown threads. Work compensation stitches of different lengths to make the front, back and side edges straight.

At the front and back edges of the roof overhang, along marked lines, leave two free threads of canvas and fill the underneath portion with the same satin stitch. Now fold the canvas back on itself along unworked threads and cover these with a row of straight gobelin stitch to make a firm fold.

Making up the finished work

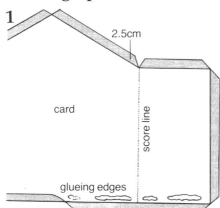

1

2.5cm

card

score line

glueing edges

If you've made the chalet or other house as a flat picture, stretch the canvas and mount it on a panel of hardboard cut to fit (see page 99). Do not cover the piece with glass – use a deeply-recessed frame to protect it.

Three-dimensional projects
Here is the method for making up a square or rectangular house, like the chalet, which is made up in two pieces, plus the roof.
1 Cut two pieces of firm card to the exact size and shape of the front plus side and back plus side. With a craft knife, score the card down the two corners of the house. Trim canvas around needlepoint to 2.5cm/1in and lay over pieces of card. Turn spare canvas to the

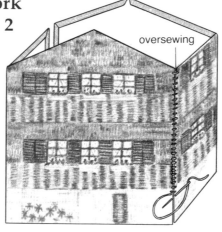

2

oversewing

underside and glue firmly in place. Mount the roof piece in exactly the same way, scoring the card along the roof centre.
2 Using matching wool, oversew the two wall pieces together along the two opposite corners.
The filling depends on the intended use. For a sturdy doorstop, fill the house with a standard brick bonded to blocks of wood cut to form a base for the house.
Glue wood in place.
For a lightweight, purely ornamental piece, use a block of firm foam cut to the exact shape, or thick polystyrene tiles glued together and cut to shape.
Place the bent roof in position and catch it in place at intervals along upper edges of house walls.

Making up the town house
The town house doorstop shown on page 146 is made up in a slightly different way and you may find it a slightly simpler project as well as being closer in style to your own home. As before the front and one side wall are worked as one piece, the back and the other side wall as another. This time, however, half the roof is included with the front and half with the back. The roof pieces are straight continuations of the canvas with a fold where the roof meets the wall at the eaves, and the side walls are peaked.

When making up, mount the canvas on firm card as described earlier and score the card down the two corners of the house and along the eaves. As before, join the side walls first and then stitch the short edges of the roof to the side walls. Finally, oversew along the ridge to join the roof.

A rectangular piece of canvas mounted on a piece of card the dimensions of the base of the house can be stitched to the bottom to form a box. Fill a strong plastic bag with sand and insert it into the house before the base is finally stitched into place to make a stable and attractive doorstop.

Quilting and appliqué

The ancient craft of quilting was devised to add warmth to bed covers and clothes. A layer of soft wadding was sandwiched between two layers of fabric and anchored with lines of basic stitches. In time stitching patterns were created to add interest and texture to the quilting, and elaborate, all-over designs can be found on many of the old English quilts.

Today traditional hand-sewn methods can be replaced by the sewing machine, and the introduction of lightweight, synthetic wadding means you can wash quilted fabrics more easily so that the techniques are available for a far wider range of items, including fashion jackets and waistcoats, table linen and cushions. Quick-to-make projects with small amounts of quilting can be just as effective as the traditional, full-scale bed cover. Try making some simple quilted bags or add some quilted relief to a garment by emphasising the pattern on a dress fabric.

Explore quilting variations such as trapunto, where varied amounts of wadding are inserted into a stitched design to give a subtle, three-dimensional effect; Italian quilting, where a cord is inserted between parallel lines of stitching to create a raised, linear design; or contour quilting, which uses the design printed on the fabric as a stitching guide.

Quilting combines particularly well with appliqué, which is the name given to the technique of stitching pieces of fabric on to a background, either as simple, outline shapes or more complex designs built up from several pieces. They can be hand-stitched or machined into position and a variety of trimmings, such as braids, ribbons and beads, can be added for interest.

You do not have to buy special fabric – a look through your scrap bag can inspire you to add that individual touch to soft furnishings and clothes. Patterns for the motifs can be copied from magazines. Or you can create your own pictures and designs in fabric.

The simplest forms of appliqué use patches of fabric to build up a picture which can be framed or used as a cushion cover. It can also be used to create a motif to highlight a jacket. In appliqué perse motifs are cut out from patterned fabrics and arranged in a pleasing design to decorate clothes or soft furnishings, and shadow appliqué adds a subtle hint of colour on a fine see-through fabric.

This is one of the most versatile of needlecrafts. Whether stitched by hand or machine, it is restricted only by the limitations of your own imagination.

CHAPTER 34

Quick quilting on a sewing machine

Wadded machine quilting is fun to do and gives a luxurious padded look to both clothes and home items. Try making some of these deliciously pretty bags for a bathroom or dressing table. Pick a fabric with ready-made lines to sew along, and make the job fast and easy.

Quilting is the stitching together of two or more layers of fabric. It is decorative and adds another dimension to the fabric by altering the surface, giving it texture and relief. It is also of practical use, providing warmth, strength and body for clothing and household articles.

One of the most popular uses of quilting is as an enhancement for bed covers, often those worked in patchwork or appliqué. The quilting makes them thicker, warmer and more hardwearing.

Wadded quilting

There are several different types of quilting, but one of the most useful is wadded quilting. The method involves making a sandwich of a top layer which can be plain or patterned fabric, a middle layer of wadding, and a bottom layer of lining fabric. The sandwich of three layers is tacked securely and then quilted – either on your lap or on a frame. Once tacked, the three layers can be quilted by hand or by machine in a series of small running stitches.

Machine quilting

This chapter deals with wadded machine quilting – a quick technique which gives a professional finish. The fabric is quilted first and then made up into the finished item.

Although quilted fabrics are available commercially, colour ranges are limited. Using your machine and a little imagination, you can make your own individually quilted fabrics.

Once you have perfected the technique, you can make tablecloths, mats, bags, jackets, cushions and all sorts of small household accessories and gifts like those in the picture.

Fabrics, threads and wadding The top fabric for a quilted layer is usually cotton, cotton blend, silk, satin or wool, with similar lining fabric.

Use a matching shade of Sylko machine twist, or silk twist for silk fabrics. The fabrics in this chapter have been quilted with transparent nylon thread, which is almost invisible. It should be used only for machine quilting.

Most people use bonded terylene wadding available in 2oz, 4oz and 8oz weights, which can be bought in 1m/1yd wide rolls in most fabric departments. Cotton and wool domette (a soft interfacing) is sometimes used for machine quilting and is less bulky to use.

Right: These quilted bags look expensive but are economical to make (see instructions overleaf).

Step-by-step machine quilting

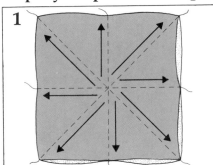

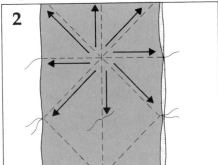

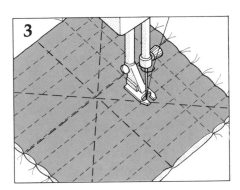

Preparing the fabric
Take a piece of fabric at least 5cm/2in larger all round than the amount needed for the pattern pieces of the project. Cut lining and wadding to same size. Press fabric to remove wrinkles. Lay the lining fabric flat with the wadding on top. Next lay down the top fabric, right side up, and smooth out, keeping all layers aligned.

Tacking fabrics and wadding
1 Tack through all layers using a contrasting thread, which is easy to

spot when removing. Stitch in a starburst pattern – first sew centred horizontal and vertical lines, then sew equidistant lines radiating from the centre to the outer edges. Use long running stitches. The spokes should be no more than 15cm/6in apart along outer edges of fabric.
2 If the piece of fabric is long and narrow, you may need to tack several smaller starbursts along its length.
This tacking distributes the wadding evenly and prevents it from bunching. Do not tack round

the outer edges of the fabric – this can cause puckering during quilting.

Stitching
Loosen tension and pressure on the sewing machine. Set a medium stitch length and try out on a scrap 'sandwich' of fabric and wadding.
3 Small pieces of fabric can be quilted with consecutive rows of stitching, beginning at one side. All the rows must be stitched in the same direction. If quilting a grid pattern, work parallel rows, turn

Machine quilting designs

Fabrics quilted by machine are often stitched in straight-line or grid patterns. These include diamonds, squares, vertical or diagonal stripes, and zigzags, which divide the fabric into neat, padded compartments.

A quilting guide-bar on your machine will place the stitching accurately. Stitch one straight guide-line, set the guide-bar to a suitable width, and stitch the second row with the bar following the first row. Work successive rows in the same way.

Quilting lines can be marked on to fabrics using a ruler and chalk pencil (brushes off after stitching) or a water-erasable marker (easily removed from most fabrics with a little water – test on fabric scrap first).

Simplest of all, use the design of a geometric print fabric to place the quilting lines. Stripes, trellis designs and checks are ideal, teamed with a plain or non-geometric print fabric as the backing.

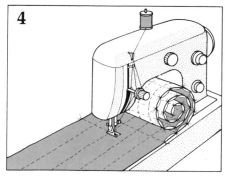

fabric and work the crossing rows. Begin stitching with the bulk of the fabric on the left of the needle.

4 If quilting a long length of fabric, roll the quilted portion of the fabric up under the machine arm to keep it out of the way while you are working the remaining portion. Leave a short length of thread at the end of each line of stitching to prevent unravelling. These threads do not need finishing off – they will be secured by seams or bound edges.

Above: A selection of effective quilting patterns for plain or printed fabrics.

Quilted bags make perfect gifts

All-over machine quilting is particularly suitable for small items such as these pretty cosmetic bags.

The four bags described in this chapter are made up in trellis fabrics specially chosen to give a suitable quilting design of diamonds or squares. For each bag, first quilt the fabric as shown on page 154. Graph patterns are given for the small and larger cases. To enlarge, copy on a grid of 5cm/2in squares. Cut required pattern pieces first from paper, then use these to cut shapes from quilted fabric or plastic lining. For sewing linings with plastic, see below. All seam allowances are 1cm/½in unless otherwise indicated, and are included in the pattern pieces.

Buy top fabric and lining of any width. They should tone in colour.

Two drawstring bags

These come in two sizes and each bag incorporates a pair of eyelet holes. Follow the kit manufacturer's instructions for inserting the eyelets.

You will need
40cm/½yd printed cotton fabric
40cm/½yd polyester wadding (4oz)
40cm/½yd cotton lining fabric
2 large eyelets (12mm/⅝in available in kit with insertion tool)
1m/1yd cotton cord to fit eyelets
1 card bias binding (25mm/1in wide or buy 12mm width and join)
Transparent nylon thread or matching sewing cotton

Making up the bag
Cut fabric pieces as follows:
Large bag, one rectangle 40.5cm× 28.5cm/16in×11in. Small bag, one rectangle 40.5cm×18cm/16in×7in. Both bags one circle radius 7.3cm/ 2⅞in. Cut drawstring casing strip from leftover lining fabric 3.4cm ×40.5cm/1¼in×16in. Tack close to edge of quilted pieces to reduce bulk. Insert eyelets 2.5cm/ 1in apart in centre front of main bag piece, 9cm/3½in from top (long edge) of large bag, 5.5cm/2¼in from top of small bag. Join short edges of main piece; neaten seam allowance with bias binding. Press seam open.
Turn in 7mm/⅜in seam allowance along both edges of casing and tack. Join ends to make a circle. Turn bag to wrong side and tack

Small cosmetics case

One flat pattern piece folds up into an envelope-style case. The pattern is given far right, 1 square = 5cm/2in.

You will need
25cm/¼yd printed cotton fabric
25cm/¼yd polyester wadding (4oz)
25cm/¼yd cotton lining fabric
25cm/¼yd opaque shower curtaining
5cm/2in strip of Velcro (20mm/¾in wide)
1 card bias binding (12mm/½in wide)
Transparent nylon thread or matching sewing cotton

Making up the case
Cut one pattern piece from quilted fabric and one from plastic lining. Stitch loopy side of Velcro strip to centre front of quilted fabric

piece, 2cm/¾in from the straight end of the fabric. Stitch fuzzy side of Velcro strip to plastic lining, 2cm/¾in away from rounded end of the plastic. Place lining on fabric with right sides facing. With a fine needle, tack together 5mm/⅜in in from edge. Machine the tacked pieces together along seamlines leaving one of the case side seams unstitched.
Carefully clip to stitching at each inward corner. Trim allowances close to stitching on all but the open edge of the case. Turn to right side and push out all corners with closed scissors. Tuck in edges of unstitched side along seamline and tack close to edge. Topstitch all round 6mm/¼in from edge. To assemble, place side and

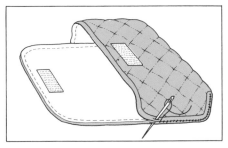

bottom edges together and join by hand with overcasting stitches. Continue up side seams and finish off at top of bag. Stitch over first stitching, reversing direction. Make tie with 65cm/25in of bias binding. Stitch to centre of front flap on stitching line so that 20cm/7¼in extends below flap, 40cm/15¼in above it. To seal case, close Velcro and tie bow.

PROFESSIONAL TOUCH

Sewing with plastic
Give your cosmetic bags a practical and professional-looking plastic lining with a soft, pliable plastic such as shower curtaining.
Once a puncture is made in plastic, it's there to stay, so avoid using pins on it. Cut out pattern pieces by fixing the pattern to the plastic with adhesive tape. When tacking, use a fine needle and stitch along the *outer* edges of

seam allowances.
Use transparent nylon thread and a medium stitch – a small stitch could cause the plastic to tear between perforations. Plastics may pull under the machine's presser foot. If this happens, sandwich the article you are sewing between sheets of tissue paper, stitch through all layers. When the sewing is completed, simply tear away from the seams.

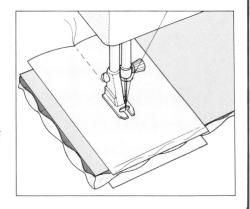

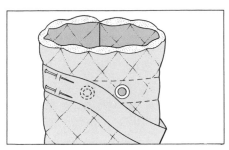

casing in place, centring over eyelets and matching seams. Machine stitch close to edges. Pin bag bottom to bag body with right sides together. Tack and stitch. seam. Finish with binding or overcast. Apply binding to top edge of bag. Insert cord through casing.

For tassels, knot cord 10cm/4in from ends, unravel below knot and trim.

The drawstring bag and small cosmetics case are cut on the straight grain, but the larger cosmetics case has been cut on the cross to give a pattern of squares.

Larger cosmetics case

This larger sized cosmetics case has a convenient Velcro closure at the top and a plastic lining. The pattern is given below, 1 square=5cm/2in.

You will need

20cm/¼yd printed cotton fabric
20cm/¼yd polyester wadding (4oz)
20cm/¼yd cotton lining fabric
20cm/¼yd transparent shower curtaining
22.5cm/¼yd strip of Velcro (20mm/ ¾in wide)
1 card bias binding (12mm/½in wide)
Transparent nylon thread or matching sewing cotton

Making up the case

Cut paper pattern from graph. Cut two fabric and two plastic pieces from this pattern.

Trim 6mm/¼in off top edge of each piece of plastic. Aligning bottom edges, tack a piece of plastic to wrong side of each quilted piece, sewing close to outer edges and along top edge of plastic. Fold top 6mm/¼in of quilted fabric to back and tack it down; stitch through all layers. Separate Velcro strip and tack each piece near top edge of case pieces on wrong sides. Stitch top and bottom edges. On right side of each case piece, tack bias binding so the top edge aligns with the bottom edge of the Velcro (on wrong side of case piece). Stitch binding in place.

Position a strip of 12mm/½in bias binding flush with curved outer edge of each case piece. The binding should run along each outer edge and extend 4cm/1½in at each top edge. Stitch inner edge of binding. Trim away fabric and lining below the newly-stitched edge. Turn top ends of binding to wrong side of each piece, turn under when level with bottom edge of Velcro on inside, and tack in place. With wrong sides together, tack case pieces together, sealing Velcro and aligning outer binding edges.

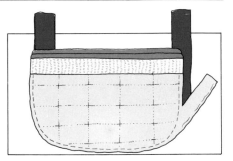

Stitch along outer edges of binding. For bow trim, cut a 28cm/11in strip of 12mm/½in binding. Fold in half lengthwise. Sew along open edge. Knot ends, trim excess, tie bow and hand sew to case front.

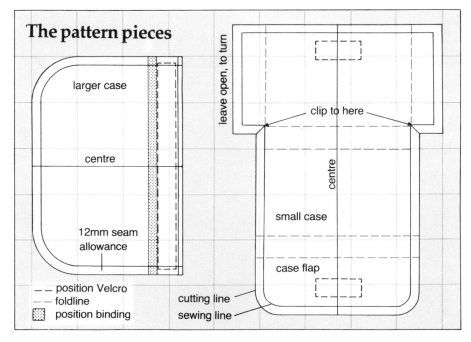

The pattern pieces

leave open, to turn

larger case

centre

12mm seam allowance

clip to here

centre

small case

case flap

- - position Velcro
- foldline
- position binding

cutting line
sewing line

CHAPTER 35

English quilting: a hand-stitched technique

*Quilting was originated for the purely practical purpose of
adding warmth, but its effect is so decorative
that top designers now use it to decorate not only household
items, but high fashion. And with these
basic techniques at your fingertips, so can you . . .*

Quilting by hand is relaxing and satisfying because you can watch the design grow as your needle goes in and out.

Wadded quilting, sometimes known as English quilting, is traditionally worked by hand in running stitch. Often the designs are very intricate and seen to best advantage worked on large quilts; particularly beautiful examples come from Wales and the north of England.

Popular quilting designs and motifs have been passed down through the generations and you will find these old patterns available commercially – some in the form of templates or stencils.

Many geometric or pictorial motifs are adaptable to quilting, too, so there's plenty of scope for designing your own.

English quilting materials

Most of the fabrics, waddings and threads used for machine quilting are suitable for hand quilting.

Fabrics Plain cotton fabrics are the easiest to work with because you can see the quilting design more clearly than on patterned ones. Shiny fabrics, which catch the light, give the most relief to the design.

The backing fabric for hand-stitched work should either be the same type as the top fabric, or it can be muslin or

*Below: A perfect present for a new baby,
this hand-quilted cover is fully washable.*

calico – the latter is the traditional backing for English quilting.

Needles must be fine to avoid marking the fabric, and this applies to tacking needles, too. Betweens in sizes 7-9, even as fine as 10, are in common use and crewels are sometimes used. You will also need a box of fine lace pins.

Threads Quilting threads should be strong, and of the same type as the fabric. Strong, poly-cotton quilting thread is available in white and some colours, but if you need a thicker thread, good choices are DMC Cordonnet Spécial coton 20, 30, 40 or 50, Coats crochet cotton, or DMC pearl cotton. If the thread does not have a glazed finish, run it through a block of beeswax before quilting to help it to pass smoothly through the layers of fabric and wadding, and to make it stronger.

Thimbles It is well worth persevering to learn to use a thimble, to protect the finger constantly pushing a needle through several layers of fabric. Choose a large, comfortable thimble with a flat, indented head and wear it on the middle finger of your sewing hand. Some quilters use a second thimble on the hand underneath the quilt to guide the needle back up again when it has passed down through the three layers. Others use a leather finger guard or masking tape on the working finger.

Transferring designs

The design must be marked on the fabric before it is attached to the wadding and backing. It is important not to use a permanent marker as the design may show between stitches.

For fairly intricate quilting designs such as the one overleaf, traditional methods used for transferring embroidery designs are suitable. These include the trace and tack method, dressmaker's carbon paper (following manufacturer's instructions) and the window method.

If the fabric you are using is translucent against the light, the window method is the simplest. Make sure the design tracing is marked in clear, black lines and trace it off on to the fabric with a dressmaker's chalk pencil, a well-sharpened hard pencil or a blue water-erasable marker (test it first on a fabric scrap).

Some geometric or repeat motif quilting designs can be transferred by making card or plastic templates of sections of the design which can be traced around. Another method is to make a stencil.

How to begin

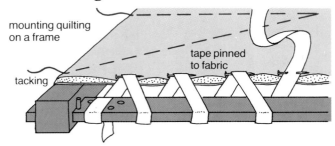

mounting quilting on a frame

tacking

tape pinned to fabric

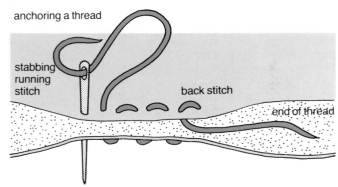

anchoring a thread

stabbing running stitch

back stitch

end of thread

Small items such as cushions can be quilted using only your lap as a support. For larger work, use a rectangular embroidery frame or a special quilting hoop with a stand, to liberate both hands. To mount fabric on the hoop, simply lay the work over the smaller hoop and press the larger hoop over it to hold the surface flat, but not taut. If you stretch it too tightly the stitches will not sink deeply into the layers of fabric and the design will lack definition.

Mounting quilting on a frame An embroidery frame acts as a small quilting frame for a cushion or cot cover.

Attach the top and bottom of the tacked layers to the rollers on the frame. If the quilting is longer than the side stretchers, roll part of it over the rollers so it can be wound on as work progresses. Fix the rollers and stretchers so that the work is held firm but not taut.

To attach the sides of the work to the stretchers, tie a length of cotton tape to one end of one stretcher. Pin to the edge of the quilting, turn tape back over pin, wind round the stretcher and pin to the quilting again, 7.5-10cm/3-4in further along. Continue to the end of the quilting. Repeat on other side.

Basic stitching techniques

As with machine quilting, the three layers – fabric, wadding and backing – must be well tacked before the quilting stitches are worked, especially when you are not using a frame. Lay the layers down in the correct order and smooth them out. Pin together with fine pins and tack in straight lines, radiating out from the centre.

The main quilting stitch is hand-sewn running stitch. Keep the sewing hand above the fabric, with the other hand underneath to guide the needle back into the fabric.

Running stitch can be worked either with a stabbing motion, one stitch at a time, or by picking up groups of four or five stitches – usually possible only on thinner layers, not with wadded quilting.

It is the evenness of the stitches that makes quilting pleasing to the eye, so make sure that your stitches (and the spacing between them) are all of equal length – about 2mm/⅛in for most projects. Begin stitching at the centre of the design and work outwards.

With each new length of thread, insert the needle into the top fabric and wadding some way from the stitching line. As shown above, bring the needle up where you wish to stitch, leaving a long thread in the wadding, and backstitch through the first stitch to anchor it securely. To finish off, make a small back stitch through the last stitch and run the thread through the wadding before snipping it off.

Hand-quilted cot cover

A delightful design of doves, hearts, leaves and flowers adorns this cot cover. The stitching is worked in white thread but you could use colours to create a bolder effect. All materials are made of polyester, so the quilt is fully washable.

You will need
1.80m/2yd white polyester satin or similar (122cm/48in width) *or*
2m/2⅛yd of 112cm/44in width
3.20m/3½yd polyester wadding (4oz weight) 122cm/48in width *or* 100cm/39in width

1m/1⅛yd muslin 122cm/48in wide *or* enough to cut a piece 116cm × 100cm/46in × 40in
Square or rectangular embroidery frame or quilting hoop to fit fabric
1 reel Coats Drima polyester thread
Crewel or between needle size 8

Working the design

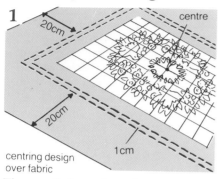

centring design over fabric

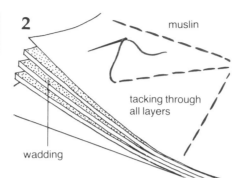

tacking through all layers

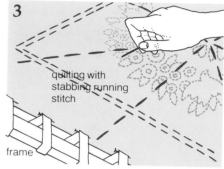

quilting with stabbing running stitch

The small chart gives the complete quilting design. Enlarge it on to a grid of 5cm/2in squares on tracing paper, copying it square by square. The dove, heart and leaf motifs are given full size to help you.
1 Trace off the motifs and, using the small diagram as a guide, position the tracings under your enlargement of the design and trace them in at the appropriate points to complete the full-size design.
Preparing the fabric Cut a piece of satin fabric 116cm × 100cm/ 46in × 40in. Fold it in half both ways, creasing lightly to make folds which cross at the centre point of

fabric. This will help you to place the quilting design centrally. Transfer the design to the fabric matching the design and fabric centres.
Measure 20cm/8in from all four edges of fabric and tack or mark a border line all round the rectangle. Then tack or mark a second line 1cm/½in inside the first. Cut three 116cm × 100cm/46in × 40in pieces from the length of wadding.
2 Lay them one on top of the other on the wrong side of the top fabric. Lay the muslin centrally over the wadding and tack thoroughly through all layers.

Working the quilting Mount the quilting on the frame, if you have one. If necessary, roll part of the design round the roller bars, but make sure you are able to begin the quilting at the centre of the design. (If you do not have a frame, work the quilting on your lap.)
3 Work the quilting in stabbing running stitch (two movements) using the polyester thread – the wadding is too bulky to allow you to pick up several stitches at once. After completing the central motifs, stitch along the double parallel lines. Remove the work from the frame.

DESIGN EXTRA

Bluebird basket cover

This pretty quilted cover can be worked on a small hoop. Pick out motifs from the cot cover.

You will need
For a round basket, diameter 20-30cm/8-12in
40cm/½yd polyester satin
40cm/½yd medium (4oz) wadding (use double)
40cm/½yd muslin for backing
Coats Drima polyester thread

Working the cover
Measure the basket diameter and add 10cm/4in to obtain fabric lengths.

To plan the design, draw round the upturned basket on tracing paper and trace off motifs in desired positions. The cover (right) has a central dove inside a ring of hearts, leaves and flowers. Draw round a saucer and position them along this line. Transfer design to fabric and work quilting as for cot cover. Cut out circle of quilted fabric allowing extra 1cm/½in all round for seam. Cut satin backing to same size. Place right sides together and sew, leaving opening for turning. Turn, slipstitching opening.

Above: A quilted cover for a basket.

Trace patterns

Chart for quilting design

centre
point

1 square = 5cm

Making up and backing

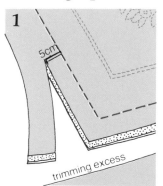

5cm

trimming excess

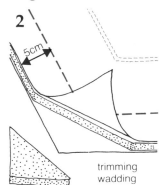

5cm

trimming
wadding

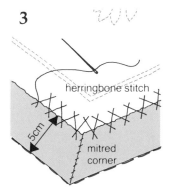

herringbone stitch

5cm

mitred
corner

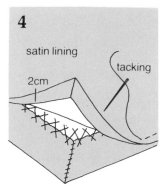

satin lining

tacking

2cm

Measure and tack all round 8cm/
3¼in outside the parallel border
lines to mark finished edge of quilt.
Remove all other original tacking.
1 Trim fabrics and wadding to within
5cm/2in of the tacking.
2 Trim the wadding only diagonally
across each corner.
3 Fold 5cm/2in to wrong side all
round, mitring corners of satin and
muslin. Tack in position. Slipstitch
mitred corners and catch raw edge
down all round with herringbone
stitch.

4 Cut a rectangle of satin fabric for
the quilt backing measuring
96cm×80cm/38in×32in. Turn
under 2cm/¾in all round and press.
Tack to back of quilt close to outer
edge and slipstitch in position all
round.

CHAPTER 36

Trapunto

Trapunto is an attractive form of quilting where selected areas of the work are padded, giving a raised effect to pictorial or geometric designs. The patterns are outlined in simple running or backstitch and the visual effect is varied by the amount of padding inserted.

The technique is sometimes known as stuffed quilting and gives the effect of a raised design on a flat background. It is usually worked on plain fabric using the same colour thread. Two layers of fabric are stitched together and padding is inserted between the layers through slits made in the backing fabric. The slits are then sewn up. The quilting is usually hand sewn, but geometric and other simple designs can be machined.

Materials and equipment

For successful trapunto, choose a closely-woven cotton or silk fabric in a pale or medium shade for the top fabric so that the design shows up well in relief. Lightweight fabrics can use the same material for the backing. Heavier or more openweave fabrics should be backed with muslin. Pins and needles should be fine, and you will also need a small pair of sharp embroidery scissors for slitting the backs of the motifs.

Use a medium-sized knitting needle to help insert the wadding.

It is best if you choose a fairly simple design without too many tiny details; at the same time make sure the areas to be padded are not too large or you will have difficulty in making the work look even. Transfer this design to the right side of the top fabric as for ordinary English quilting. Water-erasable felt pens can be useful for this, but take care to make a fine line as the stitching is delicate.

Working the trapunto

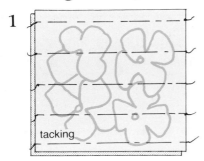

1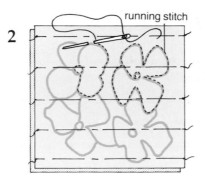

tacking

1 Place the top fabric over the backing fabric. Pin and jon the two together with lines of tacking stitches, about 7cm/2¾in apart, to cover the whole piece of fabric.

Below: These beautiful trapunto designs are worked by hand on the cushion fronts before making up.

2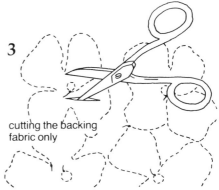

running stitch

2 This type of quilting can easily be done in the hand, but mount the double fabric on a frame if you find it easier.
Stitch along the design lines in either backstitch or running stitch, making your stitches small and neat – they will have to hold the wadding securely in place later.

3

cutting the backing fabric only

Begin each thread with a tiny knot. When the whole design is stitched, remove the tacking threads.
3 Turn the work wrong side up. With a small, sharp pair of scissors, make a small slit in the centre of each shape to be padded, cutting through the backing fabric only.

4

padding the design

wadding

4 Tease out a small piece of wadding and push it through the slit with the point of a medium-sized knitting needle; carry on doing this until the shape is evenly padded out on the right side, but not hard. Make sure you don't miss any corners.

5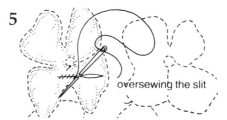

oversewing the slit

Some areas can be padded out more than others but do not insert so much wadding that the unpadded background fabric puckers. Other parts of the design can be left completely flat.
5 Sew up the edges of the slit with small oversewing stitches.

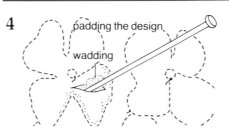

A pair of trapunto cushions

These two cushions would look attractive either end of a window seat. The two scenes show inside and outside views of a window. You could make them from glazed cotton, polyester crêpe de chine or luxurious silk, but remember to match the thread to the material used.
Choose cool pale green and shell pink colours for a delicate look. Cream, yellow or palest blue would also look lovely.
The designs are worked partly in backstitch and partly in running stitch, and the amount of padding varies in different parts of the design.

You will need for each cushion
50cm/⅝yd crêpe de chine (90cm/ 36in width, or more) in a pale shade
50cm/⅝yd backing fabric to match
1 reel pure silk sewing thread, to match crêpe de chine
10cm/⅛yd polyester wadding
18in/45cm square cushion pad
40cm/16in zip
Fine crewel or sharps needles
Tacking cotton

Preparing the fabric
Cut both pieces of fabric in half to make two pieces 45cm × 50cm/ 18in × 20in. Enlarge the design on each chart to double the size (one square = 5cm/2in). Trace over the outlines in black felt tip pen on white paper, and lay one of the crêpe de chine squares over it, making sure the fabric is centred over the design. Pin in position all round the edge.

Trace the outline of the design on to the crêpe de chine using either a finely sharpened crayon just a little darker than the fabric, or a water-erasable embroidery marker. Test on a scrap of the fabric first.

Working the trapunto cushions
Remove the pins and paper, and lay the marked fabric over one of the squares of backing fabric.

Tack the two squares together as described on the previous page and carefully stitch the design in matching silk thread, working solid lines in backstitch and dotted lines in running stitch.
Turn the work to wrong side and insert wadding in those parts of the design indicated. Some parts are lightly wadded, some more fully to give more relief and texture.

Windowbox design Insert light padding into the outer window frames and the windowbox area. The flowers and leaves should be more fully padded so that they stand out in the foreground.
Bedroom window design Again, refer to the design to see which parts of the design are wadded. Heavy padding is inserted into the brush, bottles, necklace and part of

Graph for windowbox design

◻ fully padded

□ lightly padded

——— back stitch

------- running stitch

1 square = 5cm

the curtains. Some of the curtain folds are lightly padded, while others are left completely flat.

Making up the cushion

Cut the remaining pieces of crêpe de chine and backing in half to make two pieces 45cm × 25cm/18in × 10in. With wrong sides together, tack the two pieces of backing to the pieces of top fabric.

Insert zip centrally between two long edges of these pieces. With zip slightly undone, place right side of quilting to right side of back and stitch all round with a 1cm/½in seam (the size of the finished square will be 43cm/17in). Trim seams and corners, open zip fully and turn to right side. Top-stitch round seam 2mm/⅛in from edge.

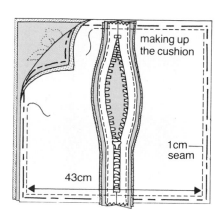

Graph for bedroom window design

CHAPTER 37

Italian quilting for raised corded designs

An intricate Celtic motif from the Book of Kells inspired this linear design which is particularly suitable for Italian quilting. Transfer the pattern to the delicate fabric by using pounce, and make an elegant cummerbund and matching bag.

Italian quilting is sometimes called corded quilting and gives an attractive raised effect which is suitable for linear patterns. It is purely decorative and cannot be relied on for warmth and body. It is often combined with trapunto (page 162) and is used, for example, in floral designs where there may be a combination of linear stems worked in Italian quilting, and larger flower areas padded out in trapunto.

Like trapunto, the stitching is worked on a double layer of fabric tacked together and then the design is padded from the wrong side. The design is worked by hand or machine in parallel lines about 6mm/¼in apart and lengths of quilting wool or cord are inserted into the tubes formed by the parallel lines. The finished quilting is lined to hide the backing.

Top fabrics Italian quilting works best on plain fabrics with a sheen which shows up the corded design to advantage and therefore satin is a popular choice. The fabric needs to have a little more give than those normally used for other kinds of quilting so a fine silky jersey is also recommended. You could equally well use lawn or crêpe.

Backing fabrics Butter muslin or lawn are often used for the backing fabric. The quilting wool or cord is easily inserted through these soft fabrics.

Cords The cord inserted between the design lines may be a soft cotton cord or a special quilting wool. Wash both these before use – any shrinkage after quilting would cause the ground fabric to pucker.

Threads Try and match thread to fabric, using silk twist for stitching on silk, cotton thread for cotton fabrics, and polyester thread for synthetics.

Right: An exquisite quilted cummerbund for straight or full-skirted outfits. Make a matching purse with a strap.

The techniques of Italian quilting

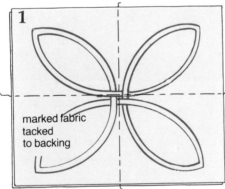

1 marked fabric tacked to backing

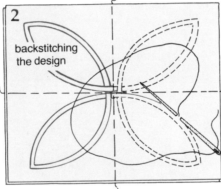

backstitching the design

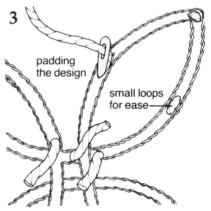

3

padding the design

small loops for ease

Transfer the design on to the right side of the top fabric using the prick and pounce method or tacking.

1 Tack the marked fabric to the backing lawn or muslin with vertical, horizontal and diagonal lines. If quilting by hand, mount the two fabrics in a rectangular frame large enough to take the whole design. This leaves both your hands free for stitching.

2 Stitch along the parallel lines of the design using backstitch or running stitch and a fine needle. If using running stitch, you may be able to pick up several stitches at once, rather than using a stabbing running stitch which takes longer. Make sure you finish off each length of thread securely on the back of the work. The cords cannot overlap – where one cord meets another the ends of one cord stop each side so that it looks as though it passes underneath the other cord.

Using your sewing machine If the design being quilted is not too complicated or curvy, it can be machined using a small straight stitch. In this case, do not mount the fabric on a frame. Work slowly and carefully, pulling all ends through to the back and finishing them off securely.

Padding the design When the entire design is stitched, remove the work from the frame. Working from the back, fill in the tubes formed by the stitching using a blunt bodkin or tapestry needle size 16 or 18 threaded with quilting wool or cord. To avoid piercing the top fabric, make the entry hole in the backing fabric very carefully using a stitch ripper. Insert the needle into the entry hole and after about 2.5cm/1in, bring it back through the backing fabric.

3 Pull the wool or cord loosely through the tubes of the design, leaving a little showing at the beginning. Re-insert the needle in the same hole. At corners or on tight curves, bring the needle out and re-insert it in the same way, again leaving a little loop of the wool showing. This helps the tubes to remain full and not flatten, and also prevents the fabric round the design from puckering.

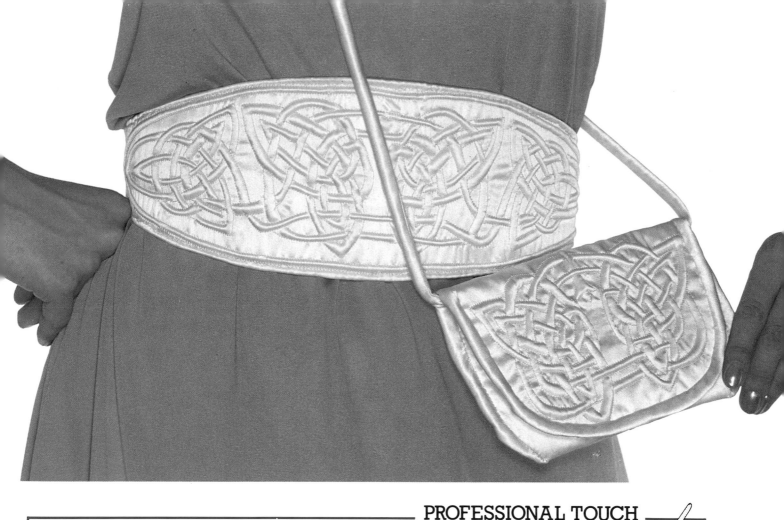

Prick and pounce

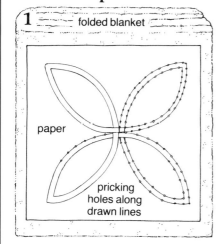

1 folded blanket

paper

pricking holes along drawn lines

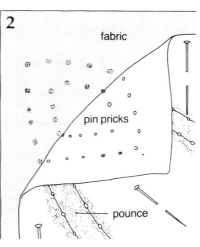

2

fabric

pin pricks

pounce

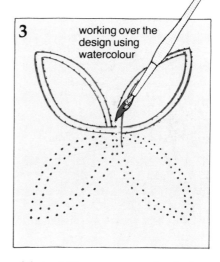

3 working over the design using watercolour

One of the best ways to transfer an Italian quilting design is the prick and pounce method. Marking with tacks is cumbersome for a delicate design, and dressmaker's carbon is indelible and may show on a light-coloured fabric.

1 Draw the design on a sheet of firm paper and place it over a folded piece of blanket. Prick a series of holes along all the design lines – using a sharp needle, a stiletto or, if the design is not too intricate, by running along them with your sewing machine unthreaded and set to a long stitch.

2 Pin the pricked pattern firmly in place on the right side of the fabric where the design is to be quilted. You will need a special marking powder called *pounce*. Take a small felt pad, or a rolled-up piece of felt, and rub pounce all over the design so it goes through the holes on to the

fabric. Lift a corner to check that the design is clearly transferred before removing the tracing.

3 Blow gently over the surface of the fabric to remove excess pounce. The design will show up as a series of dotted lines. Go over the design lines using a very fine paint brush dipped in watercolour slightly darker than the fabric or use a finely sharpened dressmaker's chalk pencil.

Italian quilted cummerbund and matching purse

Treat yourself to the luxury of silk satin and make this cummerbund and purse for a special occasion. The design has been stitched in pale pink thread for emphasis. It shows up perfectly on the ivory silk satin.

You will need
For cummerbund only
30cm/⅜yd silk satin (any width)
30cm/⅜yd matching silk lining
30cm/⅜yd muslin/lawn for backing
15cm/⅛yd craft quality Vilene
15cm/⅛yd buckram for stiffening

2 hanks quilting wool
6 reels silk twist
Fine crewel needle
Blunt bodkin or tapestry needle
Pounce and felt pad (for marking design)
Rectangular embroidery frame (optional)
Stitch ripper
For cummerbund and purse
½m/½yd silk satin, width 115cm/ 45in *or* 1m/1yd of width 90cm/36in
70cm/¾yd silk lining (90cm/36in wide)

70cm/¾yd cotton lawn or muslin
35cm/⅜yd craft quality Vilene
8 reels silk twist
25cm/¼yd polyester wadding (2oz)
All other requirements are as for cummerbund only

Cutting out the cummerbund
Follow the cutting layouts carefully if you plan to make the purse too. The 90cm/36in width fabric is only suitable for waist measurements up to 86cm/34in. Above this use 115cm/ 45in-width fabric.

Making the cummerbund

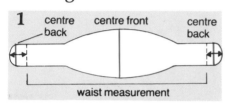

1

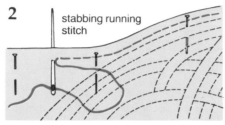

2 stabbing running stitch

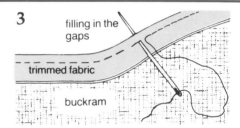

3 filling in the gaps / trimmed fabric / buckram

Make a paper pattern for the finished belt using the trace pattern outline.
1 Extend each end equally until belt is 5cm/2in longer than your waist measurement. Round off ends as shown.
Use this pattern to cut a piece of Vilene and one of buckram to the finished size and tack them

together. Pin the completed quilting with the backing fabric next to the Vilene. You will note that the quilting has 'shrunk' the design a little, leaving a small rebate between the quilting and the edge of Vilene/buckram.
Trim the quilting to about 4cm/1½in larger than the Vilene.
2 Pull the satin and backing fabric

tightly over the edge of the Vilene/ buckram and work stabbing running stitch about 3mm/⅛in away from the edge, through all layers.
3 When you have stitched all the way round the belt, cut away excess fabric at the back and work running stitch all round the edge again, filling in the gaps left by the

Making the purse

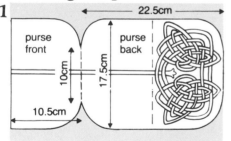

1

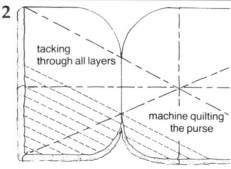

2 tacking through all layers / machine quilting the purse

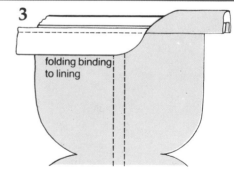

3 folding binding to lining

The purse has the Italian quilted design taken from the centre part of the cummerbund design on the front flap and a machine-quilted lining.
1 Make a paper pattern following the dimensions in the diagram. Draw curved edges by eye, or use a saucer, or dressmaker's flexicurve. Cut rectangles 25cm×45cm/ 10in×18in from the satin and the lawn backing fabric. Use the pattern to roughly mark the purse outline with tacking stitches to help you position the motif. Transfer, stitch

and quilt the design as described earlier. A single line of quilting runs down the centre of the purse, ending in a claw shape at front flap. Cut a purse shape from Vilene and cut two slightly larger ones from wadding and lining silk.
2 Tack these together, wadding in the centre, and quilt all-over pattern by hand or machine.
Trim silk and wadding flush with Vilene and cut the quilted satin to the same size. Tack satin and quilted lining, wrong sides together.

Finishing off You need an 80cm/ 32in bias satin strip, width 3cm/ 1¼in, for joining and binding the purse. This can be cut in one piece if using 90cm/36in-wide fabric, or join strips to obtain right length.
3 Bind top edge of purse front by placing right side of bias strip on right side of purse with edges matching. Stitching with a 6mm/¼in seam, turn binding to lining side, turn edge under, and slipstitch.
4 Fold bag front and back together (lining inside) matching curved

Cut a satin rectangle 30cm×90cm/
12in×36in. For waists larger than
81cm/32in, add the extra inches to
the length. Cut backing to same
size.
Fold a piece of tracing paper in half
and trace the design on one half.
Turn the paper and re-trace the
design on the other half.

Working the quilting

Transfer, stitch and quilt the design
as described on pages 166-167.
Begin at the centre and work
outwards and do not forget the line
which runs round the whole design.

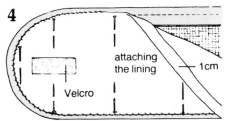

4

attaching
the lining — 1cm

Velcro

stabbing stitch. This will give the
same effect as the backstitch on the
Italian quilting.
4 Use the paper pattern to cut a
piece of lining silk, adding 1cm/½in
all round. Turn under 1cm/½in, pin
to back of belt and hem to border.
Add two 4cm/1½in pieces of Velcro
to the ends so that the cummerbund
fastens with a 5cm/2in overlap.

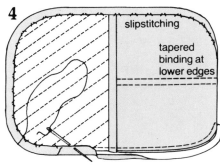

4

slipstitching

tapered
binding at
lower edges

edges. Tack down sides. Place right
side of strip on right side of back of
bag and up round front flap and
machine. Turn binding over edge
and slipstitch, continuing round
flap. Taper binding at lower edges.
To make shoulder strap Cut a
112cm/44in straight satin strip 5cm/
2in wide. With right sides together,
join long edges of strip taking a
1cm/½in seam. Trim seam, turn and
stuff with four strands of quilting
wool. Close ends and sew to lining
at base of front flap.

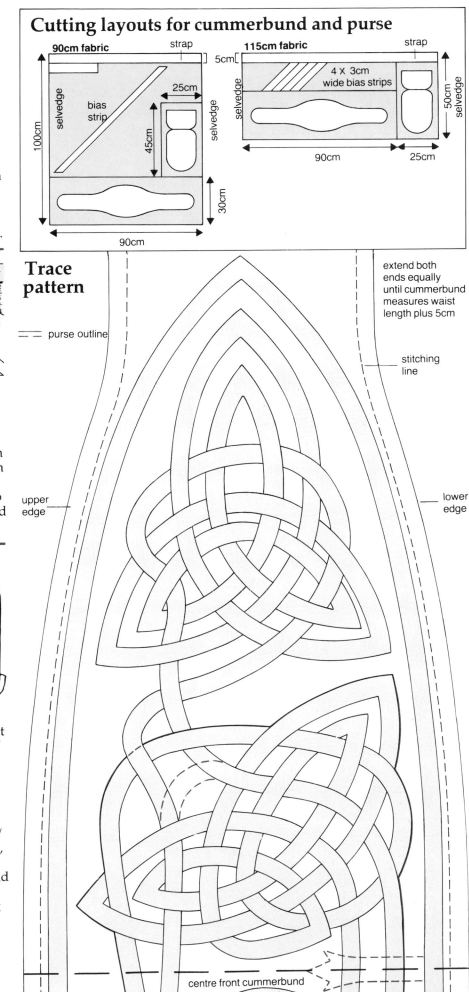

Cutting layouts for cummerbund and purse

90cm fabric strap

115cm fabric strap

5cm

4 X 3cm
wide bias strips

25cm

selvedge

bias
strip

100cm

selvedge

45cm

selvedge

50cm

selvedge

30cm

90cm

90cm

25cm

Trace pattern

extend both
ends equally
until cummerbund
measures waist
length plus 5cm

= = purse outline

stitching
line

upper
edge

lower
edge

centre front cummerbund

CHAPTER 38

Pillow and puff quilting for luxurious bedcovers

Use these simple techniques to make a luxuriously padded pillow quilt for a full-size bed or a cosy puff quilt for a child's cot. Control the thickness by varying the amount and type of filling and edge the quilts with an attractive bound border.

These two forms of quilting sound soft and soothing – and they are. Both are easy to do, and result in the most luxurious-looking, cosy throw-over quilts for beds or cots. You could also make softly padded cushion covers using both these techniques.

Below: This cosy quilt is so easy to make using the pillow quilting method. Use alternate colours as shown here, or make it all in the same fabric, to fit a single or a double bed.

Pillow quilting consists of a number of small 'pillows' (usually square) made up individually and then joined together along their finished edges. The pillows can be any size, but the smaller they are, the more stitching you will have to do.

Pillow quilting is just as neat on the back as on the front, so quilts are easily reversible.

Use firm cotton fabrics, lawn, or satin for real glamour. Fill each little pillow with a square of polyester wadding or stuff with washable polyester filling if you want to make a more heavily stuffed quilt. Remember to wash new fabrics first to avoid shrinkage. Any puckering would spoil the look of the quilting.

Puff quilting is similar to pillow quilting but it gives a slightly different effect – fuller and puffier. To achieve this look, make up pillows by stitching squares of top fabric on to smaller bottom squares to create fullness at the top. Fill the squares with polyester filling or folded wadding and seam them together. The top fabric squares can be up to 1½ times the size of the bottom ones – the top squares in the quilt featured here are 1¼ times the size.

The bottom squares can be made from muslin as the back of puff quilting needs to be lined to conceal the joins.

Although the basic patches are square, the overall finished effect is of raised rounded puffs.

Pillow quilting techniques

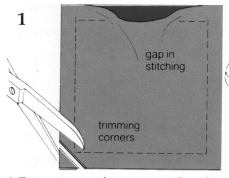

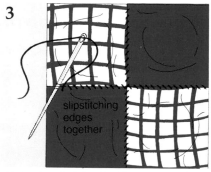

1 Cut out several square patches the same size from both fabrics.
With right sides facing, stitch top and bottom squares together in pairs around three sides, leaving an opening along the centre of the fourth. Trim corners diagonally.

2 Turn pillows to right side and stuff each pillow with polyester filling, distributing it evenly.
Do not over-fill the pillows which would make them difficult to sew together.
For a flatter-looking quilt, use polyester wadding cut to the size of the *finished* squares. Neatly oversew the opening.

3 Join the finished pillows together along their edges in the correct pattern sequence, if you have planned one. To join pillows successfully, hold two with their edges butted up together and slipstitch invisibly by hand. Alternatively, holding them firmly together, use a wide machine zigzag stitch to link them.

Puff quilting techniques

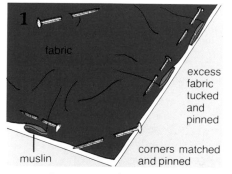

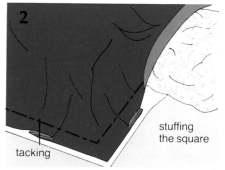

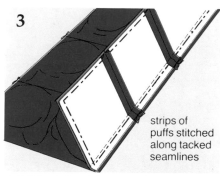

1 Decide on size of squares and make a template for both sizes. Use these to cut fabric and muslin (bottom) squares.
Lay a fabric square right side up over a muslin one, matching and pinning together the four corners. Pin at centre of each side and fit the excess fabric by making tucks each side which lie towards the corners.

2 When all four sides are pinned, tack round, 1cm/½in from raw edges, leaving one side open between the centre and one corner for filling. (Tack the tuck in place on top fabric.)
Fill the puffed shape with washable polyester filling or folded wadding, pushing it in carefully until the spare fabric is filled up. Tack opening closed.

3 With right sides together, join the prepared puffs along tacked seamlines: seam together several puffs in a strip, make more strips and join these together lengthwise. To line the work, cut backing fabric to the same size as quilt and with right sides together stitch together round edges, leaving an opening to turn through. Turn, and slipstitch opening.

Pillow quilted cover for single or double bed

The quilt in the picture is made up from five different red and white printed fabrics, plus plain red, but you could also use patchwork pieced blocks, random coloured squares or squares all the same colour.

Fabric requirements given here are based on the design of diagonal checks as shown in the diagram. For any other designs, make your own calculations for the amount of top fabric required; each patch measures 32cm/12½in.

The single bed cover measures 145cm × 232cm/58in × 93in and the double is 203cm × 232cm/ 81in × 93in.

You will need – single bed

Fabric requirements are based on 90cm/36in wide fabric (except backing and wadding)

1. 30m/1½yd fabrics A and B, 1.90m/ 2⅛yd fabric C, 1m/1⅛yd fabrics D and E, 0.70m/¾yd fabric F
2. 35m/3⅝yd of 150cm/60in wide fabric for backs of pillows
3. 15m/4½yd 4oz wadding, 1m/40in wide

You will need – double bed

1. 95m/2⅛yd fabrics A and B, 2.60m/ 2⅞yd fabric C, 1.30m/1½yd fabric D, 1m/1⅛yd fabrics E and F
2. 50m/4⅞yd of 150cm/60in wide fabric for backs of pillows
3. 50m/6yd wadding as above

Making up the quilt

Following the pattern chart for the number and arrangement of squares, cut out 40 (56 for the

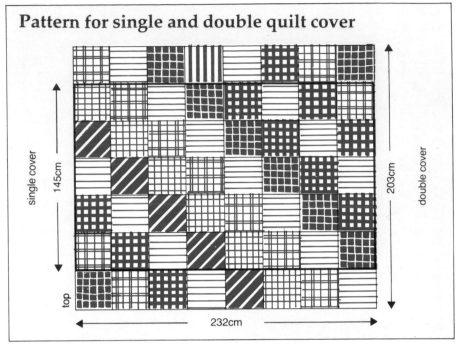

Pattern for single and double quilt cover

double bed quilt) 32cm/12½in squares from your chosen top fabric(s) and 40(56) from the pillow backing fabric.

Make up the 40(56) pillows, taking 1.5cm/⅝in seams when joining fronts to backs. Now cut 40(56) 29cm/11¼in squares from the piece of wadding and insert one into each pillow. Slipstitch openings and join pillows by hand, forming pattern as given in diagram.

Optional binding Cut binding strips for long edges from fabric B and C, 13cm/5in wide and slightly longer than the quilt – join strips if necessary to obtain this length. Lay binding strip wrong side up along right side of quilt with raw edges

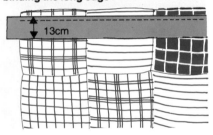

binding the long edge

3.5cm/1⅜in from edge of quilt and stitch with a 1.5cm/⅝in seam. Turn binding to wrong side of quilt, turning ends and remaining long edge under, and slipstitch in place. On top and bottom edges of quilt, machine along 5cm/2in from edge to balance side borders.

Puff quilting for a pretty cot or pram quilt

Try out puff quilting by making a pretty quilt for a baby which is warm but extremely light and has a padded border. Use medium weight printed cottons – the ones used here are printed but you can choose plain fabrics in pastel shades.

You will need

To make a quilt measuring about 60cm/24in square

25cm/¼yd each of 5 cotton print fabrics (any width)

90cm/1yd plain cotton fabric for backing and border (90cm/36in wide)

50cm/½yd muslin

1m/1⅛yd polyester wadding (4oz weight)

Matching thread

Making up the quilt

Make two templates – 12cm/4¾in and 15cm/6in square. Cut 25 muslin squares using the smaller template and five squares from each of the printed cottons using the larger one. Join each cotton square to a muslin square taking 1cm/½in seams and leaving an opening in one side of each.

Cut 25 squares of wadding, 17cm/

6¾in square. Fold the corners to the centre on each of these and slip one into each puff before sewing up the opening. Stitch the puffs together scattering the prints evenly.

From the plain fabric, cut a 62cm/ 24½in square for the backing. Lay the puff quilting right side up on the centre of the wrong side of this and machine all round, along outer seamline of quilting.

Cut four strips of plain fabric 8cm × 62cm/3¼in × 24½in. Join them together with mitred corners to form a 'frame', and leaving 1cm/½in unstitched at each inner corner

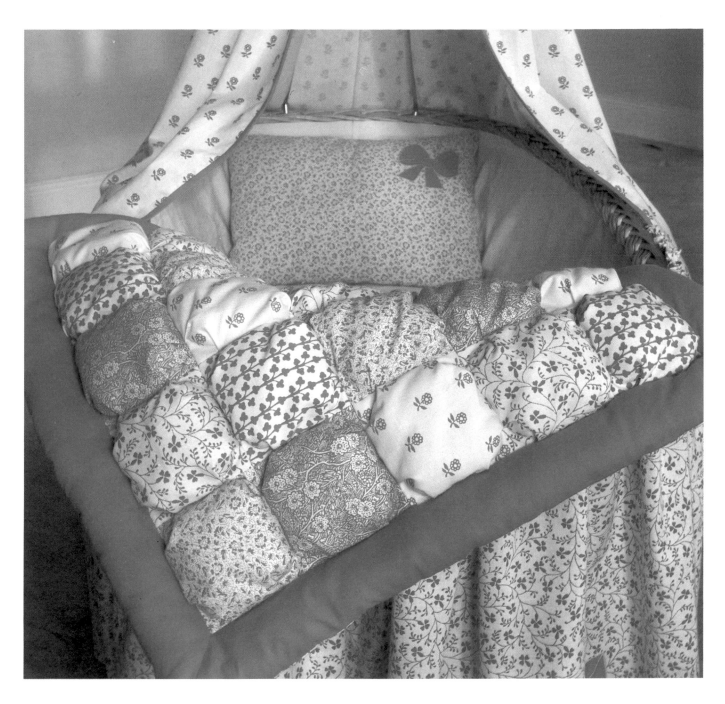

Above: It's a good idea to pre-wash all the fabrics to check colour fastness.

seam. Trim mitred seams.
Lay the frame right side down on the back of the quilted piece and machine round, 1.5cm/⅝in from outer raw edges. Trim corners and turn to right side.
Finishing off Cut enough 5cm/2in wide strips from remaining wadding to fill the border with a double thickness all round. Lay two strips of wadding inside the border along each side, fold over 1cm/½in on border strip edges, and catch in place along quilting seamline.

making the frame

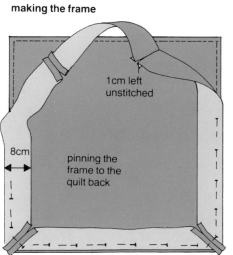

8cm

1cm left unstitched

pinning the frame to the quilt back

finishing off

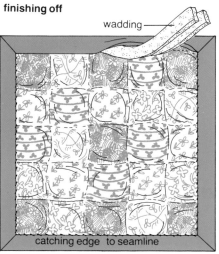

wadding

catching edge to seamline

CHAPTER 39

Contour quilting

This quilting technique adds a softly-contoured look to ready-printed fabrics. It needs no pre-marking, simply machine round the motifs to add definition to the shapes or hand stitch the outlines using decorative embroidery stitches if the design is more intricate.

Contour quilting gives printed fabrics a new dimension. It adds emphasis to the pattern, and if wadding is inserted between the top fabric and the backing, the outlined design becomes raised and padded.

Instead of ignoring the pattern of a fabric and superimposing it with a completely unrelated quilting design, this technique makes the most of the pattern, whether floral, abstract or pictorial.

Use contour quilting to give that designer touch to cushions matching sofas and chairs, drop-in seats and stool covers, throw-over bed covers, bedheads and mats for dressing tables. Even parts of clothes such as dress yokes, cuffs and bodices can be contour quilted for effect.

Choosing fabrics

Cotton, silk, satin or wool are all suitable for the top fabric. Glazed furnishing chintz looks particularly effective with a contour quilted design.

Lightweight fabrics such as cotton lawn or muslin are suitable for the lining.

Use a polyester wadding, or a cotton domette which is heavier, but thinner than the polyester. For articles which will require washing, choose polyester for practicality.

Examine the pattern of the top fabric carefully and decide which parts you will quilt round. With a floral design, for instance, you could outline each leaf and flower with stitches, or you could highlight other parts of the design such as a basket or some background stripes by quilting along their outlines.

Do not choose too intricate a design unless you intend to work by hand. If the pattern repeat is very large and only one or two of the motifs will fit on an item such as a chair back or a bedhead, make sure you buy enough fabric from which to cut out the correct portions of the design and are able to position the motifs so that they are balanced.

Estimate the area of quilted fabric you need for the project in hand. As all-over quilting will 'shrink' the fabric, it is wise to be generous in the amount you allow.

Right: This headboard combines two co-ordinated furnishing fabrics. Quilt a cushion cover, using any remnants.

Successful contour quilting

Follow the normal quilting procedure and cut wadding and lining fabric to the same size as the top fabric. Make a sandwich of the three layers with the wadding in the middle and pin together. Tack across the fabric diagonally, both ways, to secure the layers and avoid any puckering on the motifs.

Stitching round the motifs

Fit a transparent presser foot on your sewing machine if possible. This helps you to see the design more clearly.

Begin at the centre of the piece of work using regular machine twist in a colour to match or contrast with the fabric. Leaving long ends of thread, lower the presser foot on to the fabric and start stitching using a small to medium length stitch. Work in the long ends afterwards by hand.

For extra emphasis, if desired, stitch round again close to the first stitching line. As far as possible, try to link motifs together without removing the work from the machine. When all the motifs are outlined, raise the presser foot, remove the work and cut the two threads, allowing enough to finish off. Pull all free ends of thread through to the back, knot them together and snip off. Remove the tacking stitches.

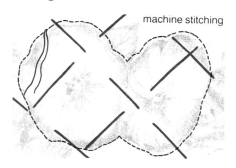

machine stitching

A contour quilted headboard

Use a length of pretty bedroom fabric to quilt a headboard to match your furnishings. Most headboards can be covered by a simple slip-on cover and contour quilting gives a softly-padded finish to the front cover.

You will need

Printed furnishing fabric
Polyester wadding (2oz weight)
Light backing fabric

Cutting out the fabric

Cutting the fabric pieces to make the headboard is easy if it is a regular rectangular shape. For curves or fancy edges, make a template of the headboard front. If the board is more than 5mm/³⁄₈in thick, it will need a gusset.

The only part of the cover which needs to be quilted is the front – remember it may shrink, so cut it out generously. Quilt the front before making up the cover.

Quilting the design

Plan the quilting carefully. Do not give yourself too much work to do. If you begin quilting round every tiny detail on the fabric you may become discouraged halfway through the project.

CHAPTER 40

Simple fabric pictures

If you have never tried your hand at appliqué, now is the time to start. It's a quick, simple and satisfying way to build wonderful combinations of shapes and colours into any design you choose. All you need to begin are some fabric scraps and basic drawing materials.

'Appliqué' is the name given to the technique of placing pieces of fabric on to other fabrics and stitching them in place. This sounds like a very broad definition, but appliqué is an art with limitless expressions. It can be pictorial or abstract, bold and colourful or pale and delicate. Simple or complex designs can be created, depending on the number of different shapes you are laying on to the base fabric. You can also quilt the appliqué or add decorative embroidery to make your work extra-special. Appliqué has close links with both patchwork and quilting – techniques with which it is often combined.

Choosing the colours and textures of the fabrics and carefully planning an appliqué design is a skill in itself, and one which develops with practice.

Using appliqué

The technique lends itself well to pictorial designs. Picture-painting with fabric is perhaps the most enjoyable and creative kind of appliqué.

As it is so quick to do, areas can be covered comparatively fast, so appliqué is also suitable for furnishings – cushions, curtains, tablecloths, towels and blinds, even bed-covers. Colour co-ordinating in the home becomes easy and fun.

Sensational effects can be achieved on clothes. Adding the right motif can turn skirt hems, dresses, T-shirts, baby and children's wear into eye-catching designer originals.

Types of appliqué

Appliqué can be hand or machine sewn. The choice will often depend on the desired finished effect or the function of the article you are making. The applied shapes can have either raw or turned edges. In the following pages, you will discover several different types of appliqué and how and where to use them. You can design your own motifs or cut shapes from

ready-printed fabrics adding embroidery, trimmings or beads for effect. This chapter concentrates on the simplest method – single and double layer appliqué without turnings – and gives patterns for a rag book.

Fabrics for appliqué

The fabrics used in appliqué are all-important. Choose them according to the project in hand. Obviously, if it is going to need washing, you must use washable, pre-shrunk, colour-fast fabrics. It would be very disappointing if parts of the design shrunk or lost their colour after one wash.

Fabrics should be of a similar weight if possible – particularly for anything which will receive hard wear or repeated washing. For wall-hangings and pictures this is not a problem, so you can go to town with pieces of silk and satin, velvets and other non-washables. Unless you want a translucent effect, make sure the fabric is densely woven. If it is too flimsy, it can be backed with a firmer fabric or with light iron-on interfacing to give it extra body and prevent the ground fabric from showing through. Firm cottons are always a good choice. Felt is very easy to work with and does not fray but unfortunately it is not washable, so its use is restricted. Ribbon, braids and other trims can also be used to great effect in appliqué designs. For a novelty effect you could use lamé and metallic fabrics, or fur and pile fabrics.

Other equipment

Scissors You will need two pairs – one for cutting paper patterns, and a sharper pair for the fabric itself.
Pins, needles and thread are also indispensable.
Stiff paper is useful for making tem-

Right: Successful appliqué needs well-chosen materials. Look out for suitable scraps of fabric, lace and trimmings.

plates (patterns), as is tracing paper.
Graph paper is needed for enlarging and reducing designs.
Tailor's chalk or a pencil is used for marking shapes on to fabric. You could also use dressmaker's carbon paper for this.
Frames A frame is sometimes useful for working appliqué, but by no means essential. If you do use a frame, do not over-stretch the base fabric –

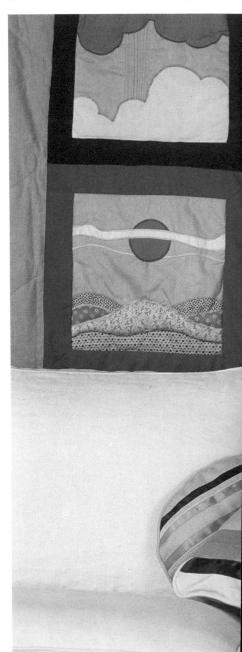

keep all the fabrics at the same tension to avoid any puckering.

Planning a simple appliqué

Shapes can be cut freely from the fabric, or else marked and cut accurately using paper patterns to enable you to repeat a design.

You can sometimes plan an appliqué design as you go along, but in general it's best to have a good idea of the effect you are after before starting work. Make sure that your chosen colours harmonize or contrast as you wish, and that none of the shapes is too complex. Remember that you can always add embroidery or machine stitching as part of the design. Books and pictures are a good source of designs for appliqué if you are not an artist. Try looking at young children's books for simple pictures with bold outlines.

Enlarging and reducing designs

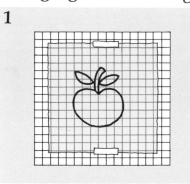

1 Trace the lines of your chosen picture on to a sheet of tracing paper. Then stick the tracing paper over some graph paper so that you have a squared up drawing. (If the squares on the graph paper are very small, take a ruler and felt-tip pen and make an evenly squared grid on a larger scale using the graph paper.)

2 Make a larger grid (smaller if reducing) on new graph paper. Copy the design on to it square by square. The design will be enlarged (or reduced) according to the relative scales of the grids. For example: copying a motif from a grid of 1cm/ ½in squares on to a grid of 2cm/ 1in squares doubles the motif size.

Appealing rag book for a baby or toddler

The everyday objects that children see at home appear on the pages of this rag book. It would make a lovely present for any baby or toddler. Alternatively, you could cut out just one of the motifs and appliqué it on to the top of a pair of dungarees.

Using simple appliqué techniques, it is quick and easy to make in brightly coloured shapes. If you do not own a sewing machine, use non-woven fabrics for the motifs and secure the edges with overcasting or a decorative stitch such as cross stitch.

Use the shapes given overleaf, or incorporate any others your child would like – your dog or rabbit, for example. Try to avoid complicated shapes and too many design 'features'. Limit yourself to about four colours per page. The fabrics which you use for the motifs should be the same weight, or slightly lighter than the pages.

Above: This brightly coloured rag book is an ideal first project in appliqué.

You will need

Eight pieces of coloured cotton fabric of similar weight, each 22cm×27cm/9in×11in
Scraps of fabric for the motifs
Cotton thread in motif colours
20cm/8in soft iron-on standard-width Vilene for backing motifs
Pinking shears to cut page edges

Making the patterns for the motifs

Outline motif shapes are shown in the diagram overleaf at reduced size. Enlarge them to the correct size as described on the previous page. Copy the square grid pattern on plain paper, making 2cm/1in squares. Or take 1cm/½in squared graph paper and mark up 2cm/1in squares with a ruler.

Cut round the outline shape of the motif to make a paper pattern for each. Cut the paper pattern into sections so that each colour has its own pattern piece. Where two sections overlap (shown by broken lines), you will need to make a tracing of one of them, and cut the other from the main pattern paper.

178

Marking and cutting out the motifs

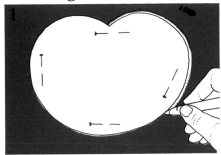

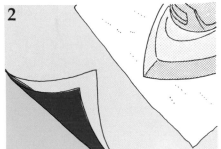

1 Pin each section of the pattern on to the appropriately coloured or patterned motif fabric and mark the outline on to the fabric with tailor's chalk or a pencil. Try to position the pieces on the straight grain of fabric so that they will match the grain of the ground fabric.
Cut the motif fabric into a square or

rectangle a few centimetres larger all round than the actual motif outline.
2 Lay this fabric right side down and position on top a piece of soft iron-on Vilene interfacing, cut to the same size. The rougher, adhesive side of the Vilene should be facing the fabric. Cover with a

damp cloth and press with a hot, dry iron. The Vilene will stiffen the fabric slightly and will also help prevent the raw edges from fraying when the fabric is cut.
3 Carefully cut out the sections of the motif design round the marked cutting lines using an ordinary pair of scissors.

Making the pages and fixing the motifs

To make pages, use pinking shears to cut out eight pieces of fabric, each 19cm×24cm/7½in×9½in. Choose different coloured cotton fabrics for each page, or very simple patterns such as checks or stripes. Position each motif centrally on the page, noting that sections with partly dotted lines must be laid down first. When the motif is complete tack sections in place. Using a small zigzag stitch, machine

round all the raw edges with a matching sewing cotton to secure. Remove tacking. Add stitching lines for features such as the cat's whiskers, the hands on the watch, and the tips of the coloured pencils. Pull ends of thread through to the wrong side.

Putting the complete book together

1 Lay two pages right sides facing, and tack together down one short side. Sew, making a 1.5cm/⅝in seam. Trim seam to 5mm/¼in. Turn to right side and press to make a complete page with wrong sides inside. Repeat for remaining six page pieces to make three more pages. If necessary, iron with spray starch.
2 Lay the four pages together, one on top of the other with pinked edges matching and tack through all eight layers of fabric on the unstitched short side. Sew through all layers with a 1cm/½in seam. Remove tacking.

No pinking shears?

If you don't own pinking shears, proceed as above, but cut the pages to 22cm×27cm/9in×11in with ordinary scissors. Complete step 1 of *Putting the complete book*

together and then press a 5mm/¼in hem to wrong side on raw page edges. Turn a further 1cm/½in to wrong side and machine with matching thread. Lay the four back-to-back pages together as for step 2, but join with a 2cm/¾in seam.

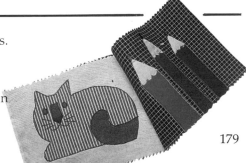

Patterns for the eight motifs

cutting line for
upper pieces

cutting line for
lower pieces

1 square = 2cm

CHAPTER 41

Quick padded appliqué using bold motifs

Develop your appliqué skills by making an amusing cushion for your favourite armchair. Add interest and relief to the design by slipping pieces of polyester wadding under some of the shapes, giving a quilted effect. Machine zigzag stitchery makes the appliqué hard-wearing.

You can add interest and appeal to all sorts of appliqué designs by padding some sections with polyester wadding. Follow all the hints given on pages 176-177, and take extra care when securing the wadded pieces of the design.

As you can see, the zigzag stitch makes the armchair design look bold, bright and well defined. However, stitching with such a wide zigzag requires careful treatment. On tight curves where you continually need to stop stitching and pivot the fabric,

work steadily so that the edges of the stitching line are smooth and even. At a right angled corner, stitch up to the edge, raise the presser foot and pivot the fabric so that you begin stitching in the new direction directly in line with the edge of the previous row of stitching.

Where more than two lines of stitching intersect on the design, do not stitch three times over the same point, as the work will look too bulky: once or twice is enough.

If you don't have a zigzag function on your sewing machine, use a regular straight stitch and then finish the raw edges by hand, using satin or buttonhole stitch and stranded cotton in the appropriate colours.

Below: The bold, appliquéd design on this cushion is simple to cut and stitch.

Cosy armchair motif cushion

This plump cushion looks even more inviting when the miniature cushions on it are padded with wadding. The entire cushion cover is backed with another layer of wadding to give it that extra bit of body.

You will need

Main (ground) fabric: 1m/1⅛yd of 90cm/36in wide *or* 50cm/½yd of 112cm/44in or wider
Lining fabric: same as above
Scraps of four other plain or patterned fabrics (at least 20cm/8in for armchair motif and 10cm/4in for leaves and each cushion)
1m/1⅛yd medium weight (4oz) polyester wadding
Thread to tone with the chair, plant and both miniature cushions
35cm/14in zip fastener
Cushion pad, 50cm/20in square

Planning the design

Choose fabrics carefully, picking firm, not translucent cottons. If a colour you need only comes in flimsy fabric, back it with iron-on interfacing before cutting out the pattern pieces. The ground fabric can be plain or patterned; here it is a fairly small red and multi-coloured print. An even smaller red and white print is chosen for the armchair, but they contrast well. Cut out the houseplant leaves in plain green fabric, or a simple,

predominantly green print like this polka dot.
Make sure that the scale of your design is convincing – for instance, do not choose a design so large for the armchair that no pattern repeats are visible. It is helpful to make a coloured sketch first to be sure it works.

Making the pattern pieces

Enlarge the armchair design given on the chart making each square 2cm/¾in to give the required size, and mark the design centre. Make a pattern piece for each section of the enlarged design by tracing this off and then cutting it into sections along the thick, black lines.

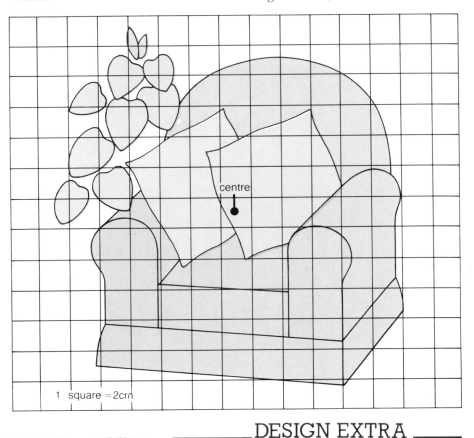

centre

1 square = 2cm

Colour and design ideas

You don't have to copy the cushion design and colours exactly. Perhaps you'd like to make one for a pale, pretty bedroom – in which case, choose pastel fabrics and pale sewing threads. Or appliqué a design of bright primary colours to a plain black or white ground fabric. If you feel adventurous, have fun with the miniature cushions by making them different shapes, cutting them in shiny satin, or adding ribbon, lace or embroidery trims.
Suit the cushion to the chair A round cushion with a Victorian chair design (add beads or knots to a wadded button-back chair)

could be trimmed with pretty lace to sit on an old-fashioned chair. And if you want to make sofa cushions, design a sofa motif and include more small cushions, or your cat sitting on it. The idea can be adapted in endless different ways.

Making the cushion cover

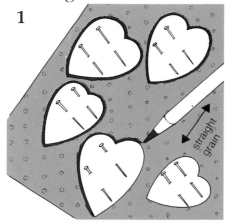

Assembling the front

1 Pin the pattern pieces on to the wrong side of the appropriate fabrics, keeping them on the straight grain as far as possible. Mark the outlines with a pencil or chalk pencil. Cut out. Cut main fabric into two 50cm/20in squares, and mark the centre of one of them by folding the fabric in half and in half again. Cut a further 50cm/20in square from the wadding.

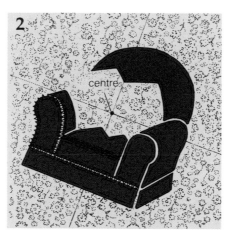

2 Attach the chair shapes first, then the cushions, then the leaves. Following the chart, arrange the chair shapes on the right side of one of the main fabric squares. Make sure the centre point of the design is positioned over the marked centre of the main fabric. Pin the pieces so that the edges just touch and tack them carefully in place, close to the raw edges. Set the sewing machine to the tightest zigzag stitch (stitch length about 4mm/¼in) and machine round edges of the shapes, guiding the fabric.

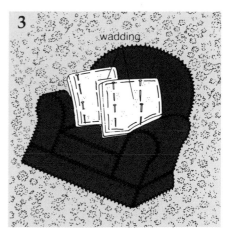

3 Before appliquéing the small cushion shapes, cut two pieces of wadding slightly smaller than the actual pieces, to fit underneath them. Tack these in place on the ground fabric first to avoid any puckering.
Finally, add the leaves of the plant, tacking and stitching them in place as before. Remember to change the thread in your machine to the correct colour for each motif.

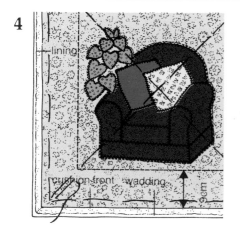

Backing the front

4 Cut lining fabric to 50cm/20in square. Lay it right side down with the 50cm/20in square of wadding on top. Place appliquéd cushion front right side up on these, pin, and tack with long stitches through all layers.
Set the machine stitch to a small straight stitch and carefully machine all round the outside of the chair and the leaves, very close to the zigzag stitching, using thread to match the ground fabric.

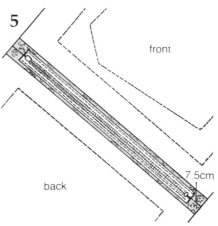

To secure the wadding, stitch all round the square, with a slightly longer straight stitch, about 9cm/3½in in from the edges.

Making the back

Make a sandwich of lining, wadding and main fabric for the cushion back. Tack them together and machine round about 9cm/3½in in from the edges.

Joining front and back

5 Place front and back right sides

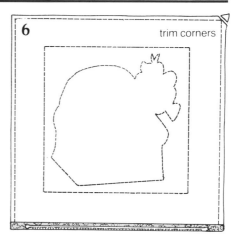

together. Along bottom edge only, tack and stitch a 1cm/½in seam, 7.5cm/3in in from each edge. Press seams open and insert zip in opening.
6 Now place the right sides of the cushion front and back together and stitch the remaining three edges with a 1cm/½in seam. Trim corners diagonally and trim excess wadding away from seams. Turn right sides out. Gently push out the corners with a closed pair of scissors.

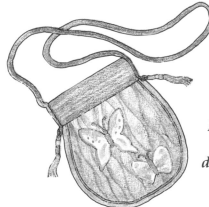

CHAPTER 42

Combining quilting and appliqué

*Machine quilt your own fabric to make a really individual
waistcoat and bag. The freestyle quilting
design needs no prior marking on the fabric and is the perfect
background for colourful appliqué butterflies.*

Quilted garments have been in vogue for hundreds of years. They are warm, often lighter than several layers of woollens, and can be stunningly attractive.

When making your own quilted clothing, remember that fabrics 'shrink' when quilting stitches are added, so never cut pattern pieces to their final size until the machine or hand quilt-

ing is completed. Either allow a few extra centimetres round the pattern piece edges when cutting out, or quilt a whole length of fabric and cut pattern pieces from this as usual.

Quilted silk waistcoat

This waistcoat with its unusual machine-quilted design and shimmering appliquéd butterflies could be a collector's piece. Add the butterflies to any basic commercial waistcoat pattern.

Antung is good, firm silk suitable for quilting, but you could use tussah or surah silk or medium-weight cotton.

You will need for waistcoat

Raspberry red silk (top) and pink silk (lining) fabric for waistcoat as stated on your pattern envelope. (Remember you need to cut the

waistcoat out twice, once in top fabric and once in lining fabric).
25cm/¼yd multi-coloured swirling print silk for butterflies
90cm/1yd polyester wadding (2oz weight)
25cm/¼yd light iron-on Vilene
3.50m/4yd pink satin bias binding
Machine quilting foot (if possible)
1 large reel silk machine twist in purple, raspberry red and pink
1 ball Anchor pearl cotton in purple for embroidery, 1 ball in bright pink for waistcoat tassels
1 skein bright coton à broder for bag

tassels
1 sheet of tracing paper

Making the pattern

Trace off the half butterfly shapes given overleaf to make paper patterns. Use pattern pieces for the waistcoat from your pattern envelope. Following the cutting layout given in your pattern, cut out one back and two fronts in raspberry red silk with 2cm/¾in extra all round to allow for shrinkage in quilting. Cut out the same pieces in the pink lining silk.

Quilting the pattern pieces

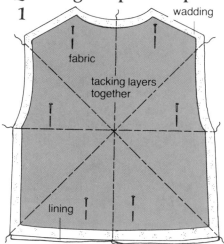

1
wadding
fabric
tacking layers together
lining

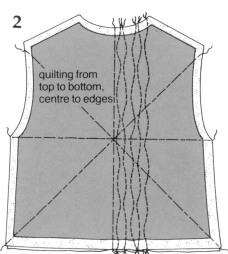

2
quilting from top to bottom, centre to edges

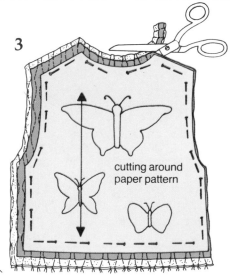

3
cutting around paper pattern

Lay the waistcoat back over the wadding, right side uppermost, and cut out the wadding slightly larger than the top fabric.
Lay down the back lining, wrong side uppermost, place the wadding on top, and the back top fabric (right side uppermost) on top. Pin.

1 Beginning in the middle, tack a central line to top and bottom, one at right-angles to each side, and four others radiating out from the centre, as shown.
2 With red thread in machine needle and pink in the bobbin, work gently curving lines of quilting on the right

side. Quilt from top to bottom: begin in the centre back and work out to one side, then go back to the centre and quilt towards the other side edge. Repeat for the two fronts.
3 Pin the paper pattern pieces over each quilted piece, and cut out to the correct size along cutting lines.

The advantage of quilting your own fabric is that you can quilt it in any pattern you like to make unique items, unlike anything available in the shops. Make sure the quilting pattern has enough stitching to anchor the fabric, wadding and lining together and give the garment stability. Garments which are to be worn often need all-over quilting designs with regular stitching.

The freestyle quilting pattern of undulating vertical lines which appears on the waistcoat and matching bag shown here is best used on a plain-coloured fabric, which will show it to its best advantage.

Wadding There are several different types and weights of wadding, so you can choose one appropriate to the project you have in mind. The two ounce wadding used for the projects shown here is very light, not too bulky and gives adequate relief to the quilting design. It is particularly suitable for decorative evening jackets, waistcoats or skirts which do not need to be particularly warm or thick.

Seams There are several ways of neatening seams on quilted garments. You can trim back the wadding by a few millimetres, turn the fabric edges under and hem to the backing fabric or you can trim the seam allowance down to 3mm/⅛in, press the seam open and stitch binding on the wrong side to cover the seam allowances. If you want to make the garment reversible, use a machine flat-felled seam.

Raw edges on the right side are best finished with binding. Choose matching or contrasting bias binding or make your own bias strips from leftover fabric.

Decorative extras Quilt a garment in a plain-coloured fabric and add appliqué, embroidery, beads or tassels.

Below: A randomly quilted waistcoat – make it with or without appliqué.

Working the appliqué

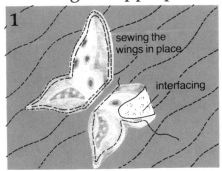
1 sewing the wings in place / interfacing

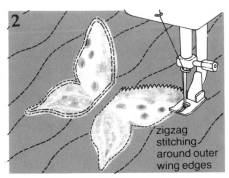
2 zigzag stitching around outer wing edges

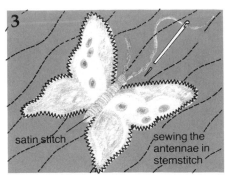
3 satin stitch / sewing the antennae in stemstitch

Cut seven butterflies from the printed fabric, cutting each wing separately but making sure that the fabric design is symmetrical for each wing in a pair.
1 Iron the shapes on to light iron-on Vilene, cut round them and tack into position on the quilted pieces. Position the butterflies by eye or

using the photo on the previous page as a guide. Machine straight stitch all round the wing edges.
2 Change to a medium-width satin stitch and zigzag round the *outer* edges of each wing.
If your machine has a speed control, set this on slow to give more control when stitching round the tight

corners on the wings.
3 Using the purple pearl cotton, hand sew the butterflies' bodies in satin stitch to cover the raw inner wing edges – you can work an extra layer on the larger bodies to give them more relief. In the same thread work antennae in stem stitch.

Trace patterns for half butterfly motifs

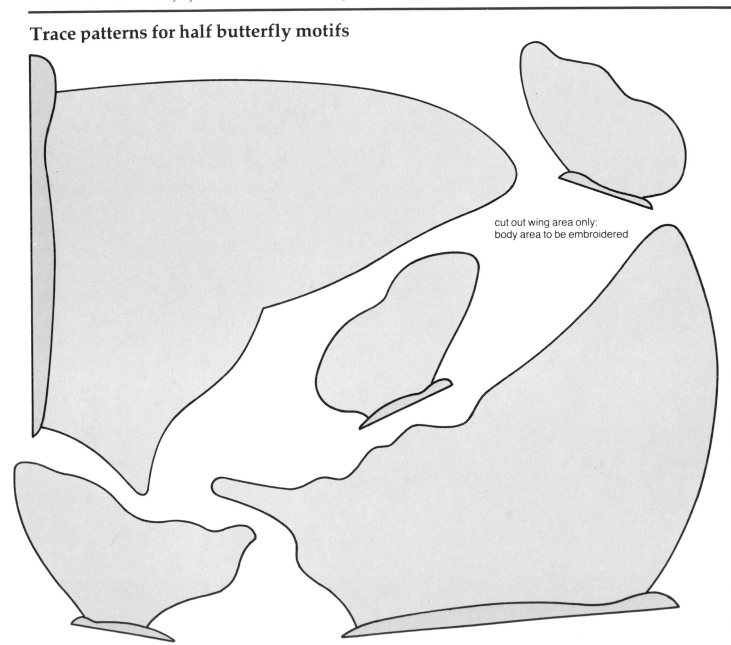

cut out wing area only:
body area to be embroidered

Making up the waistcoat

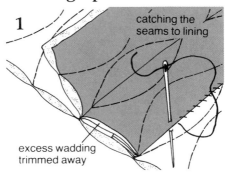

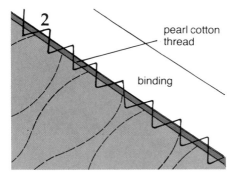

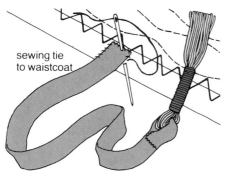

With right sides together, join the back to the fronts at sides and shoulders, with a 1cm/½in seam.
1 Press seams open and trim away excess wadding from seam allowances. Fold over raw edges of each seam allowance and hem, catching on to lining.
Binding edges With right sides together, stitch one long edge of satin binding to all raw edges. Turn binding to inside and catch hem to lining.
2 Lay one strand of purple pearl cotton along the inner edge of the satin binding and catch into place with purple thread, using a widely-spaced machine zigzag stitch.

Repeat along all the bound edges.
Waistcoat ties Cut a strip of fabric 3cm × 20cm/1½in × 8in. Fold lengthways, machine raw edges together with a 1cm/½in seam and turn inside out. Press, cut in half and neaten one end of each before looping through tassel and securing. Sew inside front edge.

Matching quilted bag

This beautifully quilted, embroidered and appliquéd bag perfectly complements the waistcoat, but you could make it on its own as a special gift.

You will need for bag only
25cm/¼yd raspberry red silk antung (any width)
25cm/¼yd pink silk antung for lining (any width)
25cm/¼yd polyester wadding (2oz weight)
Threads as for waistcoat
Machine quilting foot (if possible)
50cm/½yd pink satin bias binding

How to make the bag
Draw round a 20cm/8in plate to make a paper pattern for the bag or draw a 20cm/8in circle using the string, pencil and drawing pin method. Measure in 3cm/1¼in at any point on the edge of the circle, rule a line through this point and cut off a section of the circle to give the flat top of the bag.
Cut out two raspberry red and two pink bag shapes. Quilt the pieces and add two butterflies to one side in exactly the same way as for the waistcoat. Remember to tack the fabric securely to the wadding and lining before quilting it. Place the two quilted pieces wrong sides together and tack round curved edges.
Tack satin bias binding round

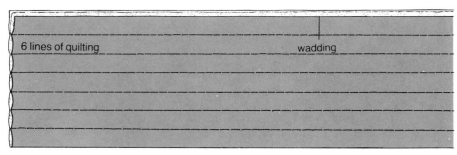

curved front edge of bag, right sides together, and stitch (do not bind top edge). Turn binding to back of bag and catch in place by hand.
Add the embroidery thread trim to the bias-bound edge as for the waistcoat.
From the raspberry fabric, cut a long strip 12cm × 34cm/5in × 13½in. Cut out a strip of wadding 6cm × 34cm/2½in × 13½in. Fold the fabric over the wadding to make the bag top and tack in place.
Quilting the bag top Machine six equally-spaced parallel lines lengthwise along the strip, using the quilting foot (if you have one) as a guide. Join end of strip with a 1cm/½in seam.
Attaching the bag top With right sides together, stitch strip round top of bag, with a 1cm/½in seam. Trim seam and neaten with overcasting zigzag stitch.
For the strap cut a long strip of raspberry silk 3cm × 115cm/1½in × 45in (you may need to join strips to obtain this length). Join long edges of strip with a 1cm/½in seam, turn

through and press. Loop each end through a tassel (see above) and stitch to each side of the bag, beginning at lower edge of quilted band.

Making tassels
Cut about 30 lengths of embroidery thread measuring 20cm/8in. Double them and pass bag strap or waistcoat tie through loop.

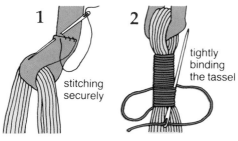

1 Neaten end of strap/tie and stitch securely.
2 Bind tassel tightly for about 3cm/1¼in from top using leftover embroidery thread in contrast colours. Finish by threading wrapping thread on a needle and sewing into tassel.

CHAPTER 43

Appliqué with towelling for a child's bathrobe

Bath and bedtime will be lots of fun for the proud owner of this towelling robe. Appliqué the bear in chunky towelling, and add toothpaste and brush in shiny fabrics. 'Real' teddy eyes and nose give the finishing touch to make him a special friend.

With its rich, soft texture, towelling offers lots of scope for imaginative and practical appliqué designs. The familiar looped pile of towelling is in fact a variation of uncut velvet weave and was first developed in Turkey. Since the first Turkish towels were exported during the late eighteenth century, towelling has quite naturally been a favourite fabric for bathroom and beach. It has unbeatable absorbent and easy-care qualities and is both warm and hard wearing.

Towelling comes in a wide variety of colours and textures with thick or thin pile, in firm, woven textures, stretchy types or velour; it is available by the metre in prints or plains. Used together with other fabrics, towelling gives depth and richness to a design, and can also be used where other thickly-textured fabrics would not be practical. It is easy to handle, and appliqué aids such as Bondaweb minimise the problems of fraying edges.

Working with towelling

Because towelling is made from cotton, it has a tendency to shrink, so it is advisable to wash all the towelling to be used in one design before cutting out. Deep dye colours are likely to run slightly too, so preliminary washing will check this as well.

Take care when working with towelling to avoid pulling the looped threads. A pulled thread spoils the appearance of the texture, so always use a pair of very sharp scissors when cutting out, and remove any pins very gently.

Stretchy velour towelling is attractive and looks good used with ordinary towelling or other fabrics. Because of its elasticity, it is important to back this towelling for an appliqué with lightweight iron-on interfacing, before cutting out the shapes.

Right: Inset showing the front pocket which is also decorated with the teddy's cheerful face. For appliqué beginners, this is a good motif to use on children's items.

Preparing the towelling bathrobe

On the back of this child's bathrobe a cheery teddy is about to brush his teeth. Use a simple pattern for the basic robe, or stitch the appliqué on to an existing one.

A teddy's face is also appliquéd on the front pocket, so if your pattern has no pocket, cut a simple patch pocket from surplus towelling. Do not stitch the pocket to the robe until you have worked the appliqué.

Cut out robe, following pattern, and stitch motifs in place before assembling.

You will need

Commercial paper pattern for wrapover bathrobe
Towelling fabric as given in pattern requirements
Matching weight towelling (90cm/ 36in wide) in the following amounts:
0.30m/⅜yd light brown
0.20m/¼yd blue
0.20m/¼yd pink
0.10m/⅛yd black
Satin scraps in white, red and grey
Cotton scraps in green, white and pale blue for brush
Matching sewing threads
2 packs Vilene Bondaweb

Preparing the teddy bear appliqué

1 Back all the fabrics needed for the appliqué with Bondaweb but do not remove the paper backing at this stage.

Make a tracing of the teddy bear outline, and keep this for reference. Make a second tracing, marking in overlaps and stitching lines around head, legs and feet. This tracing is used for marking the pattern pieces on the Bondaweb. Use carbon paper to transfer the shapes to the paper backing of the Bondaweb.

Cut out four brown head shapes – two for the teddy on the pocket and two for the teddy on the robe (the double thickness of towelling gives the faces a plump, padded look).

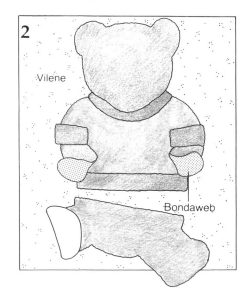

4 eyes medium size
2 noses medium size
Black and pink stranded
  embroidery thread
0.40m/½yd lightweight sew-in
  Vilene
Embroidery marker
Dressmaker's carbon paper

2 Cut out the remaining pieces.
When all the teddy shapes are cut
out, remove paper backing and
assemble them in position right side
up on the lightweight sew-in
Vilene. Press to bond in place.
Assemble the parts of the
toothpaste tube and brush on
another piece of Vilene. To make
sewing easier, these are assembled
separately and stitched in position
later.
Iron one head shape in place over
the teddy's jumper, and iron one
head directly on to the pocket.

*Right: Off to bed wearing a snug robe
complete with tooth-brushing teddy.*

Trace pattern for teddy motif

dotted lines indicate edges of underlapped fabric

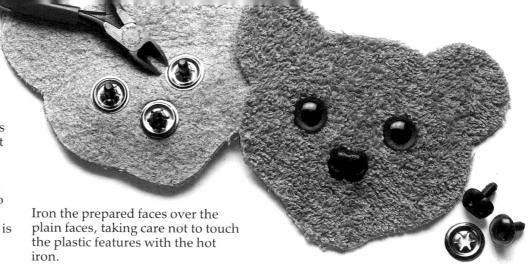

Attaching the features

Take the remaining head sections and pencil in the positions for eyes and mouth. Pierce the towelling at these marks. Insert the eyes and nose and fit the clips behind, pushing them firmly down on the back of the towelling. Use pliers to snip off the remaining stems close to each clip, checking that the clip is gripping enough stem to prevent the features from working loose.

Iron the prepared faces over the plain faces, taking care not to touch the plastic features with the hot iron.

Stitching the design

1 Use cream thread in the machine bobbin throughout, and change the top thread to match each appliqué

shape. Stitch the design with a closely-set zigzag stitch, working round each shape twice to give a

smooth satin stitch finish. Carefully cut out the toothpaste and brush shapes from the Vilene. Lift up the teddy's paws slightly and slip these shapes in place. Stitch these shapes first, using a smaller stitch than that you will use for the bear. Work small straight stitches to imitate bristles on the brush, and two lines of red satin stitch for the toothpaste stripes.

2 Cut out the complete teddy motif from the Vilene and pin it in place centrally on the back of the robe. Tack in place. Thread the machine needle with blue thread and stitch along the shoulder lines. Change to pink thread to stitch the collar, cuffs and waistband. Use black thread to stitch the foot pads.

3 With the embroidery marker, draw in the topstitching lines on the face, legs and feet.
Thread the needle with light brown and work round the teddy bear's body as follows: stitch round the ear shapes then right round the face. Stitch round the arms, then down and round the legs ending at the

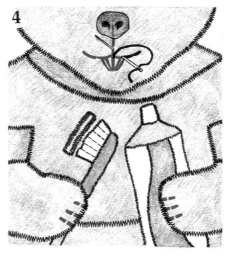

crutch. Stitch across the top of the legs and across the crutch line in one movement. Stitch round each foot.

4 Use the embroidery marker to draw in the mouth and claws, and use doubled embroidery thread to work them. The claws are simple long stitches and the mouth is

worked in backstitch. Use satin stitch for the pink tongue.

5 Embroider the mouth and tongue on the pocket bear, and fold in the pocket turnings. Pin and tack the pocket to the bathrobe front and topstitch in place.
Complete making up of robe, according to pattern.

191

CHAPTER 44

Floating balloon cushions

Confident enlarging and reducing of designs is an important part of pictorial appliqué. The larger cushion shown here tells a story in pictures – the hot-air balloon appears at a different size in each panel, getting smaller as it slowly floats away.

Beautiful appliqué work calls for a combination of skills. First, choosing suitable appliqué motifs and planning their positioning – which needs great care. Next, attaching the shapes to the ground fabric in the right order and with no puckers – thorough tacking will ensure this.

These balloon pictures include a stitched landscape. It is quite usual to embellish an appliqué with embroidery for the fine detail. Always finish the appliqué before adding any stitching either over or around the design. If your machine does not have a zigzag function, finish the edges of the motifs with buttonhole stitch then embroider the landscape by hand in stem or chain stitch, using a ring frame.

Right: These appliqué cushions in two sizes are easy to make – choose pastel or primary colours for the balloon design.

Making the small balloon cushion

This pretty little cushion in fresh pastels is an ideal exercise in placing the appliqué pieces in the correct order, before you go on to make the larger cushion.

Try to obtain glazed chintz for the cushion cover and the motifs – it has a lovely sheen and can be found in most furnishing departments.

You will need

50cm/½yd white cotton fabric,
  (width 112cm/44in or more)
35cm/⅜yd pale blue cotton fabric
20cm/¼yd cotton fabric remnants in
  pale pink, mid pink and yellow
35cm/⅜yd medium iron-on Vilene
  interfacing

Sewing thread in turquoise, white,
  yellow, pale blue, mid pink
1 sheet white dressmaker's carbon
  paper
40cm/16in square cushion pad
Tracing paper
Pencil

Cutting the shapes

Enlarge the balloon grid design (on which one square = 3cm/1¼in). Trace off each part of the enlarged design on to the non-adhesive side of the Vilene.

From the colour remnants you need to cut one large pink circle for the balloon, two paler pink stripes and a pale pink balloon base. You also

need two yellow sections for the basket, a white flag, and two white birds.

First, cut round each of the shapes on the Vilene, then iron these on to the wrong side of the appropriate fabric. Cut round the outlines carefully.

Cutting the cushion fabric

From the white fabric, cut one 42cm/16½in square for the cushion front and two rectangles measuring 41.5cm×42cm/16¼in×16½in and 20.5cm×42cm/8in×16½in for the cushion backs. From the blue fabric cut four strips 7cm×47cm/ 3in×18½in for the flat border trim.

Working the design and making up

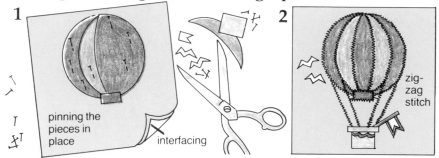

1 pinning the pieces in place — interfacing

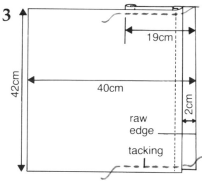

zig-zag stitch

3

42cm · 40cm · 19cm · 2cm · raw edge · tacking

1 From the blue fabric cut a 32cm/ 12½in square for the ground fabric and interface it with iron-on Vilene. Assemble the parts of the balloon design, laying down the large pink circle with the two paler pink crescent shapes on top to make the striped balloon. Use your tracing of the enlarged design to check the accuracy of positioning.
Pin all the fabric pieces in place and tack. Stitch round the raw edges

with a close machine zigzag stitch using the following colours of thread; balloon parts – turquoise; basket – yellow; birds – white; flag – pink.
2 Using dressmaker's carbon paper and your design tracing, transfer on to the fabric the balloon ropes, flag pole and scalloped line on the basket. Zigzag stitch the rope lines in turquoise and the other lines in pink.

Take the cushion front, press under 1cm/½in on all four edges of the ground fabric and pin centrally on to the white cushion front. Stitch round close to the edge of the blue square.
To make up cushion back press under 5mm/¼in, then turn under and hem 1cm/½in, on one 42cm/ 16½in edge of each of the rectangles.
3 Tack the two pieces together with

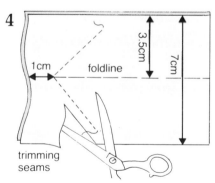

4

3.5cm

7cm

1cm   foldline

trimming
seams

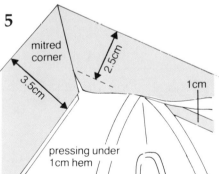

5

mitred
corner

3.5cm

2.5cm

1cm

pressing under
1cm hem

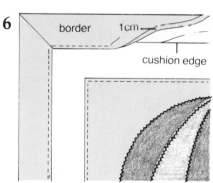

6

border   1cm

cushion edge

the long raw edge of the smaller
piece projecting 2cm/¾in
underneath the hem of the larger
piece, to form a 42cm/16½in square,
with a pocket for inserting the
cushion pad.
The finished width of the blue
border is 2.5cm/1in. Fold each blue
strip lengthways, right sides
together and press lightly.
4 Open up the strips and join
together two at a time with right-

angled seams as shown. The
corners of the right angles should
lie 1cm/½in in from the ends of each
strip. When all four strips are joined
together to form a 'frame', trim back
seams to 5mm/¼in, press open and
turn whole border to right side.
5 Press carefully and turn under
1cm/½in on all the raw inner edges.
Tack the appliquéd cushion front
and the back in place so that the
back flap opens downwards.

6 Slip the cushion edges 1cm/½in
under the border. Stitch through all
layers, close to edge of white strip
on cushion front.
Insert cushion pad through back
opening.

Making the large four-panelled cushion

Children and adults alike will love this larger version of the appliqué cushion, following the balloon as it drifts further and further away. The four panels are divided by bands of white and the whole appliqué is bordered in the blue background colour. If you are not able to obtain an 80cm/32in cushion pad, it is a simple matter to make one.

You will need

1.70m/2yds white cotton fabric (width 112cm/44in or more)
90cm/1yd pale blue cotton fabric
20cm/¼yd cotton fabric remnants in pale pink, mid pink and yellow
1.20m/1¼yd medium iron-on Vilene interfacing
Sewing thread in turquoise, pale pink, mid pink, white, yellow and pale blue
1 pack white dressmaker's carbon paper
Tracing or greaseproof paper

To make the cushion pad

1m/1yd down-proof cambric and feather or feather/down filling
or 1m/1yd calico fabric and foam chip filling

Cutting the cushion fabric

From the white fabric, cut one 82cm/33in square, one 81.5cm×82cm/32in×33in rectangle and one 20.5cm×82cm/8in×33in rectangle. From the pale blue fabric cut four strips 7cm×87cm/

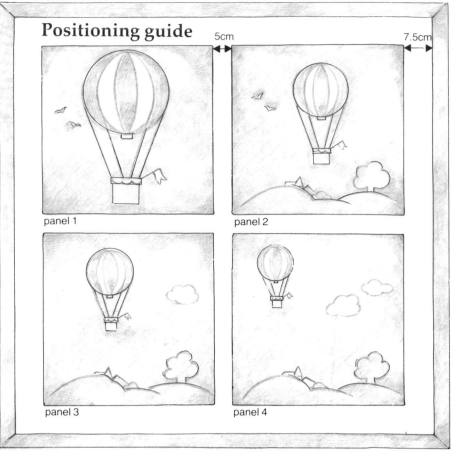

Positioning guide

5cm   7.5cm

panel 1   panel 2

panel 3   panel 4

3in×34½in.
For the appliqué ground fabric, cut four 32cm/13in squares in pale blue and interface with iron-on Vilene.

Enlarging the motifs

The cushion design contains four panels, each with a slightly different version of the balloon in the landscape. The landscape appears the same size in each panel while the balloon is a different size in each, so the two parts of the design – balloon and landscape – are given separately. Enlarge the balloon motif to four different sizes

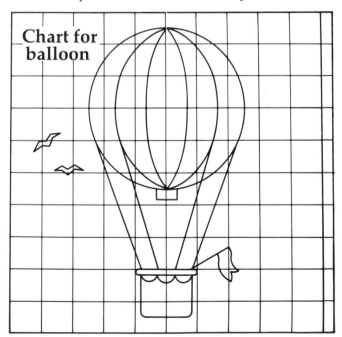

Chart for balloon

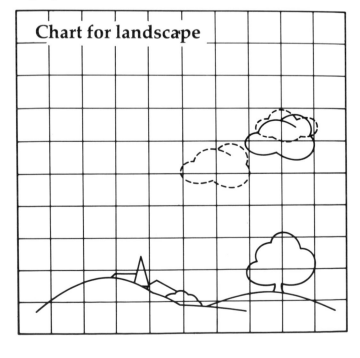

Chart for landscape

194

on to tracing or greaseproof paper as follows:

Panel 1 Enlarge balloon with one square=3cm/1¼in, no landscape.

Panel 2 Enlarge balloon with one square=2cm/¾in, enlarge landscape with one square=3cm/1¼in (no clouds). Position balloon 3cm/1¼in from top edge and 10cm/4in from right-hand edge.

Panel 3 Enlarge balloon with one square=1.5cm/⅝in. Enlarge landscape with one square=3cm/1¼in. Include one cloud (bold outline). Position balloon 3cm/1¼in from top edge and 15cm/6in from right-hand edge.

Panel 4 Enlarge balloon with one square=1cm/½in, enlarge landscape with one square=3cm/1¼in. Include both clouds (dotted outlines). Position balloon 3.5cm/1⅜in from top edge and 19cm/7½in from right-hand edge.

Working the appliqué panels

Follow the instructions for the small cushion for the appliqué designs. Position the motifs on the four blue squares as indicated in the enlarging instructions. When adding the white clouds, stitch round them using pale blue thread. In addition, all the panels except the first one include the landscape design, enlarged as described above. Transfer the landscapes using white dressmaker's carbon paper. Outline with zigzag stitch: hills, tree and bush – turquoise; church – pink; house – pale pink.

Making up the cushion

Press under 1cm/½in on all four edges of the four blue panels. Pin them to the large white square so that the distance between them is 5cm/2in and the distance of each one from the edge is 7.5cm/3in.

Stitch round each panel close to the edge.

Make the cushion back in exactly the same way as given for the small cushion, turning in 1.5cm/⅝in along one 82cm/33in edge of both blue rectangles and tacking together to form a 82cm/33in square with a flap opening.

Join and attach the blue border strips as described for the small cushion – the method is exactly the same.

Making a jumbo cushion pad

If you want to fill your cushion with feathers or feather and down, use down-proof cambric for the cover. Otherwise, use calico fabric and fill the cushion with foam chips. Simply join two 84cm/33in squares of fabric taking 1cm/½in seams all round, leaving an opening in one side. Turn right side out, stuff and slipstitch opening.

── DESIGN EXTRA ──

Framed balloon picture

For an extra decorative touch, star-shaped sequins make a dazzling balloon. The white border acts as a 'mount' for the picture.

You will need

50cm/½yd white cotton fabric
35cm/⅜yd pale blue cotton fabric
20cm/¼yd remnants in pale pink, mid pink and yellow
35cm/⅜yd medium iron-on Vilene interfacing
Sewing thread in turquoise, white, yellow and pink
Pink and silver star sequins
Carbon and tracing papers as for small cushion

To make the picture

Cut a 50cm/20in square from white fabric. Enlarge balloon design with 1 square=3cm/1¼in. Work exactly as for the small cushion. Turn edges of blue square over 1cm/½in and press. Pin centrally to white square, leaving a 10cm/4in border all round and stitch close to the edge. Now scatter the sequins on to the balloon and hand sew them in place through all layers. Have the appliqué professionally mounted and framed.

CHAPTER 45

Shadow appliqué with added embroidery

The delicate appearance of shadow appliqué has been used to great effect on this detachable organdie collar. The motifs can be hand or machine sewn and the technique is easier than it looks. A few simple embroidery stitches add detail to the design.

Shadow appliqué is just like regular appliqué except that the motifs are applied to the *wrong* side of a sheer fabric, so that they show through as pale, shadowy shapes on the right side. The stitching which secures the shapes is worked on the right side by hand or machine, and helps to give definition to the design. Decorative embroidery stitches can also be

Below: The back of this appliquéd collar is just as pretty as the front.

added afterwards to complete the design.

If the finished work is hung against the light, the motifs will show up more boldly, so it's an effective decoration for sheer curtains or light roller blinds. It is not essential to have light behind the work for the motifs to show up. Beautiful designs can also be stitched on lingerie, mats, cushion covers for a bedroom – all sorts of delicate, pretty things for home and wardrobe.

Materials and equipment

Suitable ground fabrics for shadow appliqué are organdie, voile and even gauze for very delicate work. The motifs for appliqué should be cut from plain-coloured, firm fabrics such as cotton lawn or cotton batiste. Do not choose anything too heavy or it will pull the ground fabric out of shape. The fabric must be colour fast or it will spoil the ground fabric.

Placing a coloured fabric behind a white fabric, however sheer, makes it much paler, so choose strong coloured fabrics for the appliqué unless you want a really subtle effect.

Use fine crewel needles and make sure you have a small sharp pair of scissors for snipping away the surplus fabric round the appliqué. The ground fabric can be mounted in a frame if you have one. This helps to prevent any puckering and maintains the tension of the fabric.

Shadow appliqué step-by-step

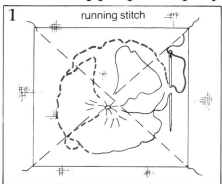

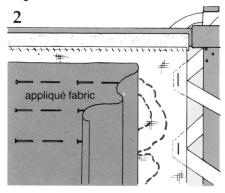

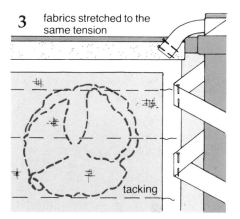

1 Tack the ground fabric over a tracing of the design. Outline the design with small, neat running stitches without sewing through the paper. Do not knot the thread but leave loose ends at the back of the fabric. These stitches will be hidden by the stitched edge of the motif but it is important to keep them neat as they are not easy to remove later on. Remove the tracing and mount the ground fabric on a frame if you have one. Trim the ends of the threads outlining the design close to fabric.

2 Pin a piece of the appliqué fabric to the back of the ground fabric, matching the straight grains of the two fabrics and covering the design.
3 Tack the appliqué fabric in place, stretching it to the same tension as the ground fabric.

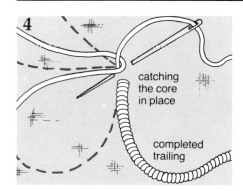

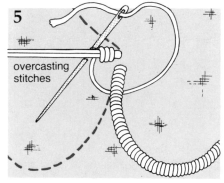

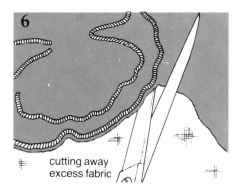

Stitching the appliqué Trailing (overcast stitch) is a good choice for work that needs to be washed. It gives a good firm outline and holds the appliqué securely in place with no risk of fraying. You could also use buttonhole stitch or, if you are using a machine, a narrow satin stitch.

Do not knot threads when starting or finishing – leave a tail of thread at the back of the work instead. Do not carry any threads across the back, from one motif to another, as they will show.

4 To work trailing, cut a length of thread for the core at least twice the length of the line to be stitched. Fold it in half and catch in place with a small stitch over the loop.
5 Hold the doubled thread in the direction of the embroidery with your left hand and work over it with small overcasting stitches. At the end, thread the core to the back of the work and snip off.

Finishing off Turn the work to the wrong side and remove the tacking holding the appliqué fabric.
6 Hold the excess fabric tautly away from the stitching and cut it as close to the stitches as possible, using small sharp scissors. Take care not to cut the stitching or the ground fabric. Snip off any untidy ends on the back.

Pin the work out, appliqué side up, on an ironing board and press lightly with steam iron or damp cloth.

Shadow appliqué poppies on a detachable collar

This beautiful organdie collar with its design of pale poppies and delicate white stitchery is surprisingly simple to make. A tie-on collar like this looks smart over a blouse, dress or jumper – tie it at the front or the back.

Organdie is a very fine fabric, so be sure to use the fine needles and tacking threads recommended. The finished collar is hand washable but you should check the red fabric for colour fastness.

You will need

Commercial paper pattern for collar
1m/1yd white organdie or voile or the recommended pattern fabric requirement
Piece of red cotton lawn or batiste, about 15cm along straight grain × 41cm wide/6in × 16in
3 skeins white stranded cotton for embroidery
White cotton sewing thread No. 50 for tacking
Fine crewel needle (size 9 or 10)

Working the appliqué

Trace off the poppy design on to the collar paper pattern piece, using a felt-tip pen. The trace patterns given are for the right and left-hand parts of the collar front. Match the dotted lines to give the design for the collar centre back. Cut two pieces of organdie to fit the paper pattern. The grain should run from the front to the back of the collar on each piece. Cut a strip of organdie 2cm × 90cm/¾in × 36in for the tie. Pin and tack one piece of organdie over the pattern. Use fine white thread and small tacking stitches to outline the cutting edge of the collar, but do not sew through the paper pattern. Outline the petals, leaves and corn with small running stitches in the same way. Try to keep the work as flat as possible as you sew. Remove the paper pattern and mount the organdie in a frame if you have one. Cut the piece of red fabric in half, lengthwise along the grain of the fabric; cut one of these pieces in half lengthwise, again along the grain, so that you have two smaller pieces for each of the collar fronts.

Pin the red fabric to the wrong side of the organdie on the collar back and both fronts, covering the poppy flowers and matching the grain of the ground fabric. Tack firmly in place.

Working the stitchery

All the embroidery is worked with two strands of stranded cotton. Start with the poppy petal outlines in trailing.

The poppy centres are worked as oval buttonhole wheels with a few straight stitches radiating from the centre of each one.

When the appliqué is complete, turn the work to the wrong side, remove tacking and cut away the surplus red fabric as described on the previous page.

Trace pattern for shadow appliqué poppies

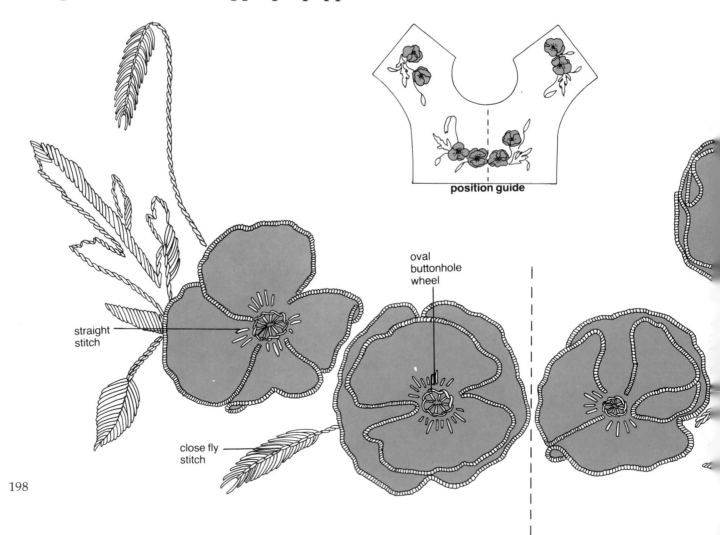

position guide

oval buttonhole wheel

straight stitch

close fly stitch

Now embroider the ears of corn, stems and poppy leaves in satin, stem and close fly stitch as indicated on trace pattern.
To give the satin stitch a firm edge, work over the outline stitches, stitching as close to them as possible.
Pin out the collar and press carefully.

Making up the collar
Cut out the embroidered collar piece along marked cutting line. Using the paper pattern, cut a second collar piece from the remaining organdie for backing. With right sides together, seam the two collar pieces together along all edges except the neck edge. Trim seam allowance to 1cm/½in, and turn collar to right side. Press carefully.
If your machine has a decorative stitch facility, you could add a machine-stitched edging on the right side of the outer collar edges, to disguise the seam allowance. Use a thread that matches the appliqué.

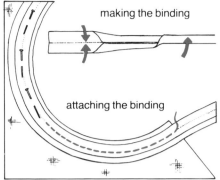

making the binding

attaching the binding

Adding the tie/binding
Take the strip of organdie for the tie/binding. Fold in long edges to meet in the centre, then fold in half lengthwise and press.
Matching the centre of the strip with the centre back of collar, open out one side of the strip and place fold on right side of collar stitching line. Pin and stitch round collar edge. Trim seam to 6mm/¼in and press seam towards strip. Fold in strip ends and then fold strip in half lengthwise over collar edge and stitch the length of the strip through all layers and collar to finish ties.

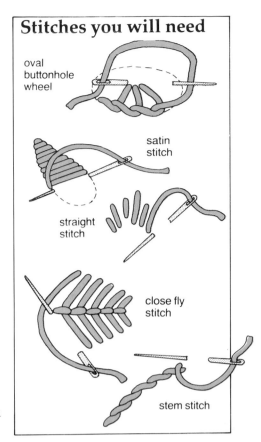

Stitches you will need
oval buttonhole wheel

satin stitch

straight stitch

close fly stitch

stem stitch

Right: The two halves of the design (left) appear on the two collar fronts.
Geometric appliqué designs could also be adapted for this type of collar.

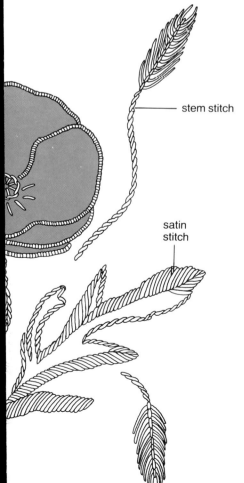

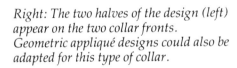

stem stitch

satin stitch

CHAPTER 46

Appliqué perse to decorate soft furnishings

This appliqué technique was very popular in the nineteenth century. It is sometimes called broderie perse or cretonne appliqué and uses motifs cut from printed fabrics to build up a rich applied design on soft furnishings such as this collection of cushions.

Appliqué was probably originally invented by the Persians or the Indians as a way of inexpensively imitating the effect of richer embroidered textiles. The particular technique known as appliqué perse (Persian appliqué) is fun to do and quicker than regular appliqué – the shapes are taken from printed fabric and so are already 'drawn' ready for you to cut out. You have to decide on the best arrangement of the cut-out motifs, and stitch them neatly in place on the ground fabric, usually with a machine satin stitch which gives a well-defined edge. If you don't have a swing needle machine, work by hand using buttonhole stitch. Traditionally, motifs were always cut from printed chintz but any printed fabric will do, so long as it has a bold enough pattern and a close enough weave not to fray.

Below: One length of fabric provides motifs for several cushions, each one using a different background colour.

Using the technique

This is a marvellous way of using up an odd remnant of furnishing fabric left over from making curtains or loose covers. You may not even have enough left to make up a cushion cover, yet you could use the remnant to create a unique design to decorate a plain cover with appliqué perse. Appliqué the motifs on to table-cloths, table mats, pillowcases, blinds and curtain hems. They can also be used to add a decorative touch to clothes and accessories.

Planning the design

Wash and press your chosen piece of printed fabric to avoid shrinkage and to make sure the colours will not run on to ground fabric when washed. Take a sheet of tracing paper and, using a thick felt-tip pen, trace off a series of motifs from the printed fabric – all the motifs which are bold enough to stitch round. Cut out the paper shapes and experiment with different ways of arranging them in a balanced design. Bear in mind the shape of the finished article when doing this. Motifs can certainly over-lap, but don't make the design too complicated for yourself to stitch – more than two layers could be too bulky, especially if you are machine stitching round the motifs.

Your design need not resemble the original fabric design – create some-thing completely different if you like. If the basic design is floral, have fun 'arranging' vases, baskets or bun-ches of flowers. Make a drawing of your completed design to refer to when appliquéing the motifs.

Working appliqué perse

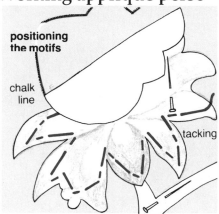

positioning the motifs

chalk line

tacking

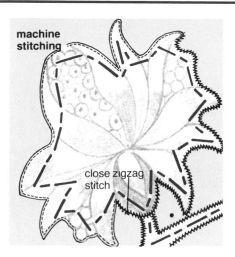

machine stitching

close zigzag stitch

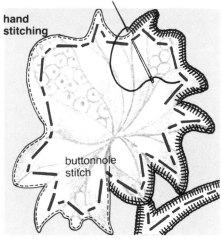

hand stitching

buttonhole stitch

Using a pair of small, sharp scissors, cut out the fabric motifs along the outlines. Where an outline is too intricate, simplify it a little by ignoring some of the fine detail. Cut the appliqué ground fabric to the desired size for whatever you intend to make.
Positioning the motifs Using your tracing paper cut-outs, roughly mark the position of the appliqué motifs on the ground fabric by tracing round the shapes with a chalk pencil. If working by hand,

mount the ground fabric in a frame if you have one.
Lay the fabric motifs on the ground fabric. Pin them in place and tack securely.
Machine stitching With the machine set to a medium straight stitch, sew all round the outside of the motif to anchor it securely. Using a close zigzag stitch and a thread to match either one of the motif colours or the ground fabric, stitch round all edges covering raw edges. Go slowly and carefully;

some corners may need careful manipulation. Make sure you attach the shapes in the correct order for the design – raw edges of fabric and ends of thread should be neatly covered.
Hand stitching Tack round close to the raw edges of the motifs. Using stranded cotton, pearl cotton or coton à broder, work buttonhole stitch round raw edges with the knots on the outside. Make sure you keep the stitches close together to cover raw edges.

Cushions with appliquéd motifs

The cushion shown here is decorated with motifs taken from a multi-coloured furnishing fabric. Plan your design to suit your cushion shape.

Making up the covers

Work the appliqué design on the front of the cushion cover before making up.
Make bolster and large square cushion covers like the ones shown opposite from a half-metre/yard of plain cotton furnishing fabric.

Ready-made covers are easier to appliqué by hand. If you prefer to use your machine, you may need to unpick one of the cover seams to enable the fabric to lie flat.

Stitching the appliqué

The appliqué is stitched using as many colours of thread as necessary to match the main colours in the design. Use a fairly wide satin stitch for leaves and flowers, making it narrower for stems.

Appliqué perse ideas for the home

Use appliqué perse to give a quaint Victorian look or a modern finish to your furnishings. Some fabrics almost ask to be used for this technique. Designs which include open background spaces can be appliquéd on to the hem of a circular tablecloth, for example, and the ground fabric cut away behind the spaces for a professional, openwork look.

If your plain cushion covers need a new lease of life, stitch yourself a vase or basket of flowers using a combination of several floral chintzes – add leaves, birds and butterflies as you wish.

Give a roller blind a boldly scalloped hem and scatter appliquéd leaves and flowers along the border.

Team this technique up with others like trapunto, English quilting and embroidery. To add emphasis to an appliquéd motif, particularly on a flat surface such as a screen or a bedhead, make a small slit in the ground fabric

behind the motif and insert some padding. Carefully stitch up the slit. Alternatively, add wadding to the background fabric after the motifs have been stitched and then add a line of quilting stitches round the motif outline. French knots or bullion knots worked in the centre of a flower can bring some life to the design – experiment with other embroidery stitches to add emphasis or surface texture.

the same furnishing fabric can be used in many ways to draw together all the elements in a room

position cut-out motifs to complement the scalloped edge of a roller blind

use appliqué perse as a central motif on scatter cushions

apply a co-ordinated border to the edge of a circular tablecloth

Patchwork

Patchwork, as the name suggests, is the craft of sewing patches or pieces of fabric together. In the days when cloth was expensive or difficult to obtain, needlewomen would save pieces of fabric from worn-out or damaged clothes and furnishings and join them together to make gaily coloured quilts. Frequently, the pieces were cut into different shapes and sewn together to create an amazing variety of patterns which were given intriguing names such as Log Cabin, Streak of Lightning, and Dresden Plate.

All you need to start this fascinating hobby is a selection of fabrics and templates. It is the arrangement of the patches which creates the pattern – the simplest square shape can be sub-divided into triangles which are then built up to make larger patterns; hexagonal patches can be pieced to form rosettes; and pieced triangles can be combined with strips to create a pleasing geometric design. Colour choice is vitally important too: a change in the colour mix can totally alter the appearance of a patchwork.

Use patchwork to make bed covers, cushions, place mats or even pictures. Add a dramatic trim to a shirt or blouse. Make up a simple jacket with a quilted patchwork fabric. Patchwork addicts will tell you that this is a wonderful way for needleworkers of all standards to express their sense of colour and design.

CHAPTER 47

Colourful creations from fabric scraps

One of the main pleasures of patchwork is the satisfaction of using humble scraps and remnants to create unique and beautiful results. Combining colours and shapes is a real art, whether you choose the quiet and restful hand-sewing methods, or opt for the quick efficiency of your sewing machine.

Down the ages, generations of busy seamstresses have pieced and patched with small neat stitches to make quilts which today are collector's items. The earliest patchwork was made from fragments of different fabrics pieced together in a random or 'crazy' design. The craft was born out of the need to make a strong or warm piece of fabric out of whatever came to hand – dressmaking leftovers or pieces of old clothes.

Patchwork became very popular in the early eighteenth century, particularly in America where quilts were often made up by groups of people working together. A young girl and her friends would often sew several patchwork quilts prior to her wedding. These quilts were made up in many patterns and vivid colours. The traditional designs are still popular today, and look every bit as fresh and individual.

The advent of the sewing machine in the mid-nineteenth century revolutionized the craft of patchwork, dramatically reducing the time spent on making up some of the larger and more complicated quilts. However, all forms of patchwork can also be done by hand.

Traditional methods

The traditional English method of assembling patchwork is to join together many small fabric shapes into striking geometrical designs entirely by hand and sewing over paper patches cut from patterns called "templates". The American way is to hand-sew the various shapes into square units called 'pieced blocks'. A newcomer to patchwork can immediately begin a pretty cushion cover using one of the simple pieced block designs. For the initiated, keen to embark on a more ambitious pro-

ject, these blocks can be built into a full-size patchwork quilt.

Your patchwork can be as large or as small as you like and range from table-mats and pin cushions to wedding quilts and wall-hangings. Whatever your choice, the secret of success lies above all in colour planning, choice of fabrics, and the accuracy of your pattern-cutting and sewing.

The pleasure of patchwork comes from its colours and patterns which create the attractive finished effect and make each piece a personal masterpiece, as you will see if you make up the pretty pram quilt cover opposite. Patchwork is a matter of colour, hue pattern, shape and texture. It is well worth taking time at the planning stage to achieve a well-balanced design.

Patchwork materials

Patchwork is traditionally made from fabrics of the same weight, strength, and even age. Heavy patches pull lighter ones out of shape, while very old fabrics may show signs of wear before their neighbours in the design. Dressweight cottons are ideal – use them plain or printed. If you wish to use luxurious silks or velvets, make sure all your patches are compatible in weight and thickness. Keep a lookout for suitable fabrics and try swapping scraps with friends, although for larger pieces of work you may need to buy fabric. Wash and press new pieces of cotton fabric before starting the patchwork to make sure they will not shrink, nor the colours run.

Ideally you need three pairs of scissors for patchwork – a sharp pair for fabric, another for cutting paper patches, and some small embroidery scissors for snipping thread. Sharp steel pins and a thimble are important pieces of equipment as well.

The paper patches that are actually used in the patchwork are cut very carefully from patterns called templates. Many template shapes can be bought commercially but it is easy to make your own – see how in the next chapter.

Colour planning patchwork

Take some squared graph paper or isometric paper (marked with triangles) depending on the shapes you plan to use. With coloured felt-tip pens or crayons, experiment with combinations of squares, triangles and other geometric shapes. The isometric paper is ideal for designs based on triangles or hexagons. Try

Above: Patchwork can make cushions, quilts and other furnishings into focal points for any room.

Right: A rough sketch shows how, by altering the positions of key colours, you can dramatically alter the effect.

out several versions – playing around with different dominant colours or light and dark tones of the same colour. You can mix plain and printed patches if you like. Consider adding a border or central medallion in toning or contrasting colours. When you are happy with the scheme, make a scaled-down plan of the whole design as a guide to work from.

CHAPTER 48

The tradition of patchwork

Many of the beautiful patchwork quilts made in Victorian times and earlier were stitched together using hundreds of hexagons. This popular six-sided shape makes a decorative honeycomb effect and is a simple and satisfying introduction to English patchwork.

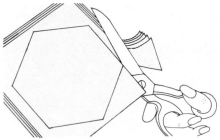

Traditional English patchwork is made of patches which are very often all the same shape, such as clamshells, diamonds or hexagons. Each patch is made by covering a paper or card shape with a piece of fabric secured by tacking. The patches are joined by handsewing the edges and the papers are then removed.

Pins, needles and thread

Fine white cotton thread is usually the best for preparing patches for English patchwork. Use fine matching thread for joining them. Sharps, betweens or crewels in sizes 8, 9 or 10 are the most suitable needles. Make sure your pins are small and slender to minimise the risk of marking the fabric.

Templates

You can make your own templates. Two methods for hexagon templates are given below. The compass method is the more traditional, but if you can obtain isometric paper, the shape can be drawn more quickly.

You can buy metal or plastic templates in a limited range of sizes. These are long lasting and will not become worn at the corners.

Solid templates are often sold with a corresponding window template. This looks like a frame – an empty or transparent centre portion (actual finished size of patch) bordered by a strip measuring the same as the seam allowance. It is useful for cutting patches – especially on patterned fabric where you may be creating a

Typical English patchwork templates: hexagon, clamshell and diamond.

decorative effect with the motifs, for instance, using the direction of stripes. The finished patch area can be seen through the window.

Working with hexagons

Traditional hexagon designs such as Grandmother's Flower Garden which is based on rosette shapes make striking heirlooms. Random hexagons of every pattern and hue give a homely look.

Today's patchwork enthusiasts are no less fascinated by the many different effects possible with hexagons. They combine well with squares and triangles in many design variations.

Making your own hexagonal templates

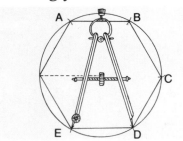

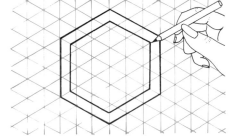

Making papers

Using a pair of compasses

You can draw hexagons of any size you like simply and accurately using a pair of compasses. Set the compass width to the measurement of one side of the hexagon, and draw a circle on to a stiff piece of card. Place the point of the compass anywhere along the circle and draw an arc to cut the circle at point A. With the compass point on A, draw another arc to cut the circle at B. Place the point on B and draw another arc. Continue in this way around the circle until you have six points which, when joined up, form a hexagon. Cut out with a craft knife.

Using isometric paper

On isometric paper (marked out in triangles), draw the outline of the required size of hexagon using a ruler. Stick the isometric paper on to a piece of stiff card and cut out the shape using a craft knife and a metal ruler if you have one.

To make a window template, mark two outlines on the paper, one inside the other, 6mm/¼in (or whatever the seam allowance) apart. Carefully cut out the centre hexagonal portion with the craft knife to leave a frame. The window template is invaluable for cutting fabric patches which include the seam allowance.

The next step is to use the template for cutting the papers which go into the patches. Use firm paper such as cartridge or writing paper, magazine covers or thin card. Many people use old greetings cards. The choice will depend on the strength of the fabrics. Be very careful to cut accurately – an uneven patch will cause the work to pull out of shape. Lay the template on the paper and draw round it with a hard, sharp pencil. Cut along the pencil lines and check that all the papers are exactly the same. By folding the paper, it is possible to cut several patches at a time.

Making patches

If you have a window template, hold this against the piece of fabric and cut round the edge, or use it to mark a cutting line. It will help you to get the seam allowance accurate. Otherwise, pin the papers to the wrong side of the fabric, leaving space for turnings, and cut out. Have two sides of the shape on the straight grain unless a particular pattern effect is desired. Pin two opposite sides of the fabric over the paper with fine pins. Fold the seam allowance over the paper all round and tack in place through the paper, catching the folds well down on

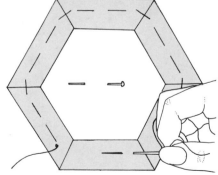

each corner. Press prepared shapes before joining to give crisp edges. Hexagons have wide-angled corners which are easy to work with.

Above: This beautiful bright bed cover is made up entirely of 2.5cm/1in hexagons. A patchwork like this brings a child's bedroom alive. Red, yellow, blue and multi-coloured patches are assembled in diamond shapes, joined with plain green hexagons and bordered in green. Use scraps left over from a little girl's dresses to make her a cover full of memories. Shortcut idea: Make up some diamond or rosette shapes in plain or printed hexagons and appliqué them on to a plain background for a patchwork effect.

Plump patchwork cushions

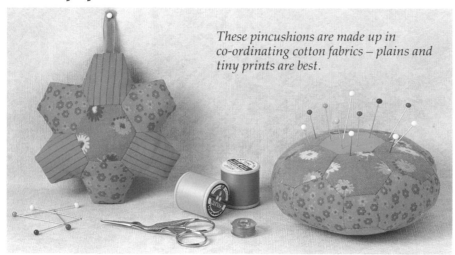

These pincushions are made up in co-ordinating cotton fabrics – plains and tiny prints are best.

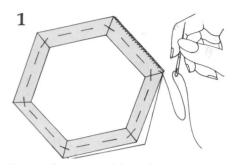

1

Scrap of narrow ribbon for rosette
  pincushion (optional)
Kapok or polyester fibre stuffing
Thin card or stiff paper
Preparing the rosettes Using the
template, cut 14 hexagons from the
card or paper. Make up the 14
patches – seven for each rosette as
described.
1 Take the centre patch and one
other. Hold them right sides
together and join with tiny
overcasting stitches, trying not to
catch in the paper. Strengthen each
corner with two or three extra
stitches.

Rosette pincushion

This slightly smaller pincushion is
formed of two rosettes joined
around the edges. The centres of
each rosette should contrast well
with the surrounding patches. It is
helpful to make a small diagram of
the colour scheme before you start.

The finished diameter of the
pincushion is about 12.5cm/5in.

You will need
For this pincushion and the
  rounded pincushion (far right)
Hexagon template, 2.5cm/1in sides
Plain and printed cotton fabric
  scraps (similar weight)

Rosette appliqué cushion cover

This quick and simple cushion cover
consists of a double rosette in hexagons appliquéd to a plain backing. It
fits a 45cm/18in square cushion pad.
Suitable fabrics for this and the
striped cushion (left) are polyester
satin, acetate taffeta or dress lining
material – back this with iron-on
interfacing if it is very flimsy and note
fine fabrics technique below.

You will need for either cushion
Hexagon template (4cm/1½in sides)
50cm/½yd fabric (90cm/36in wide)
  in main colour (used for backing)
20cm/¼yd each of three contrast
  colours (five for striped cushion)
Matching polyester sewing threads
Thin card or stiff paper
Making the double rosette Cut 19
hexagons with 4cm/1½in sides from
the card or paper.
Cut out the fabric hexagons with a
1cm/½in seam allowance in colours
as follows: 1 cream centre patch,
6 pink inner petals, 12 turquoise
outer petals. Make up the patches.
When sewing with fine, silky
fabrics, use masking tape to

*Left: Plain hexagons in toning colours
create a dramatic effect.*

2

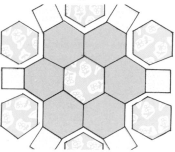

Rounded pincushion

2 Take a third hexagon and join to the centre hexagon along one edge; join to the other hexagon.
Add the remaining 'petals' in the same way, making sure you have them in the correct order if they are in different fabrics. Make an identical rosette for the other side of the pincushion.
3 To join the completed rosettes, place them right sides together, and join them round the edge with tiny overcasting stitches, leaving two adjoining edges of the last two petals open for inserting stuffing. If desired, attach a loop of narrow

ribbon to the outer edge of one of the petals so that it lies between the two rosettes on the inside, raw ends flush with hexagon edges.
Finishing off Remove tacking and papers from all the hexagons. The papers can be used again if the corners are still sharp.
Tack the turnings of the last two petal edges in place, and turn the pincushion right sides out.
Stuff tightly with kapok or polyester fibre, packing it well into all the corners. Sew up the opening neatly on the outside with small stitches and remove the tacking.

This larger pincushion needs 20 hexagons and six squares, all with 2.5cm/1in sides. There is an extra row of shapes in a new contrast fabric around the centre.
Make two rosettes with contrast centres as for rosette pincushion. Leaving the papers in, take one of the rosettes and attach six squares and six hexagons to the outer edges of the 'petals' as shown. (Join the shapes with right sides together.) With right sides together, join on the second rosette, remembering to leave an opening for the stuffing. Finish off as for rosette pincushion.

DESIGN EXTRA

stick seam allowances to back of papers to avoid marking the fabric.
Beginning at the centre, join the hexagons into a double rosette. Remove papers from centre and inner petals. Press carefully on the wrong side using a cloth. Remove papers from outer petals.
Assembling the cover front Cut two 45cm/18in squares from blue fabric for the front and back of the cover. Position the made-up double rosette in the centre of one of the 45cm/18in squares. Pin in place and secure with neat slipstitches round the outer edge.
Making up the cover With right sides together, join the back and front with a 1cm/½in seam, leaving a 30cm/12in opening along one edge. Trim seam (trim corners diagonally) and overcast to prevent fraying. Neaten raw edges of opening. Turn to right side, push out corners and insert cushion pad. Sew up the opening with neat slipstitches.

Hexagon patterns

Sketch your hexagon design ideas on isometric paper. The top two patterns are those you need for the pair of cushions (far left).

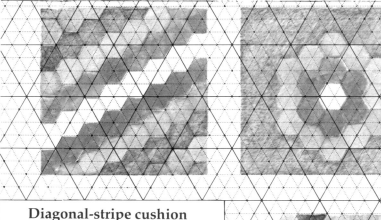

Diagonal-stripe cushion
The cover front is made up of 56 hexagons (4cm/1½in sides) joined to form the pattern above; you need about 30 papers. To finish, press patchwork carefully on the wrong side.
Press seam allowances out flat on outside hexagons before tacking back of cushion centrally in place, trimming patchwork and seaming.

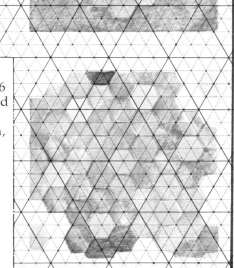

CHAPTER 49

Pieced patchwork quilts

*In days gone by, making a beautiful patchwork quilt entailed
hours of painstaking hand stitching. Now
you can use your sewing machine to join together the square
patches to form strips, then quickly seam the
strips to make a covetable square or rectangular quilt.*

A pieced quilt is one made of fabric patches seamed by hand or machine. No paper patches are involved. Individual fabric patches are either assembled into square design units, which are joined together as pattern repeats, or else they form a single design covering the quilt area.

Square patches joined randomly can also look effective, especially if several muted-tone patches are interspersed with the odd flash of bright colour such as red or orange.

Planning the design

Decide on the size of the finished quilt before designing the pattern.

Adapting a design may be just a question of altering the size of the patches. You will find that square patches lend themselves to all kinds of striking geometric designs, particularly those which use light and dark shades to create an effect. This type of design has always been popular with the Amish people (a religious sect in Pennsylvania) whose characteristic use of very bright colours with muted ones, sewn in bold geometric patterns, always results in spectacular quilts. One of their favourite designs is *Sunshine and shadow* – sometimes known as *Trip around the world*. The quilt shown overleaf for you to make

is a simplified version of *Sunshine and shadow*, which traditionally is made up in at least seven plain, brightly coloured cotton or wool fabrics. The overall design fills a square shape and has the square patches set in a pattern of concentric diamonds.

Another traditional Amish design is *Streak of lightning*. It is always made up in two plain colours – a bright one and a dark contrast – to create a vivid design of diagonal zigzags. This is an all-over design, which you can easily adapt to any size or shape.

Having decided on your design, make a scale drawing with coloured felt-tips on graph (squared) paper and calculate the size the finished squares should be. Colour in the design of the whole quilt – this gives you a good basis on which to calculate the amounts of fabric you need. Square or rectangular shapes are both easy to plan, but if you wish to enlarge or reduce a design, make sure you do it evenly – adding or subtracting the same number of squares from each edge. You can add a plain border of any width you like, to provide a frame for the design, and to cut down on the area of patchwork you need to make up. Or pick out two or three of the colours in the patchwork and plan a striped border. (You can make this by joining strips of the appropriate fabrics.)

How to estimate fabric

Use cotton or light woollen fabric, plain or patterned. Several firms supply ready-cut cotton squares, up to 12cm/4¾in square, in packs of contrasting colours. To make a rough estimate of the amount of fabric needed for a quilt, divide the area of the finished quilt by the number of colours you plan to use, and add extra for seams. If you use 10cm/4in squares, for example, cut them with 12cm/4¾in sides.

Once you have a scale plan of the design, count up the squares in each colour, then calculate how many squares will fit across one width of the fabric to make an accurate estimate of the fabric requirements.

For example, twelve 9cm/3½in squares fit across 115cm/45in fabric, but only ten across 90cm/36in fabric.

*Left: Joining the squares into strips first
makes the patchwork easier to do and
helps you form the pattern correctly.*

Assembling patchwork

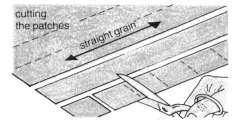

cutting the patches

straight grain

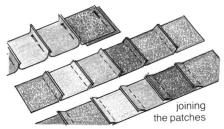

joining the patches

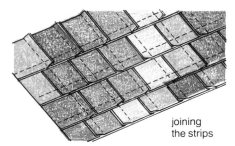

joining the strips

Cutting the patches
It is important that you cut your patches absolutely accurately. For squares smaller than 4cm/1½in, add 6mm/¼in seam allowances, otherwise add 1cm/½in seam allowances. Cut (or tear) the fabric lengthwise along the straight grain to make strips of the required width, which you then cut into squares.

If you intend to join the patches by hand, or if your machine footplate does not have a 1cm/½in mark, then it is best to mark the cutting lines and seamlines of the squares on to the wrong side of the fabric with a sharp pencil. Make a square window template to mark both the cutting line and the seamline.

Joining the patches
To avoid confusion, lay out the squares in the correct pattern on a large flat area. At this stage you may decide to make some minor changes to the design. Keep the squares on the flat surface until they are safely sewn.

Pin each square to its neighbour to form widthwise rows, matching raw edges and pencil seamlines if marked. Make sure you join them in the correct order and the right way up for one-way designs. When a complete strip has been pinned, machine along the seamlines, using the 1cm/½in mark on the machine footplate. Press all the seams in the same direction with a hot iron. This makes the

finished work stronger.

Now pin the next strip and machine in the same way. Press the seams in the opposite direction to those on the first strip. Pressing in alternate directions lessens the bulk where the seams meet.

Joining the strips
Once all the squares have been joined into strips in the correct order, join the strips along long edges, beginning at the top of the quilt and working downwards. Be careful to join the strips accurately so that the corners of the squares meet neatly. Press all horizontal seams in the same direction.

Traditional designs and borders

A scheme is shown below for a square quilt made up in the *Streak of lightning* pattern. It makes a stunning wall-hanging. Add a plain border made up of four strips of fabric – two long and two shorter, as shown.

The pattern on the right shows how squares and rectangles of different sizes can be used to make a colourful and effective border, creating a large pieced quilt around a smaller piece of patchworked squares.

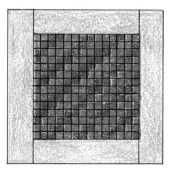

Above and right: Quilt designs made from squares, showing two different methods of dealing with the border.

Elegant quilt in machined squares

A patchwork quilt in a bedroom is an inspiring finishing touch to the rest of the furnishings. Make one that incorporates curtain and cushion fabrics, or the colours of the carpet. The pattern of squares used here is created with four printed fabrics and one plain.

Amounts are given here for both standard single and double quilt sizes. If you want to adjust the basic plan, remember that this design must have an odd number of squares both ways. First measure the bed, deciding on the drop you want, and measuring the length and width of the area on top of the bed. Then work out the design, based on 10cm/4in finished squares.

To add extra warmth and body, and to make the cover reversible, you can invest in some pre-quilted fabric for the lining.

Below: Brown and white is refreshing, but you could choose any colour scheme – make a scaled-down colour plan first.

You will need

For a single quilt 170cm×250cm/
67in×98in:

1.10m/1¼yd each of five different
cotton fabrics, 120cm/48in wide
or 1.60m/1¾yd each of five 90cm/
36in wide fabrics
Matching sewing cotton
5.10m/5⅝yd lining fabric (any
width) or pre-quilted fabric
1 sheet graph (squared) paper
For a double quilt 250cm×250cm/
99in×99in:

1.50m/1⅝yd each of five different
cotton fabrics, 120cm/48in wide
or 2.30m/2½yd each of five 90cm/
36in wide fabrics
7.60m/8⅜yd lining fabric (any
width) or pre-quilted fabric
Matching sewing cotton
1 sheet graph (squared) paper

Making up the patchwork

First choose your fabrics and colour
scheme, then make a scaled plan on
the graph paper with the help of the
chart. Planning and measuring will
be easy if you make each square on
the plan represent 10cm/4in.
Alternate the diagonal rows of dark,
light and plain patches to create the
prettiest effect.
Cut the patches as described on page
211, remembering to allow for the
seams. Join the patches in strips,
beginning with the top horizontal
row of the plan and working
downwards.

Finishing a quilt

Consider whether you would like to
add a border to the patchwork, or
whether it is already the right size.
Adding a border Join strips of plain
or patterned fabric to each edge of
the patchwork with right sides
together, pressing seams towards
the border. Many traditional quilts
have large squares and rectangles in
contrasting colours incorporated in
their borders, which help to set off
the finished patchwork.
Lining a quilt Back the quilt with
plain, patterned, or ready quilted
fabric for extra weight and warmth.
You will probably have to join two
or more widths of lining fabric.
Lay the patchwork on the lining,
wrong sides together, and turn in
both raw edges 1cm/½in. Tack, and
machine round close to the edge.
This is the traditional English
method of finishing a quilt.

Chart for double and single quilts

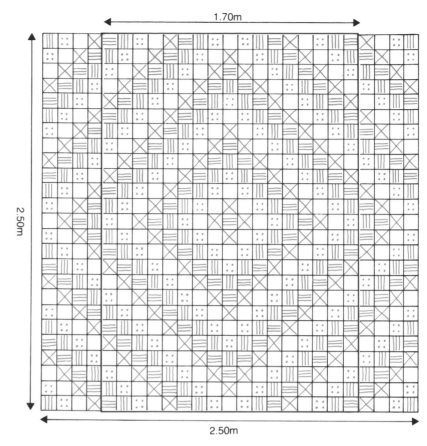

1.70m

2.50m

2.50m

Working from the chart

Use the chart for the single and
double version of the patchwork
quilt. The single version is outlined
in red. The five fabrics are
denoted by different symbols on the
chart. Cut patches 12cm/5in square
to give 10cm/4in finished squares,
and count the number you need in
each fabric from the chart.

Quick mitred corners

1 tack on fabric strip

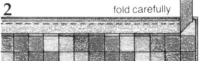
2 fold carefully

3 resume stitching at same point

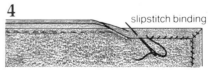
4 slipstitch binding

1 To make a bound edge with neat
mitred corners, cut a strip of plain
fabric 7cm/2¾in wide and a little
longer than the quilt's perimeter.
Tack this round the edge, right
sides together, raw edges of strip,
patchwork and lining matching.
2 When you reach a corner (1cm/
½in from two edges), stop sewing
and fold fabric strip diagonally up,
and down again so that top fold lies
flush with raw edges of strip and
quilt. Now the continuation of the
strip is parallel with next quilt edge.
3 Resume stitching at exactly the
same point on the other side of the
fold. Repeat at each corner.
4 Remove tacking and turn strip
round to wrong side. Turn raw
edge of strip over and slipstitch
neatly in place, pushing corner
folds to inside and slipstitching the
diagonal corner openings on both
front and back of quilt.

Stick-and-stitch pram quilt

Modern materials and methods have revolutionized patchwork. To achieve an effect quickly, you can now assemble patches directly on to iron-on Vilene – a light and versatile fabric normally sold for interfacing in dressmaking. One side of the Vilene will bond with another fabric when the two layers are pressed with a hot iron.

By arranging fabric patches in a patchwork design on Vilene, pressing, and oversewing the joins with a zigzag machine stitch, you can make beautiful 'patchwork' much more quickly than by traditional methods.

If you need to put any shapes on to larger ones, you can fix them in place using small pieces of Vilene Wundaweb – a light adhesive tape which bonds two layers of fabrics together when pressed.

Experiment with the stick and stitch technique by making up this pretty cover for a standard pram quilt. The cover is shown here in pink, blue and white, but you could adapt the design to any colour combination you choose using your colour planning know-how.

The shade of the thread you choose for the machine stitching will make quite a difference to the overall colour effect of the finished article. The patches in the photograph are over-sewn in blue thread to tone with the border.

You can use the stick-and-stitch method for making cushion covers, tablecloths, wall hangings – anything where you want a patchwork effect in next to no time. The addition of the Vilene adds body and keeps the patchwork looking crisp and smart.

You will need

For a quilt cover 50×58cm/20×23in:
Cotton fabric colour A 60×120cm/ 24×48in (Cut 52×60cm/20×24in for back of cover.)
30cm/12in colour B (Cut 2 pieces 30×60cm/12×24in – one for patches and one for the border strips.)
20cm/8in colour C
10cm/4in colour D
1m/1yd lightest iron-on Vilene (Light Supershape) width 84cm/33in. (Cut 2 pieces – one 40×48cm/16×19in and one 50×58cm/20×23in.)
3 standard reels polyester thread in chosen colour for oversewing
Card, 8×16cm/3×6in (not too stiff)
1 pack Vilene Wundaweb *or* tacking thread
Sewing machine (zigzag function)
2 plastic press studs *or* 25cm/10in piece white Velcro

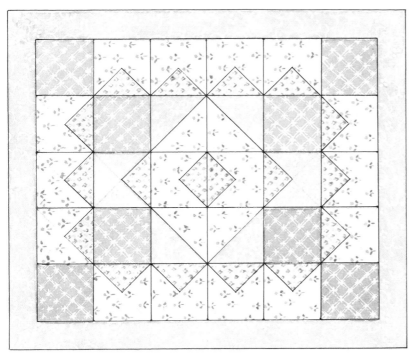

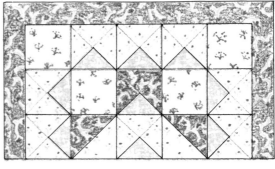

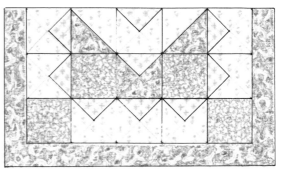

A   B   C   D

Above: Use this colour code to position the patchwork pieces as in the diagram, or choose a colour scheme from the suggestions above right.

Left: This charming pram quilt covered in quick Vilene stick-and-stitch patchwork will keep baby snug in his pram. It is shown here made up in the following Laura Ashley furnishing cottons:
A: L571 white/rose
B: R143 white/sky blue
C: P767 rose/moss/white
D: P754 sky blue/ multi/white

Preparing the patchwork pieces

1
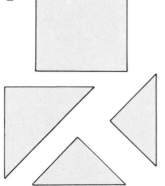

2
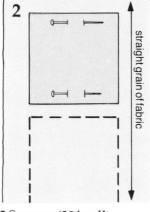

3
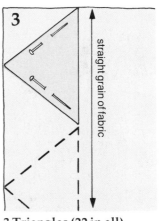

1 Making the templates
Cut 2 squares 8cm×8cm/ 3in×3in from card. Cut one of these in half diagonally to form 2 triangles, and cut one of these triangles in half again to make 2 smaller triangles. These form the templates from which you cut the fabric pieces.

2 Squares (30 in all)
Pin the square template on to colour A, making sure that two of the edges are parallel with the straight grain of the fabric. Cut round the card, allowing 1mm extra all round for a tiny overlap. Remove the card and repeat until you have 8 squares in colour A. Cut out 16 squares in colour C, and 6 squares in colour B.

3 Triangles (22 in all)
Pin the large triangle on to colour C, making sure one of the sides lies along the straight grain of the fabric, and cut round it. This time leave no extra allowance. If it suits the design of your fabric, you may prefer to place the longest side of the triangle so it runs across the straight grain.
Remove the card and repeat with each shape facing the same way, until you have 4 large triangles. Cut 18 small triangles from colour D in the same way.

Assembling the patches

Positioning the squares Pin squares on to Vilene 40×48cm/16×19in (adhesive side up), arranging them to form the pattern as on the chart on page 215. If you find this tricky, use a ruler and tailor's chalk or a pencil to mark the shapes on the Vilene. Use only one pin per piece, placing it in the centre. Overlap the patches a fraction at the edges to make neat joins and prevent gaps.

Bonding the fabrics With a warm iron (set for wool/rayon), press lightly on the fabric side over a damp cloth to bond the fabric and Vilene together. Remove pins and press again firmly on the Vilene side with a hot iron (set for cotton). Now position all the triangles as in the diagram. Lightly fix in position using small pieces of Wundaweb between the two layers of fabric and pressed with a hot iron. Alternatively, pin in place and tack around the edges.

Joining the pieces Programme your sewing machine to close zigzag for a satin stitch effect (stitch width 3mm/ ⅛in). Test this on a scrap of fabric first to check that it will cover the seams nicely without being too dense and bulky. Machine along the joins with polyester thread. Sew along all the long straight seams first, in the same direction each time. Now sew all the crosswise ones, also in the same direction. Next sew the long diagonal sides of the large triangles and finally the short sides of the small triangles. (These can be sewn in a continuous line.) Keep the fabric taut as you sew but do not stretch the patches.

Right: Zigzag stitch gives a neat finish.

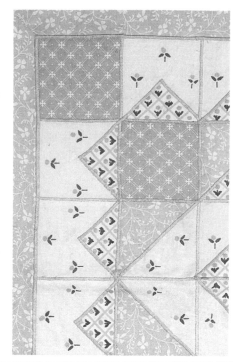

Adding the border

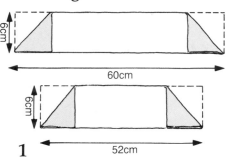

1

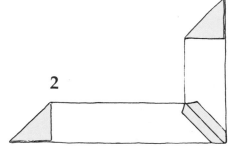

2

3

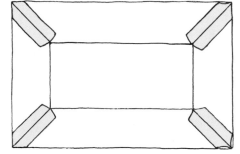

1 Cut two strips of fabric B 6cm× 52cm/2¼in×21in, and two strips 6cm×60cm/2¼in×24in. At each end of each strip, fold the corners on one side to the opposite edge as shown, forming a diagonal fold. Press flat. The resulting fold lines will be the seamlines for joining the pieces together.

2 Pin one of the short strips to one of the long strips along the seamline

fold with right sides together. Tack the seam and sew along it so that the two pieces form an L-shape. Trim seam allowance to 1.5cm/⅝in and press the seam flat. This diagonally seamed corner is called a 'mitred corner'.

3 Join the other two pieces in the same way and join the two L-shapes to form an oblong frame.

Lay the made-up patchwork section on to the centre of the other piece of Vilene (50×58cm/20×23in) leaving a 5cm/2in border. Vilene should be placed adhesive side up.

Then lay your border 'frame' in place. It should just overlap the patchwork by 1–2mm/⅛in. Press to secure. Then sew all round the inner edge of the border with zigzag stitch using the machine as before.

Backing the cover

Take the piece of backing fabric A. Place it on the front of the quilt cover with right sides together. Sew around edge with a 1cm/½in seam allowance. Leave a 25cm/10in opening in the centre of one of the shorter sides. Trim the corners diagonally and neaten the raw edges with zigzag stitch.

Turn through to right side and press

seams carefully, gently pushing out the corners with a closed pair of scissors. Neaten the raw edges of the opening and close with two medium size plastic press-studs (see diagram right) or pieces of Velcro sewn along the opening edges.

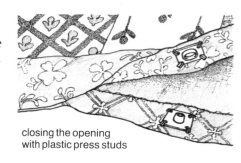

closing the opening
with plastic press studs

CHAPTER 50

Geometric wallhanging from simple pieced blocks

Many patchworks are made up from units called pieced blocks – usually identical squares of patchwork.
When they are joined together, the most beautiful geometric patterns appear, suitable for quilts, cushions or wallhangings such as the one featured here.

One of the most rewarding aspects of patchwork is that you can 'paint' a geometric masterpiece in fabric squares, even if you've never painted a picture in your life. Even the most simple of shapes can be combined to make conversation pieces.

Sometimes pieced blocks are made up by hand from patches tacked over papers. Sometimes the patches are seamed together by hand or machined without using papers. (The advantage of pieced blocks is that they do not use cornered seams, so papers are not essential.)

The simple blocks in the wallhanging shown below are made up from two basic shapes – a triangle and a series of strips of equal width which are joined by machine. They could also be sewn by hand, without papers, using running stitch.

The square pieced blocks can be treated like regular square patches – joined into long horizontal strips, then seamed together along their length.

Choosing colours

Colour plays an important part, as always in patchwork – particularly when you are working with strips. The way each strip interacts with the one next to it can make a big difference to the look of the finished work. For predominant colours and wide borders, it is a good idea to choose a muted colour – black, grey or beige, for instance – which will not fight brighter shades such as the vivid diagonal stripes in the design shown below.

Below: Traditional American patchwork designs can have a contemporary look.

Striking geometric wallhanging

This wallhanging in a dramatic colour combination looks contemporary but in fact, it is based on a traditional *Amish* design called Roman stripes, with its typical combination of bright and muted colours in plain cotton fabrics. The hanging is machine pieced and hand quilted and measures 83cm/32¾in square but you could make it whatever size you like by planning the design on graph paper and marking the measurements of squares and border.

You will need
1.30m/1⅜yd firm cotton fabric in black (A)
1.30m/1⅜yd in purple (E)
0.50m/½yd in red (B)
0.50m/½yd in deep pink (C)
0.50m/½yd in pale pink (D)
0.50m/½yd in mid brown (F)
0.30m/⅜yd in light brown (G)
1m/1yd black cotton lawn for lining
Note: all fabric requirements are based on 90cm/36in-wide fabric
1 large reel Sylko 40 thread (black)
Card *or* thin plastic sheet
For the quilting
0.90m/1yd polyester wadding (1oz or 2oz weight)

1 ball DMC pearl cotton size 12 (black) if hand quilting
1 reel black poly cotton thread if machine quilting
Betweens needles size 7
Tailor's chalk or pale crayon

Making the templates
You need one right-angled triangle with two 12cm/4¾in sides, and one strip 1.5cm/⅝in wide and 19cm/7½in long for cutting the coloured stripes. To obtain the triangle shape, either use a set-square, or graph paper, draw two 12cm/4¾in lines at right angles and join. Cut out the shapes from card, or thin plastic sheet, using a craft knife. Some patchwork specialist suppliers stock transparent plastic sheets with a square grid marked on them, specially for making templates.

Preparing the patches
Wash and press the cotton fabrics to remove any excess dye or finishing. Mark the triangle and stripe shapes on the wrong side of the fabrics by drawing round the templates with a soft lead pencil.

This pencil line will be the seamline. Allow for a generous seam of 1.5cm/⅝in (to be trimmed later) all round each shape – do not cut along the pencil lines.
Draw the triangles with one of the 12cm/4¾in sides on the straight grain, and draw the stripes running diagonally across the grain. The finished piece will then hang straight.
Following the cutting layout for the black fabric (A), draw two border strips 85cm×7cm/33½in×2¾in, two 75cm×7cm/29½in×2¾in and 25 triangles. Again, allow generous 1.5cm/⅝in seams.

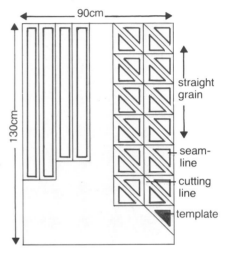

Assembling the wallhanging

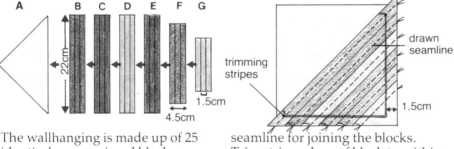

The wallhanging is made up of 25 identical square pieced blocks joined together in a square surrounded by a double border and edged with binding. To make up each block use a straight machine stitch. Pin the black triangle A to stripe B matching marked seam lines and seam, taking care not to stretch the stripes. Join B to C, C to D, D to E, E to F and F to G, as shown. Trim seams to about 8mm/⅜in and press each towards black triangle. Using the triangular template as a guide, draw another triangle on the wrong side of the sewn pieced stripes to complete the square block. This pencil line is the

seamline for joining the blocks. Trim stripe edges of block to within 1.5cm/⅝in of pencil line. Assemble 24 more blocks in this way.

Making up the panel
Machine five blocks together to form a strip, making sure that all the coloured stripes are lying in the same direction. Press all the seams towards the black triangles. Make four identical strips of five blocks each. Join all the strips together along the long edges, to make a large square. Be careful to align the corners accurately – uneven joins will affect the straightness of the diagonal lines. Trim seams and

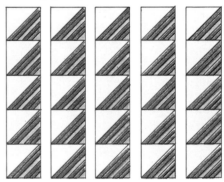

making up the panel

press towards black triangles. Press the entire panel well, unpicking and adjusting any points that do not meet properly.

Adding the borders
Join the two shorter purple side border strips (fabric E) to the sides of the patchwork along marked seamlines. Trim seams and press outwards.
Now attach the longer top and bottom border strips along marked seamlines. Again, trim seams and press outwards. Repeat with the

Next, mark and cut the purple pieces (E) – see cutting layout. This fabric is used for the thinner border strips and for binding the finished work, as well as for one of the stripes.

Draw four border strips – two 70cm×3cm/27½in×1¼in and two 65cm×3cm/25½in×1¼in (add seam allowances). Mark the binding strips – 12cm/4¾in wide. You will need about 3.50m/3¾yd in length, so cut two strips the full length of the fabric and a third strip 1m/40in long. Cut the ends diagonally for mitred seams. Now mark 25 stripes, across the

grain of the fabric in this and each of the other five colours. Make the stripes longer than you need – they can be trimmed to the required size. Obviously the red and pink ones

need to be slightly longer than the brown and purple ones. Leave 3cm/1¼in between the marked seamlines (for two seam allowances). Cut out all the pieces.

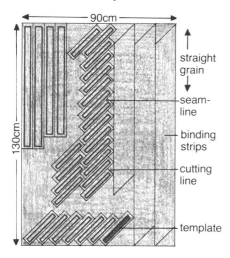

straight grain

seam-line

binding strips

cutting line

template

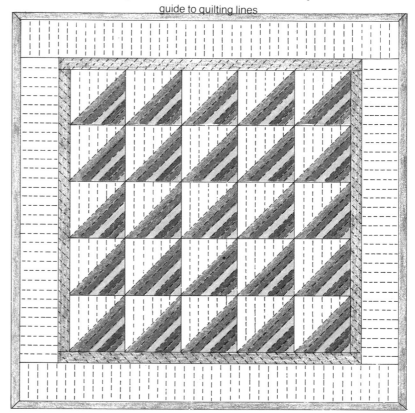

guide to quilting lines

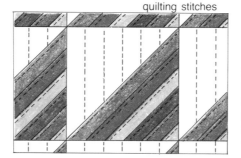

quilting stitches

four black border strips, joining the two shorter ones to the sides, and finally adding the two longer ones to the top and bottom edges. The pieced top is now complete. Press it well on both sides.

Quilting the hanging

Cut the lining and wadding slightly larger than the pieced top. Tack the three layers together, beginning at the centre and working outwards, smoothing out the wrinkles as you go. The quilting can be worked by hand (using black pearl cotton thread) or by machine (using black poly cotton thread).

By hand Mount the tacked layers on a frame if you have one, otherwise support the work on your lap. Run the lengths of pearl cotton through a block of beeswax for extra strength.

The lines of quilting which follow each stripe should run very close to the seams on the stripes – about 2mm/⅛in away on the lower (non-seam allowance side). On the black

triangles, the quilting lines should run in five equally spaced vertical lines (2cm/¾in apart).

Mark the quilting lines on the black fabric with a ruler and tailor's chalk pencil or a pale crayon. The lines on the coloured stripes can be easily judged without marking. On the purple border, the quilting lines run diagonally and are 2cm/¾in apart. On the black border, the lines run straight – vertically at the top and bottom, horizontally at the sides. Remove the work from the frame and brush off quilting marks. Remove all tacking stitches. Trim lining and wadding flush with the patchwork top.

By machine Position the lines of quilting as described for the handstitched method. Set the machine to a medium straight stitch, and begin quilting in the middle of the work. When the quilting is complete, work any loose thread ends in to the back of the work with a needle.

Binding the edges

Join purple binding strips with diagonal seams to obtain a long strip slightly longer than the perimeter (length all round) of the quilt. Fold the strip in half lengthwise so that its width is 6cm/2¼in, and press. Stitch binding to right side of quilt with raw edges matching, and allowing a 1.5cm/⅝in seam. Mitre the corners (see Quick mitred corners, page 213), and slipstitch folded edge in place on the back.

To hang Attach two small rings, or fabric tabs to the back of the quilt through which you can insert a piece of dowel for hanging.

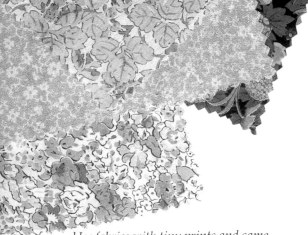

CHAPTER 51

Patchwork cushions from pieced triangles

Here is a method for joining triangular patchwork which ensures a neat finish for those tricky corners. At the same time, learn how to mix and match fabric remnants to make this set of pretty colour co-ordinated cushions in traditional designs.

Use fabrics with tiny prints and same-sized designs for patchwork cushions.

Part of the skill of professional-looking patchwork is knowing how to choose the right colours, prints and weights of fabric. For cushion covers such as the ones shown here, make sure you use good-quality cotton fabrics which are completely non-stretchy and do not fray easily.
Remember to wash and press all the fabrics before using them in case of shrinkage.

Choosing the colours

There's an art in mixing patchwork prints – tiny prints are more suitable than large, bold ones. These cushions have a predominant colour in pale and dark tones, plus two secondary colours.
The predominant-colour prints each include a little of the secondary colours giving a harmonious effect – each of the blue prints here has a little pink and green in it.
Instructions are given in this chapter for a pair of cushions in pinwheel and lattice designs with all the small triangles in pale and dark blues, and pale green outer triangles. By switching the colours around and substitut-

ing the pale for dark fabrics, different parts of the design predominate and a totally different effect is produced.
A pair of cushions can be made up to match a room's colour scheme and it is worth taking the trouble to make a coloured sketch of the design first. You may need to change the colours round to get the best effect.

Right: Carefully chosen prints combined in pairs for toning patchwork cushions will add softness and style to a bedroom or sitting room. Or you could make up just one of them for a pretty present.

Pinwheel and lattice-patterned patchwork cushions

This pair of cushions, one of each design, are made up in the same fabrics and look most effective together. Alternative colourways are shown right.
The cushions are machine sewn and machine quilted. The quilting is not essential but it is simple to do and does make all the difference to the finished patchwork.

You will need

For a pair of cushions, one lattice and one pinwheel design
25cm/¼yd each of four 90cm/36in cotton print fabrics dark blue, pale blue, pale green and pink
50cm/½yd extra of one of these or a plain toning fabric for cushion backs
50cm/½yd polyester wadding (4oz weight)
Cotton threads to match each print
Two 40cm/15in cushion pads
Two 30cm/12in zips in a colour to match cushion backs
Graph paper and stiff card, at least 20cm×30cm/8in×12in
Pencil, ruler, craft knife and glue

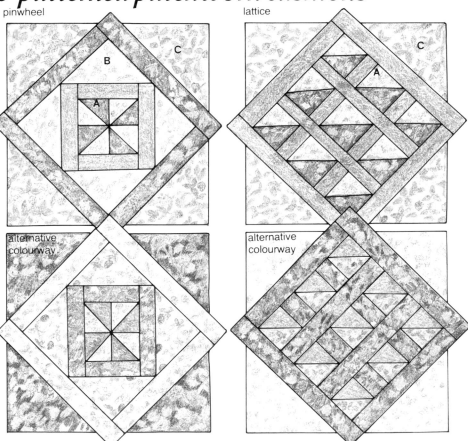

Making templates and cutting out

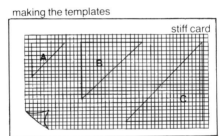

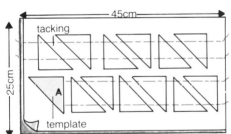

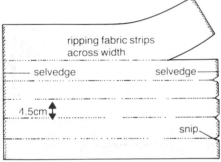

The templates

You need three triangular templates of varying sizes. On graph (squared) paper, mark three isosceles triangles – each with one right angle and two equal sides of 9cm/3⅝in (A), 15cm/5⅞in (B), and 20cm/8in (C).

Paste these on to stiff card and cut out very carefully using a ruler and craft knife. These templates include a seam allowance of 6mm/¼in.

Triangles Cut one piece 45cm/18in wide from the lengths of pale and dark blue fabric. With right sides together, press and work four rows of tacking about 7cm/3in apart. Trace 13 times round template A on the wrong side of the paler fabric, using a ball-point pen or pencil. These are the cutting lines and will not show on the front of the patchwork. Be very accurate and do not pull the fabric.

Cut out all the triangles using sharp scissors – do not remove the tacking. From template C, trace and cut eight corner triangles in the green fabric, using a single fabric thickness. For the pinwheel design only, cut four B triangles in pale blue.

Strips For both of the designs you need lengths of pink strips 4.5cm/1¾in wide and totalling 3m/120in. For the pinwheel design only you also need 1.25m/50in of strips the same width in dark blue. Three widths of the remaining 25cm×45cm/10in×18in piece of blue fabric should be sufficient. Mark 4.5cm/1¾in intervals along the fabric selvedge. You may have to waste the first few centimetres at the top to get the first strip straight. Snip the marks with scissors and rip quickly and firmly across the width of the fabric – you may have to snip through the other selvedge, too. Steam press the strips to flatten the edges.

221

Assembling the pinwheel design

1 stitching the A triangles

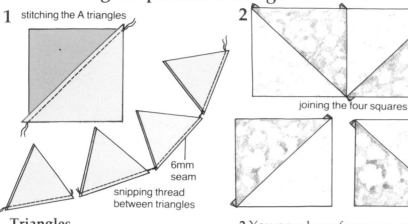

6mm seam

snipping thread between triangles

2

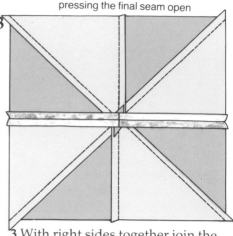

joining the four squares

pressing the final seam open

3

Triangles

1 Take four of the 13 pairs of A triangles. With dark blue thread in the machine needle and bobbin, stitch each pair together along long edges, with a 6mm/¼in seam. It is most important to keep the seam an even 6mm/¼in but it is not necessary to snip off the thread between each pair – just stitch them in a 'chain'.
Cut the four pieces apart, remove tacking and press seams towards the darker triangles.

2 You now have four squares – arrange them on the table in a pinwheel. Stitch them together in two pairs, with right sides together, again taking a 6mm/¼in seam. Press seams towards the darker triangles.

3 With right sides together join the two pairs, matching centre seams exactly to give a neat centre where the eight seams meet. This is more important than matching edges. Press this final seam open on the wrong side. Steam press the whole piece on the right side, pulling it into a perfect square shape if necessary.

Assembling the lattice design

7 stitching the C triangles

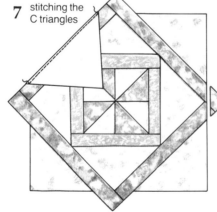

joining squares to strips

1

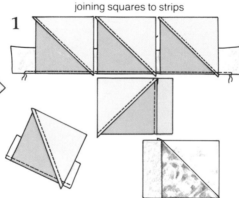

joining to make three strips

2

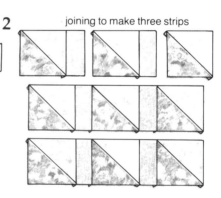

7 Finish off by adding the four large green C triangles. The patchwork now measures about 43cm/17in square. Snip off the protruding corners of the blue strips, steam press and spray starch the patchwork, ready for quilting.

Triangles

Take the remaining nine pairs of A triangles and stitch each pair together as for the pinwheel design. Open out and press seams towards dark triangles to form nine squares.
1 Take a length of pink strip and right sides together, stitch six squares along the edge, taking a 6mm/¼in seam. The squares should be close to each other but not overlapping, with all the dark triangles in the same position. Cut the strip between each square, open out and press seams towards strip.

2 You now have six squares with pink strip borders, and three without. Join these nine pieces into three strips, taking 6mm/¼in seams as usual and pressing seams towards pink strips. Take care to keep all the squares the same way up.

4

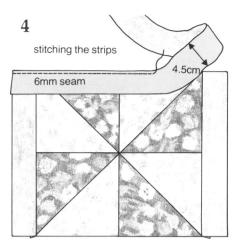

stitching the strips

6mm seam

4.5cm

Strips

Take one of the pink strips and lay it right sides together along one of the edges of the square. Sew the strips with a 6mm/¼in seam, then cut the strip off flush with the patchwork before opening it out.

4 Join the strip to the opposite edge in the same way and cut it off. Press seams outwards. Now sew the strip to the other two sides as shown, trim ends flush with first strips, and press seams outwards.

5

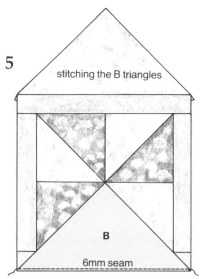

stitching the B triangles

B

6mm seam

Outer strips and triangles

5 Join on the pale blue B triangles two at a time, on opposite sides of the square. Make sure you keep the outer points of the triangles in line with the central seams of the pinwheel square. Press the first two seams outwards (towards the triangle) before adding the other two triangles.

6

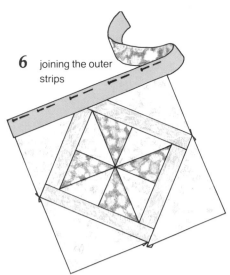

joining the outer strips

6 At this point, you may find that the edges of the patchwork do not look absolutely straight. Do not worry about this, but continue by adding the dark blue strips to the edges of this larger square. Proceed exactly as before, but cut and pin the strips in place *before* stitching to make sure all the pieces align correctly. In some places, the seam allowance may need to be wider than 6mm/¼in. Make sure you sew each strip parallel to the one opposite. Press seams outwards as you sew each strip.

3

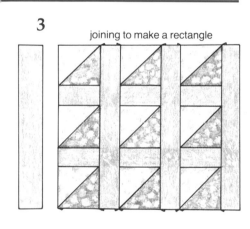

joining to make a rectangle

3 Cut four pink strips to the same length as these pieced strips, and stitch strips and squares alternately to form a large rectangle. Keep the squares aligned across the rectangle and make sure that all the pale and dark triangles are in the same position in each row. Press all seams towards pink strips.

Right: Here's the lattice design worked in apricot and rust with a touch of blue. Notice how the paler triangles stand out from the other prints.

Outer strips and triangles

4 Cut two more lengths of the pink strip to the length of the longer side of the rectangle and join these on as shown. Press seams outwards.
5 Add the four green C triangles to each edge as for the pinwheel design, making sure the outer points are centred. Open out the triangles and press seams outwards. Snip off the protruding pink corners. The finished square measures about 43cm/17in. Steam press and spray starch.

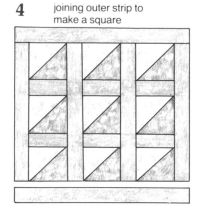

4 joining outer strip to make a square

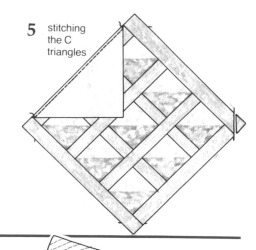

5 stitching the C triangles

Quilting the cushions

For each cushion, cut a square of wadding the same size as the patchwork. Pin the patchwork pieces over the wadding. Quilt the parts in the same colour on both cushions at the same time to save having to change the colour of thread too often.

It is a good idea to test the machine tension on a scrap of fabric and wadding before quilting the actual covers.

Using pale blue thread in the needle (the bobbin colour does not matter) set the stitch to a medium straight stitch.

Beginning at the centre of the pinwheel cushion, quilt along each seam of the central wheel.

Quilt in the seamline, stitching steadily and taking care not to waver over to the bulkier side of the seam. Finish off by pulling the needle threads through to the back

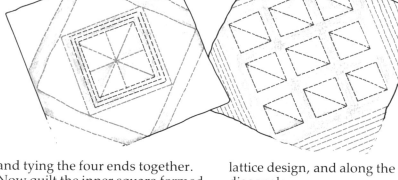

pinwheel

lattice

and tying the four ends together. Now quilt the inner square formed by the long edges of the larger pale blue triangles and finally the outer square formed by the other two edges. Finish off the ends on the back as before.

Using pink thread in the needle, add three or four parallel lines round the square pink strips on the pinwheel cushion. Now quilt round each of the nine squares on the

lattice design, and along the diagonals.

Using green thread in the needle, quilt across the long edges of the green corner triangles on both cushions. If you like, carry on quilting to the outer corners in parallel lines about 8mm/⅜in apart to give added relief and texture. There's no need to tie off the ends as they will be caught in the seam when the back is attached.

Making up

Cut a piece of fabric measuring 42cm×45cm/16½in×17½in for each cushion back. Fold over a third of the fabric, right sides together, along the longer edge.

Mark and stitch a 1.5cm/½in seam leaving a central gap of 30cm/12in for inserting the zip. Cut right across on fold and press seam open. Set zip into opening using a zip foot if your machine has one. Steam press the back.

Joining back and front Using a light pencil or water-erasable marker, draw a 38cm/15in square on the wrong side of the back. This is the seamline. (A square template cut from card is useful for doing this.) Open the zip a little and place the

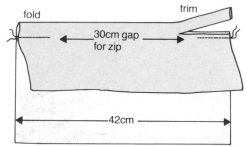

fold   trim

30cm gap for zip

42cm

cushion back and front right sides together, centring the design carefully on the backing. Pin, and sew round on the seamlines, rounding off the corners a little if you wish. Make sure there is no puckering on the patchwork. Trim seam to about 6mm/¼in to reduce bulk of wadding. Turn, steam press edges lightly and insert cushion pad.

Alternative quilting

If your machine has a decorative machine embroidery feature, this can be used instead of a straight-line stitch for the quilting. Worked in a contrasting colour, it really adds a professional touch to the work (see below). Check that the bobbin is full before starting to quilt because thread is used up very quickly in decorative stitches.

224

CHAPTER 52

Dresden Plate: a patchwork pattern in a circle

*This old American patchwork design is so called because the
circular motifs worked in floral prints
remind one of china plates. One motif pieced and quilted
makes a striking place mat while several
motifs backed on squares make a traditional quilt.*

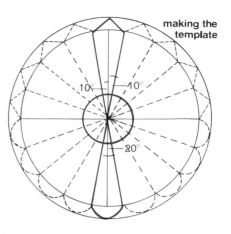

making the
template

This American pattern is a combination of pieced patchwork and appliqué and was particularly popular in the 1930s. It derives from an older pattern called Friendship Ring, so named because people used to exchange bits of fabric to make up their designs.

The circular Dresden Plate motif can be divided into as many petals (segments) as you like. The petal tips can be rounded or pointed and the ends are covered by a central circle of fabric which is stitched on last. Any number of different patterns can be used within the motif – tiny patterned prints are most effective – and the central circle is sometimes cut from a plain fabric for contrast. The petals can be stitched by hand or machine and traditionally the flower shapes are then appliquéd by hand on to squares of contrasting or complementary backing fabric to form blocks which can be made up into a highly attractive quilt.

Making your own template

Dresden Plate templates are available from craft shops but only in a limited number of sizes.

To cut your own accurate templates first decide on the size of the circle you want. If you are making a quilt you should also consider the size of the square blocks you plan to use.

Take a piece of strong card and draw a circle to the required size using compasses and a hard, sharp pencil. With the same centre point draw a smaller circle about 1cm/½in within the first circle.

Using a metal ruler draw horizontal and vertical lines at right angles to each other through the central point to cut the circle into quarters.

Decide on the number of petals you wish to divide the circle into. There are 360° in a circle so it is a good idea to choose a number which divides easily into 360. For example, if you choose 18, this would mean that each petal requires 20°.

Using a protractor, measure and mark 10° either side of the central vertical line. Draw two lines from the centre through the two marks to the outer circle. Re-set the compasses and draw a small circle for the centre. The petals can be pointed or curved. Join the edges of the petal where they cut the inner circle to the central line at the edge of the outer circle for pointed petals, or draw a freehand curve to touch the outer circle at the same point for curved petals.

If you wish to increase or decrease the overall size of the circle, then simply lengthen or shorten the outside edges of the petal.

Carefully cut out the two templates using a craft knife. Mark the straight grain along the central line of the petal template.

Right: These red and white prints make pretty, fresh-looking mats but you could equally well use a selection of multi-coloured cotton scraps.

Dresden Plate place mats

Each of these mats is made from one Dresden Plate motif using two pretty matching prints, one light, one dark. The 20cm/8in diameter mats are machine pieced, quilted, and the edges neatly bound with bias strips of the darker fabric, so there is no need to finish the outer edges of the petals before you join them.

You will need for a pair of mats

30cm/⅜yd light printed cotton
  fabric A
50cm/½yd dark printed cotton
  fabric B
30cm/⅜yd white cotton fabric
30cm/⅜yd 4oz polyester wadding *or*
  60cm/⅝yd cotton wadding (used

  double thickness)
Note: fabric and wadding
  requirements are based on 90cm/
  36in width fabric
Matching sewing thread
Firm card and soft pencil
Tracing paper, scrap of plain paper

You will need for four mats

50cm/½yd fabric A
80cm/1yd fabric B
60cm/⅝yd white cotton fabric
60cm/⅝yd polyester wadding *or*
  90cm/1yd cotton wadding
Other materials as above

Preparing the patches

Make your own templates or trace

the petal and circle template shapes from the page and cut them out in firm card.

Place the petal template on the wrong side of fabric A, positioning it upright on the straight grain of the fabric. Draw carefully round the edge of the template with a soft pencil.

Allowing a 1cm/½in seam allowance all round, mark five more petals on fabric A for each mat and six petals on fabric B.

Cutting out the patches

Carefully cut out six petals from fabric A and six from fabric B. The outlines drawn round the templates on the wrong side of the fabric will be the seamlines.

225

Assembling the mat

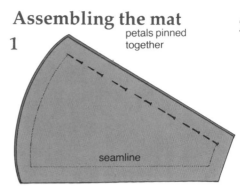

1 petals pinned together

seamline

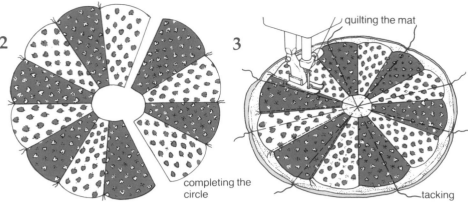

2 completing the circle

3 quilting the mat

tacking

1 With right sides together, pin the petals in pairs along long edges. Each pair has one fabric A piece and one fabric B piece. Make sure the pencil lines are aligned as you pin. Machine each pair along one seamline using a small stitch. Each mat needs six pairs of petals.
2 Join the pairs into fours in the same way, then join the three sets of four into the 12-piece circle. Press seams in the same direction.

Quilting the mat Use the pieced motif as a guide to cut a circle of wadding and a circle of white fabric, both a little larger than the motif. Make a sandwich of the wadding between the motif and the backing. Pin and tack the three layers.
3 Using a small machine stitch, quilt along each petal seam on the top (patchwork) side. Work from the outside to the centre and keep as close to the join as possible, without

catching in either of the neighbouring petals, so that the quilting line is 'sunk' between the petals. Stop stitching 1cm/½in from inner edges and fasten off threads.
Adding the centre circles Using the circle template, cut out two circles in fabric A remembering to leave a 1cm/½in seam allowance. Use the same template to cut out two paper circles without seam allowance.

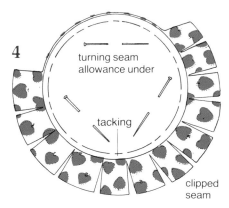

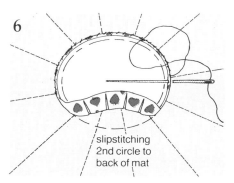

4 Centre a paper circle on the right side of a fabric circle. Pin and tack round the edge. Clip the seam allowance almost to the edge of the paper and press allowance to the wrong side. Tack down the seam allowance using the edge of the paper circle as a guide to ensure a neat circular edge. Press with a hot iron.

Tack a neatened circle to the centre front of the mat to cover the raw inner petal edges and seam ends.

5 Stab stitch close to the edge of the appliquéd circle.
To work stab stitch make tiny invisible running stitches on the top layer of fabric, and longer ones on the back, stabbing the needle vertically up and down through all layers. Remove all tacking and paper.

6 Prepare a second circle in the same way and slipstitch to the centre back of the mat. Remove tacking and paper.
Binding the edges Cut bias strips from a 30cm/12in deep piece of fabric B. Each strip should be 3cm/1¼in wide. You need about 90cm/36in of binding per mat so join strips diagonally. To join two strips, fold under a corner of each at 45° and press. Place strips right sides facing. Match creases, stitch and trim.

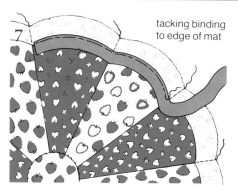

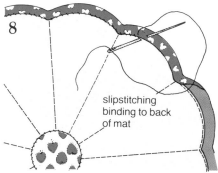

7 With right sides together, tack binding round top edge of mat, easing it carefully round the scalloped edge as you go. Machine stitch all round, about 6mm/¼in from the edge of the patches. Trim

off surplus wadding and backing neatly, flush with the patchwork.
8 Fold binding to the back of the mat, turn under raw edge and slipstitch in place.

Matching basket cosy

Make a matching basket cosy to cover an existing basket, adjusting the two templates as described below.

You will need
20cm/¼yd fabric A
30cm/⅜yd fabric B
50cm/½yd wadding
50cm/½yd white cotton fabric
All other materials as given for mats

Making up the cosy
Cut templates and patches to the required size. The finished motif is larger than the place mats, but has

the same number of petals, so extend the long edges of the template accordingly at both ends. The circular template is also larger. Make up in exactly the same way as the place mats, except for the top centre patch. To make a padded button for picking up the cosy, hem one of the larger circles with small tacking stitches, using a doubled thread. Draw the thread up slightly, insert pieces of chopped wadding to pad firmly, and draw it up tight into a knob. Stitch in place to cover all raw edges at centre.

Trace pattern for templates

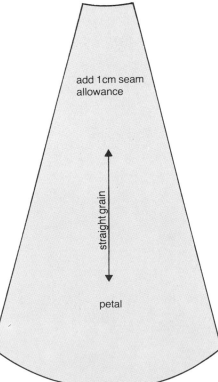

centre circle

add 1cm seam allowance

add 1cm seam allowance

straight grain

petal

CHAPTER 53

Log cabin pattern for patchwork

Log cabin originated in Britain, but is an important part of the North American patchwork tradition. The simple strip shapes create stunning colour effects which can be combined to make a variety of overall patterns for quilts, cushions and clothes.

Constructing a basic block

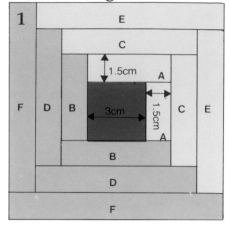

Log cabin is a very well-known pieced block patchwork pattern which is built up by laying strips – the cabin logs – around a central square patch. The use of dark and light strips in the same block is strikingly effective. Usually, half the block is worked in dark colours and half in light creating an effect of light and shadow.

The finished blocks can be joined together to produce a number of different overall patterns, and many of the early American patchwork quilts use this pattern in delightfully original ways.

Traditionally the patches were stitch-

Below: Single block in toning colours.

ed together by hand, but they can also be pieced together quickly by machine. Although templates were not normally used, a quick method using a template strip guide to make the blocks is given right.

Choosing fabrics

Dressweight cottons are the most suitable for this kind of patchwork. For the strips you will need an equal number of dark and light fabrics with the colours shading from light to medium in the first group and medium to dark in the second.

The central square should be plain and unrelated to the strip fabrics to help highlight the design.

This quick method is ideal for large projects as several blocks can be under construction at once which saves time.

1 Make a simple diagram of a finished block to help you calculate the ideal strip size. The centre square can be any size but twice the width of a strip looks about right. The block in the example has three strips each side of the centre square. Cut two templates from card or plastic, one 3cm/1¼in square and one 1.5cm/⅝in wide and the length of the block – in this case 12cm/5in.

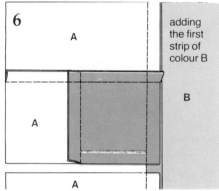

6 Now take a strip of colour B (the first of the darker colour group) and lay several of the three-piece blocks along it as before, right sides together, edges matching. The side laid flush to the long edge of the strip of colour B should be the side of the block with the centre colour and the *second* strip of colour A. Mark the seamline and machine along it. Join on as many blocks as necessary, cut apart and trim edges flush.

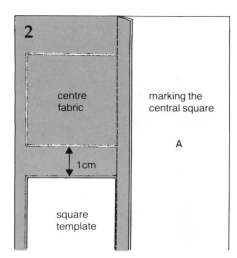

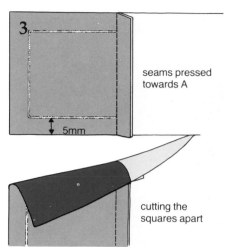

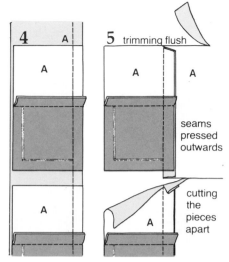

The block is made up of six different fabrics, A-F, plus the contrast fabric for the centre square. Divide them into two colour groups, A, C and E are the lighter fabrics and B, D and F are the darker fabrics.

Cut a series of strips 4cm/1½in wide across the grain using the whole width of the fabric. This includes seam allowances. Cut strips from all the fabrics including the centre square fabric.

Take one of the strips of colour A and lay it right sides together on a strip of the centre colour, matching the edges. Using a ruler and a

washable embroidery marker, draw a line along the strip, 5mm/¼in from one long edge and machine along this line. Press seam towards colour A.

2 Lay the square template on the wrong side of the centre colour strip with one side of the template butting up to the machined seamline. Mark out a series of squares at 1cm/½in intervals along the whole length of the strip.

3 Cut the squares apart, exactly halfway between each one. You will now have a series of pieces made up of the centre colour and colour A.

4 Lay up to four of these two-colour pieces right sides together on a further strip of colour A making sure one of the two-coloured sides is flush with one long edge of the new strip. Extend the marked line on the centre square across the pieces and machine in place. Continue adding pieces along the strip as necessary.

5 Cut the pieces apart as before, trimming the edges flush with the first two pieces to be joined. Press seams outwards from the centre.

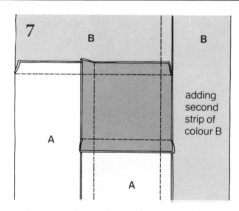

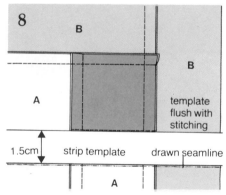

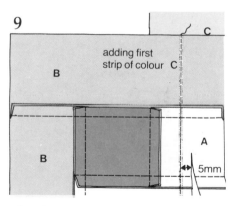

7 Lay the last edge of centre colour on a further strip of colour B, mark, machine and cut apart. Press seams outwards and trim the finished pieces to a square. The centre square is now completely surrounded.

8 Take the strip template and lay it on the wrong side of the block, with one edge along the stitched line of the centre square and on the side of the block with *three* patches and two seams. Draw a line along the other edge of the template. This gives the seamline for the next strip to be added.

9 Lay two or three blocks on to a strip of colour C, right sides together and edges matching and machine along the marked seamline. Cut blocks apart, trim seam to 5mm/¼in pieces and press outwards. Add a second strip of colour C in exactly the same way using the template strip to mark the seamline.

Continue adding on strips outwards, working round the square and trimming and pressing seams outwards after stitching until you have completed the block. There

should be the same number of strips on all sides of the centre square. Always remember that the first strip of a new round should be added to the side with *two* seams, using the template strip to mark the seamline.

Joining the blocks

When joining log cabin blocks try to avoid joining two identically coloured outer strips together. Either vary the outer strip fabrics or simply use a single outer strip to join the blocks together.

Chunky kimono-style jacket

The edges of this cosy quilted jacket are bound with the brilliant red fabric used for the centre square patches. It is worked almost entirely by machine, with a little hand finishing. The jacket shown here is made up in the largest size, for a medium/large jacket, make smaller blocks using colours A to J only (J and I will be the dividing strips) and for a small/ medium jacket, make blocks with colours A to H only (H and G will be the dividing strips). The instructions are based on making up the large jacket, you may need to add an extra row of blocks to the ends of the sleeves and bottom of the jacket to obtain the required length for the small size. This can easily be calculated by using the·diagram right.

Calculating fabric

The log cabin blocks used in this jacket have strips with a finished width of 1.5cm/⅝in. The centre square is 3cm/1¼in wide.

Draw an accurate diagram of one log cabin block for whatever size you are making to calculate how much fabric you need in each colour. Multiply the length of strips required for each colour (add about 9cm/3½in for seams) by the total number of blocks in the jacket (48). Now divide by 90cm/36in (being the width of the fabric) and multiply by 4cm/1½in (the width of each strip including seam allowances). The result will be the length of 90cm/36in-wide fabric you need. Round it up to the nearest 5cm/⅛yd.

You will need

For a large jacket:
1m/1⅛yd plain fabric in contrast tone for block centres and trim
2½m/2¾yd extra of one of the strip fabrics for lining
Light fabrics A: 30cm/⅜yd, C: 40cm/½yd, E: 55cm/⅝yd, G: 70cm/ ¾yd, I: 75cm/⅞yd, K: 80cm/⅞yd
Dark fabrics B: 35cm/⅜yd, D: 50cm/ ½yd, F: 60cm/⅝yd, H: 75cm/⅞yd, J: 85cm/1yd, L: 80cm/⅞yd
(All fabric allowances are based on 90cm/36in wide fabric)
3m/3¼yd Terylene 2oz wadding
3m/3¼yd firm Vilene interfacing
1 reel Sericum mercerised machine

twist No 60 (1000 metres) in medium shade of main colour
1 reel thread to match lining fabric
65cm/25½in open-ended zip

Making a pattern for the jacket

Cut the piece of Vilene in half, widthwise and join the two pieces halfway (for centre back) with a 1cm/½in seam. Mark and cut out the jacket cross shape to full size using the diagram to help you. Pin the side and underarm seams and try on to check size and sleeve and jacket length. Adjust as necessary. Open out pattern and mark the position of each log cabin block in pencil on the Vilene. You can then pin the finished blocks on to the Vilene as they are completed.
The jacket front and back each have sixteen blocks and each sleeve has eight blocks. Four blocks make up a pattern square.

Above: The log cabin pattern is an ideal choice for square-cut garments like this jacket. It is made up from tones of blue cotton prints, with a contrasting centre square.

Making up the blocks

Cut out all the 4cm/1¼in wide strips across the grain of the fabric. Lay out strips to see how the finished square will look. You may wish to change a fabric or alter the order. Make two card or plastic templates – one 3cm/1¼in square and one strip 1.5cm/⅝in wide and the length of one block, in this case 21cm/8¼in. Thread up a number of machine bobbins with the medium-shade thread – log cabin uses a great deal of thread. Stitch the fabric strips together using a fine needle and following the sequence given on the previous page until you have four blocks completed as far as colour J.

Joining the blocks together

1

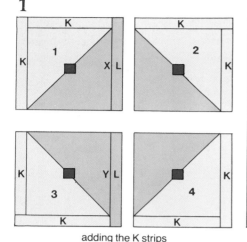

adding the K strips

2

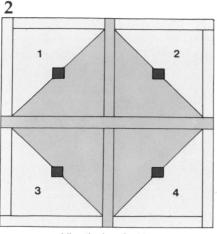

adding the long L strips

3

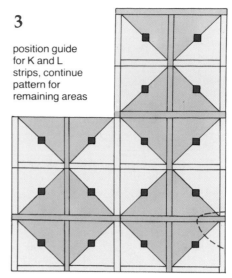

position guide for K and L strips, continue pattern for remaining areas

These blocks are to be joined into a square with the dark corners on the inside. To avoid having a double band of colour L only one strip is added to join the blocks together.
1 Add colour K on two sides of each block in the usual way. Lay the blocks out in a square as shown. Blocks 1 and 2 are separated by a single strip of colour L and similarly blocks 3 and 4.
Add a strip of colour L to block 1 on the side marked X and to block 3 on the side marked Y.
Lay the strip template on the wrong side of block 1 with the edge along the seamline joining strips J and L. Mark the new seamline on strip L.

With right sides together, match inner seamline of strip J, block 2, to outer seamline of strip J, block 1, and stitch along marked seamline on strip L.
Join block 3 and 4 in the same way, trim and press seams outwards.
2 Now join a long strip of colour L to the bottom of blocks 1 and 2 along the second colour strips J. Mark with the template, machine and press. Join this strip to blocks 3 and 4 by marking and stitching as before. You now have a block of four squares with a dark cross in the centre.
Similarly, when joining four light corners, join on only a single strip

of colour K (the darkest of the light colours) between blocks.
3 Make up all remaining blocks as far as colour J, and pin out on the Vilene jacket shape to see where the single strips of colours K and L are needed. The dividing strips of colour L (the darkest blue) should run continuously vertically and horizontally across the patchwork, interrupting the dividing strips of colour K. So join the K strips first. When you have assembled the completed blocks in a cross shape, remembering to leave centre front open, cut away half of the two blocks along each underarm edge as shown using the Vilene as a guide.

Positioning guide for strips

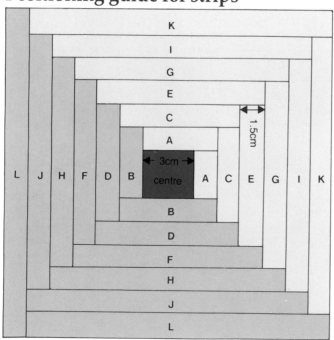

Positioning guide for blocks

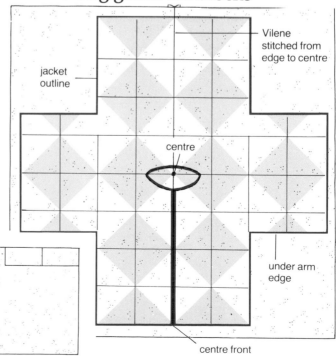

jacket outline

Vilene stitched from edge to centre

centre

under arm edge

centre front

231

Making up the jacket

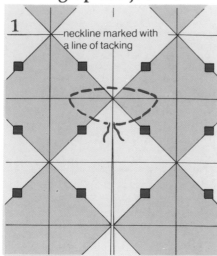

1 neckline marked with a line of tacking

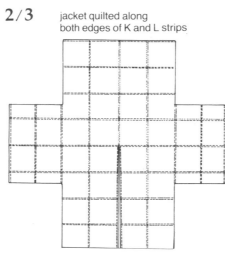

2/3 jacket quilted along both edges of K and L strips

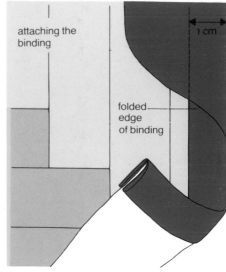

attaching the binding

1 cm

folded edge of binding

1 Mark the position of the neck edge with tacking. Mark a gentle curve from the centre top to the centre side of the two upper centre front blocks. Dip neckline down slightly at back. Use the Vilene pattern to cut out the jacket shape in lining fabric and wadding. Lay out the lining, wrong side up, and place the wadding and patchwork, right side up, on top. Pin carefully in the centre of each block, tack all layers securely together with a series of diagonal lines.

2 Thread the bobbin with thread to match the lining, set a medium stitch and quilt along all the horizontal strips of colours K and L on both edges of each strip, except for the outer edges of the lower edge strips. You will have to roll up part of the jacket under the machine arm to do this.

3 When the horizontal quilting is complete, begin at the centre back and quilt along both edges of all the vertical strips of colours K and L except for the outer edges of the front and sleeve edge strips. You can also quilt round the edges of each centre square by hand if you wish to.

Remove tacking, trim edges neatly and trim neck edge to within 1cm/ ½in of tacked edge. Fold jacket in half along shoulder line so that front and back right sides are together and tack the two side and underarm seams. Try on and make any fitting adjustments at this stage. Machine side/underarm seams with a 1.5cm/⅝in seam..Trim all fabrics close to stitching except back seam allowance of lining. Lap back lining allowance over raw seam and hem.

Trim centre front, cuffs and bottom edge to neaten.

Finishing off

Cut bias strips of centre square fabric 6cm/2¼in wide and fold and press in half. Apply bias trim round bottom edge by tacking binding to jacket with raw edges matching, and machining 1cm/½in from the edge. Hem folded edge to seamline on inside. Repeat for neck, front and cuff edges.

To close the front, use an open-ended zip (or see Design Extra). Tack zip in place so that bias-trimmed edges meet exactly when it is closed. Stitch zip in place by hand along bias trim seamlines. Hem edges of zip webbing to jacket lining on inside.

DESIGN EXTRA

Log cabin pattern variations

You can assemble finished log cabin blocks in all kinds of ways. Many traditional quilts are made up in patterns which radiate out from the centre point – these are not so suitable for smaller items.

If you think of each block being made up of a light and a dark triangle, you can design your own jacket pattern. Here are three ideas which show how you can give an effect of diagonal stripes, bold zigzags, or all-over triangles. Instead of an open-ended zip you could use fabric ties to close the jacket – or simply wrap it over and tie with a bold sash.

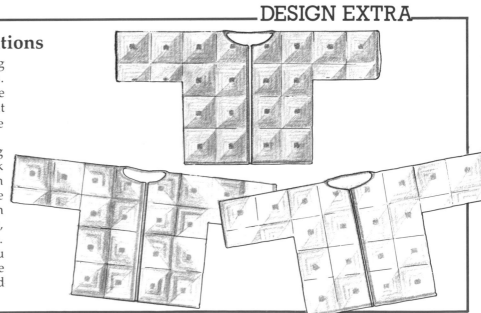

CHAPTER 54

Pattern variations in Seminole patchwork

*This traditional form of patchwork can be speedily assembled
by machine although accurate measuring
and cutting are essential. Simply by joining straight strips
of fabric, cutting and rearranging them
you can create a wealth of dramatic geometric patterning.*

Although Seminole patchwork is based on traditional designs, it has always been a technique most suited to the machine. By joining together strips of bright fabric, cutting the strips into pieces and reassembling them in an offset position, a wide range of decorative bands of patchwork can be created.

The Seminole Indians used this form of patchwork to decorate clothing and it is best used for straight bands of decoration either inserted in or applied to a garment.

By varying the number and width of the strips and the way in which you cut and reassemble the pieces, you can make numerous patterns.

Join a series of different bands together with banding strips to form a panel for the bib front of a child's dress or dungarees. Try incorporating ribbon or narrow lace on your fabric strips and as well as clothing, use Seminole patchwork on all kinds of bags, cushions, quilts, purses, pincushions, tablemats and other home projects.

Right: The ideal way to match up your separates: add a Seminole patchwork trim made from co-ordinating prints. The top and trousers make a smart, but casual, outfit.

Equipment
Apart from your sewing machine, you need an iron, pins, sharp scissors, a clear plastic ruler and a fabric marker – either a soft pencil, dressmaker's chalk pencil or a water-erasable marker.

Fabrics should be non-stretchy and firmly woven. Choose non-slip fabrics of a similar weight. Do not choose fabrics which are bulky when seamed together, or difficult to press. Pure cotton, Tana lawn and cotton/polyester blends are all suitable. For best results, use strongly contrasting fabric – plain colours and small, all-over prints.

Cutting and marking the fabric
Press the fabric and fold with right sides together, selvedge to selvedge. Use a ruler to mark the straight crosswise grain at right angles to the selvedges. This will help you to cut all the strips straight from that piece of fabric.

Stitch all pieces with 5mm/¼in seams (this means you should cut all strips 1cm/½in wider than the required finished size.) Check the width of your machine presser foot as these often measure 5mm/¼in and can be used as a seaming guide.

It is very important to cut fabric accurately and make all seams straight.

Chain sewing
When machining pieces together, save time by chain sewing (see pages 222-223, Assembling the pinwheel design). When all the cut pieces are joined in pairs, snip the joining threads and join pairs of pairs together in the same way. Proceed with this method until you have assembled a complete Seminole band.

Careful pressing is essential. Wherever possible, press all seams in one direction and check that the right side of the patchwork is perfectly smooth.

Finishing the patchwork
As your pieced strips will end up with jagged edges, you need banding strips to finish and neaten them. This provides a firm edge along which to attach the patchwork. Always cut banding strips on the straight grain of the fabric.

Stitching a simple Seminole pattern

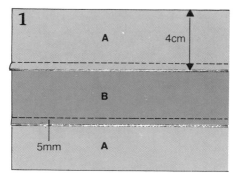

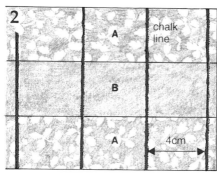

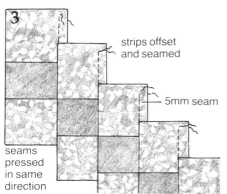

strips offset and seamed

5mm seam

seams pressed in same direction

1 On the crosswise grain of both fabrics, cut two strips of fabric A, 4cm/1½in wide and one strip of fabric B, also 4cm/1½in wide. Seam these three strips together with fabric B in the centre, taking 5mm/¼in seams, and press both seams in the same direction.

2 On the right side of the fabric, mark strips at 4cm/1½in intervals. Make sure your marked lines are at exact right angles to the seamlines. Cut along all the marked lines.
3 Place two joined pieces with long sides together, right sides facing. Slide the top piece along so that the

area of colour B diagonally adjoins the area of colour B on the lower piece. Seam the pieces together in this position and chain sew all the other pairs at the same time. Continue joining until the required length is reached. Press all seams in the same direction.

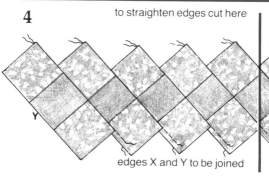

to straighten edges cut here

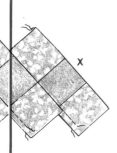

edges X and Y to be joined

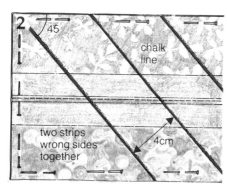

two strips fabric C joined to patchwork

4 To straighten the ends of the strip cut straight across the strip cutting one of the colour B squares diagonally in half. Now join the two diagonal-edged ends together, leaving the two straight edges at

either end of the patchwork.
5 Cut two banding strips in colour C, the length of the patchwork. Lay one strip along one side of the patchwork, right sides together and stitch in place. The stitching line

should touch each outer corner of the colour B squares. Repeat on opposite side and trim away points of colours A and B. Press these seams outwards.

Chevron pattern variation

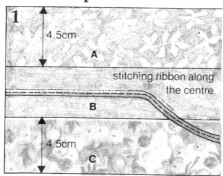

4.5cm

A

stitching ribbon along the centre

B

4.5cm

C

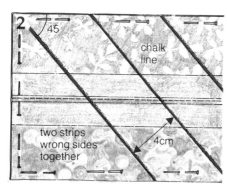

45

chalk line

two strips wrong sides together

4cm

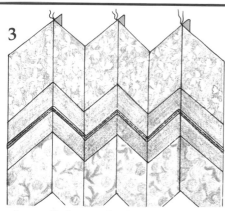

1 Cut strips of colours A and C, 5cm/2in wide. Cut a 4cm/1½in wide strip of colour B and join the three strips together with colour B in the centre. Appliqué a length of contrasting 3mm/⅛in ribbon along the centre of the strip of colour B for added decoration. Press seams.

Make a second identical pieced strip in this way.
2 Lay one pieced strip on top of the other, wrong sides together, matching seamlines, and pin in place. Mark a 45° angle across the top strip and then mark a series of parallel lines, 4cm/1½in apart. Cut

along all the marked lines, giving mirror-image pairs of strips.
3 Join the pairs along their long edges, matching seams and ribbon carefully, to produce a striking zigzag pattern band. Trim the outer edges to straighten and apply banding strips of colour B.

Diamond pattern variations

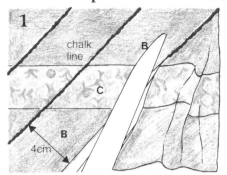

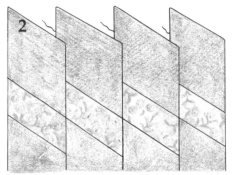

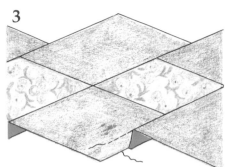

Using only two colours, it is possible to create some pretty diamond effects. It is very important to be accurate with these patterns, so pin horizontally along seamlines before stitching.
1 Cut two strips of colour B, width 4cm/1½in, and one strip of colour C, width 3cm/1¼in. Join the strips with colour C in the centre. Mark a 45° angle as before. Mark a

series of strips 4cm/1½in wide and cut out.
2 There are several different ways in which you could offset the pieces to make patterns. To make a wide border, join strips along long edges so that pointed ends are level along both sides. Colour C appears as a series of parallelograms in the centre.

3 Alternatively, join the strips so that the upper corner of one strip of colour C coincides with the lower corner of the next one. This gives a much narrower border with colour C appearing as a row of horizontal diamonds in the centre.

Up-and-down blocks design

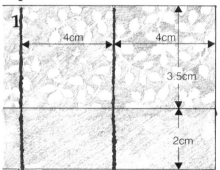

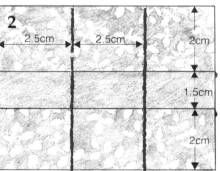

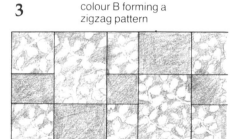

colour B forming a zigzag pattern

This simple pattern uses two sets of joined strips.
1 Cut a 4cm/1½in strip of colour A and a 2.5cm/1in strip of colour B. Seam together and press. Mark and cut into pieces 4cm/1½in wide.

2 Cut two 2.5cm/1in strips of colour A and one of colour B. Seam together with colour B in the centre. Press seams, mark and cut into pieces 2.5cm/1in wide.

3 Turn alternate pieces of the first strip upside down, placing pieces of the second strip between them. Seam together, carefully matching corners of colour B so that a zigzag pattern of boxes forms. Press all seams in the same direction.

Seminole trim for blouse and skirt

An attractive bib-fronted blouse and lightly gathered skirt are the perfect partners for the simple Seminole patchwork band trim. Try to choose patchwork fabrics which introduce a new shade, as well as providing a link with the main colour of the outfit. Two small-scale prints and a plain lawn have been used to make this Seminole trim.
The amount of patchwork you need to make depends on the garment you are trimming. The pattern shown

here makes a 76cm/30in long band from strips cut from 90cm/36in wide fabric (ie 15cm/6in approximately are lost). The skirt shown here has a band of patchwork set in about 9cm/3½in from the hem. Measure round the skirt to find out how much patchwork you need. Measure the shirt front, yokes, cuffs etc in the same way. You may wish to join completed strips together to cover a larger area. Make outer seams of patchwork panel equal to those on the pattern.

You will need
30cm/⅜yd each of three fabrics, width 90cm/36in
Soft pencil, ruler, sharp scissors
2m/2⅛yd matching prepared piping

Preparing the patchwork
Read the instructions for Seminole patchwork first. This design is similar except that three different fabrics are used instead of two. The centre colour is also used for the banding. Cut all strips 4cm/1½in wide, except the outer colour strips which should be cut 5cm/2in wide.

Choose simply constructed clothes for adding Seminole patchwork. You could use any of the patterns shown here for bands on a skirt. Add banding strips to reach required width for a blouse panel.

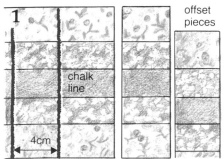

1 Join strips of centre, second and outer colours with 5mm/¼in seams. Press all the seams in the same direction.

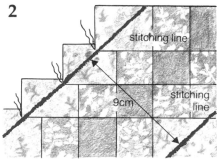

Mark and cut crosswise strips of 4cm/1½in width. Offset the pieces and stitch with 5mm/¼in seams so that the centre colour squares touch

at the corners. Continue joining pieces until you have the required length. Straighten ends of strips as described on page 235.
Press all the seams in the same direction.
2 Now mark a stitching line along either side of the strip to give a strip 9cm/3½in wide. Join banding strips of the centre colour to either side, using this seamline.
Appliqué or set in patchwork to blouse and skirt as required, using prepared piping along all seams except neck edge.

Index